LEADING BY DESIGN

An Action Framework for PLC at Work™ Leaders

Cassandra Erkens

Eric Twadell

Solution Tree | Press
a division of
Solution Tree

555 North Morton Street
Bloomington, IN 47404
800.733.6786 (toll free) / 812.336.7700

FAX: 812.336.7790
email: info@solution-tree.com
solution-tree.com

Printed in the United States of America

15 14 13 12 11   1 2 3 4 5

Library of Congress Cataloging-in-Publication Data

Erkens, Cassandra.
  Leading by design : an action framework for PLC at Work leaders / Cassandra Erkens, Eric Twadell.
       pages cm
  Includes bibliographical references and index.
    ISBN 978-1-935542-29-2 (perfect bound : alk. paper) -- ISBN 978-1-935542-30-8 (library edition : alk. paper) 1. Teaching teams. 2. Teachers--Professional relationships. I. Twadell, Eric. II. Title.
  LB1029.T4.E75 2012
  371.14'8--dc23
                        2011047147

Solution Tree
Jeffrey C. Jones, CEO
Edmund M. Ackerman, President

Solution Tree Press
President: Douglas M. Rife
Publisher: Robert D. Clouse
Vice President of Production: Gretchen Knapp
Managing Production Editor: Caroline Wise
Copy Editor: Rachel Rosolina
Text and Cover Designer: Amy Shock

ACKNOWLEDGMENTS

We would like to thank the many remarkable educational leaders who took the time to share their understandings and experiences regarding leading the work of professional learning communities. We were blessed to interview some of the finest leaders in education today. Specifically, we would like to thank the following individuals who made themselves available to us: Alan Addley, Leslie Butz, Bernice Cobbs, Scott Ferguson, William Ferriter, Lynn Fuller, Dana Ginsburg, Jayne Hanley, Susan Hintz, Marc Johnson, Janel Keating, Janet Malone, Mike Mattos, Anne Meredith, Jadi Miller, Pam Moran, Pam Moser, Garrick Peterson, Steve Pierce, Ed Rafferty, Lyn Rantz, Ross Renfrow, Jeff Ronnenberg, John Thorson, Tom Trigg, Steve Troen, Matt Wight, and Pete Zak.

We would also like to thank those who work tirelessly in the field, striving daily to make a difference with each leadership action. We have loved working and learning alongside you, and though we did not formally interview all of you, we have most certainly learned with and from you. You will note that we have included some of your inspirational stories and examples in the book as case studies; you have shown us what works, as well as when, why, and how. We would like to add a special note of thanks to John Carter and Joe Flanagan for their thoughtful suggestions and feedback, as well as to the administrative team, faculty and staff, board of education, and students of Adlai E. Stevenson High School in Lincolnshire, Illinois, for providing us with a constant reminder of what it truly means to be a high-performing professional learning community.

Of course, none of this would be possible without the foundational work, contributing insights, and keen attention of the PLC architects, Richard DuFour, Robert Eaker, and Rebecca DuFour. We can never thank you enough for all you have contributed to the field at large, for all you have offered us as resources and ideas for this specific project, and for your infinite kindness and generosity as friends. We are immeasurably blessed.

We are grateful to the team at Solution Tree, specifically Rachel Rosolina, Gretchen Knapp, Douglas Rife, and Jeff Jones. Each of you believed in us as writers long before we imagined a book for ourselves, and your faith, support, and even pressure at times (always appropriately placed) have provided the encouragement and assistance we needed to launch as writers. You were right, and we are eternally grateful!

Those in our professional lives inspired and encouraged us at strategic points along the way; those in our personal lives endured, tolerated, nudged, and believed in us in the day to day. We would be remiss if we did not acknowledge our families. Our loved ones have been nothing short of amazing. So Anne, Kaitlyn, Lauren, Dave, Calvin, Ethan, and Elise, we are forever grateful for your undying love and commitment to our success. We most certainly could not have done this without you!

Solution Tree Press would like to thank the following reviewers:

Tom Bailey
Principal
Hailey Elementary School
Hailey, Idaho

Dan Chacon
Principal
Sanger High School
Sanger, California

Mark Greenfelder
Principal
Thoreau Middle School
Vienna, Virginia

Ken Grindstaff
Principal
Snow Creek Elementary School
Penhook, Virginia

Margaret Harris
Associate Professor, Department of
    Education
Southern New Hampshire University
Manchester, New Hampshire

Kimberly Kappler Hewitt
Assistant Professor, Department of
    Education
University of North Carolina at
    Greensboro
Greensboro, North Carolina

Cathy Huemer
Instructional Specialist, K–5 Reading
Newport News Public Schools
Newport News, Virginia

Sue Mayernick
Principal
Helen Keller Junior High School
Schaumburg, Illinois

Audrey F. Murphy
Assistant Professor, Department of
    Human Services and Counseling
St. John's University
Queens, New York

Emily Poag
Associate, Delaware Academy for School
    Leadership
University of Delaware
Newark, Delaware

Lyn Rantz
Principal
Prairie Star Middle School
Leawood, Kansas

Janna Smith
Math Specialist
Far Hills Country Day School
Far Hills, New Jersey

TABLE OF CONTENTS

ABOUT THE AUTHORS

Cassandra Erkens is the owner of Anam Cara Consulting, Inc. She works with teachers and administrators nationally and internationally to advance the work of school improvement, leadership development, professional learning communities, and quality assessment design and use. As a consultant, she partners with Solution Tree and other education-based companies, such as the Assessment Trainers Institute.

Cassandra is a contributing author to *The Collaborative Teacher, The Collaborative Administrator, The Teacher as Assessment Leader,* and *The Administrator as Assessment Leader* anthologies. She has also authored many professional development curricula and training programs for education-based companies. Cassandra has served as a high school English teacher, a local union president, a regional school improvement facilitator for the Minnesota Department of Education, a district-level director of staff development, and a director of educational services in the corporate culture. She currently serves as an adjunct faculty member at Hamline University in Minnesota, where she offers master of arts courses in education. Cassandra has served on the board of the Minnesota Staff Development Council and on the commissioner-appointed Statewide Staff Development Advisory Council.

Eric Twadell, PhD, has served as social studies teacher, curriculum director, and assistant superintendent for leadership and organizational development, and currently he serves as the superintendent of Adlai E. Stevenson High School in Lincolnshire, Illinois. Stevenson High School has been described by the United States Department of Education (USDE) as "the most recognized and celebrated school in America" and is one of only three schools to win the USDE Blue Ribbon Award on four occasions. Stevenson was one of the first comprehensive schools designated a New American High School by the USDE as a model of successful school reform. In the popular press, Stevenson High School has been repeatedly cited as one of America's top high schools and the birthplace of Professional Learning Communities at Work™.

Eric has written multiple professional articles and is a contributing author to *The Collaborative Administrator* and *The Collaborative Teacher*. As a dedicated PLC practitioner, he has worked with state departments of education and local schools and districts throughout the United States to advance the successful implementation of the PLC model and achieve school improvement and reform. An accessible and articulate authority on PLC concepts, Eric brings hands-on experience to his presentations and workshops.

In addition to his teaching and leadership roles, Eric has been involved in coaching numerous athletic teams and facilitating outdoor education and adventure travel programs. He is a member of several professional organizations, including Learning Forward and ASCD, and he earned a master's degree in curriculum and instruction and a doctorate in educational leadership and policies studies from Loyola University Chicago.

To learn more about Eric's work, follow @ELT247365 on Twitter.

To book Cassandra or Eric for professional development, contact pd@solution-tree .com.

FOREWORD

For the past decade Cassandra Erkens and Eric Twadell have worked with educators throughout the United States to help them transform traditional schools and districts into high-performing professional learning communities at work™ (PLCs). They soon discovered that some districts with few financial resources were able to successfully implement the PLC process in all of their schools while others rich in resources were unable to bring the process to life in a single school. They learned that one school could become a model professional learning community while another school in the same district with a similar student body and operating under the same board policies floundered. They worked in schools where a single department or grade level became its own high-functioning collaborative team despite the indifference of the principal. They witnessed these remarkable differences in schools throughout the country—elementary, middle, and high schools; in urban, suburban, and rural settings; in small schools and in big schools; in affluent communities and high-poverty communities.

The stark contrasts they witnessed in the ability of hard-working, well-intentioned educators to implement the PLC process led them to the question that has resulted in this book. Why is it that some districts, schools, and teams are able to bring the PLC process to life in ways that powerfully impact student and adult learning while other educators working in the same organization, serving similar students, having access to the same resources, and receiving the same training were unable to meet that challenge?

Their answer to this question should come as no surprise: effective implementation of the PLC process requires effective leadership. In fact, they argue that leadership is "*the* single most important ingredient in successfully reculturing and restructuring our schools to operate as PLCs," and that "the *lack* of effective leadership at all levels—from teacher leaders to superintendents—is the defining variable in schools that fall short of being able to successfully implement important PLC practices."

The authors acknowledge that their conclusion about the importance of leadership "may appear as nothing more than a penetrating glimpse into the obvious," and if their book had merely reiterated this commonsense observation, I would agree with them. Fortunately for those who read *Leading by Design*, Erkens and Twadell delve deeply into the question of effective leadership in PLCs. They identified districts, schools, and team leaders who have been highly successful in creating model PLCs and have the results to prove it. The authors then studied the educators behind the transformation to discover both the very specific behaviors and the thinking behind those behaviors that led to the success.

Readers of this book will be delighted to find that the authors consistently move beyond morally impeccable bromides such as "leaders create a shared vision," "leaders communicate effectively," "leaders build trust," and "leaders are willing to confront those who violate the organization's core values" to offer specific steps that can be taken to bring those elusive generalities to life. This book is all about taking action, and the authors consistently come back to the question of, "What is it that effective leaders of the PLC process actually do?" The authors certainly support their ideas, assertions, and recommendations with a tremendous amount of research from both inside and outside education. This book, however, is clearly written by expert practitioners, for practitioners, and is based on lessons learned from highly effective practitioners. It is emphatically about collaboratively *doing*.

The authors recognize the complexity and challenge of educating students, and they honor contemporary educators for their ongoing efforts to meet that challenge. They make it clear, however, that working hard will not improve our schools unless people are clear about and focused on the right work, and then are given the ongoing support to be successful in that work. As they write, "clarity precedes competence, but competence demands capacity building." They challenge educators at all levels to engage in the ongoing learning necessary to increase their own capacity to lead. Furthermore, they insist that educational leaders define their roles as developing the capacity of others to succeed in what they are being asked to do. The authors point out that one important strategy in providing this service to others is helping them to understand the indicators that define high-quality work, and Erkens and Twadell provide examples throughout the book of what those specific quality indicators look like in the real world of schools.

One of the things I appreciate most about this book is that it not only offers powerful insights into beginning the PLC process, but even more importantly, focuses on the practices that sustain that process over time. The authors make a compelling case for the assumptions that drive this book, including:

- There is abundant evidence regarding what educators must do to help transform their districts and schools into PLCs.

- Despite knowing what needs to be done, many educators seem unable or unwilling to do it.

- Creating PLCs requires educators to acknowledge and ultimately to bridge this knowing-doing gap.

- Bridging the knowing-doing gap will require effective leadership at all levels of the organization.

- People throughout the organization have the capacity for leadership.

- Effective leaders nurture and develop this leadership capacity in others.

- Educators may be unable to sustain the PLCs they have created when key leaders leave the organization unless leadership is widely dispersed throughout the organization.

- The ultimate test of effective leadership is ensuring that other leaders remain after you have left who can help the organization become even more effective than when you were there.

Perhaps I reacted so favorably to *Leading by Design* because I repeatedly found myself agreeing with points the authors were making, and like most of us, I am always impressed by the wisdom of those with whom I agree. But there were many times as I was reading that I thought, "That is a great point. I wish I had written that." For example, they wrote, "Teachers must work collaboratively to demystify teaching, and leaders at all levels in PLC organizations must work collaboratively in PLCs to demystify leading." That sentence captures a fundamental premise of the book, and to their immense credit, the authors do a wonderful job of providing educators with the tools and strategies to demystify leading in their districts, school, and teams. I am certain that readers of this book will benefit from their insights, as I know I did.

—Rick DuFour
Educational author and consultant

INTRODUCTION

> The challenge of leadership is to be strong,
> but not rude; be kind, but not weak; be bold,
> but not bully; be thoughtful, but not lazy;
> be humble, but not timid; be proud, but not
> arrogant; have humor, but without folly.
>
> —Jim Rohn

Effective schools require effective leaders. Though we admit this may appear as nothing more than a penetrating glimpse into the obvious to many educators, we believe the point cannot be understated. Furthermore, we believe that a hefty dose of common sense, in addition to all of the supporting research and literature in our profession, answers the question, Does leadership affect the quality of learning and schools? The answer is a definitive "Yes!" Educational leaders do matter—a lot.

As practitioners and students of the professional learning community (PLC) process, we have been amazed and humbled by the many wonderful transformations that schools are making as they redefine their mission to ensure learning for all students, rather than simply working to ensure that all students have been *taught*. At the same time, however, the inability of some schools to either recognize the need for change or implement the needed improvement initiatives deeply saddens us.

A quick review of literature reveals there is no shortage of information on what leaders must understand about PLCs to develop a strong focus on vision, mission, values, and goals; formative and summative assessments; collaboration; effective teaching and learning; and response to intervention (RTI) and interventions. As Kegan and Lahey reflect on many well-known best practices in education, "Ninety-five percent of what we need to know to provide excellent learning opportunities for all of our children is probably already known. We are already well informed, and it is maddeningly insufficient" (2001, p. 232). The question of what effective leaders must *know* to lead their PLCs haunts us less than the question of what effective leaders actually *do*. This compels us as authors to actively search for answers, and whenever we work with educational systems striving to become PLCs, they too ask us these questions.

Any number of factors can determine whether improvement initiatives will prove successful. Through both our personal experiences of working with effective leaders across North America and the overwhelming supporting research for this project, however, we have come to the conclusion that leadership is *the* single most important ingredient in successfully reculturing and restructuring our schools to operate as PLCs. We also have come to believe that the *lack* of effective leadership at all levels—from teacher leaders to superintendents—is the defining variable in schools that fall short of being able to successfully implement important PLC practices.

Since 2000, we have been blessed to work with hundreds of schools and school leaders as they worked to implement PLC practices in their districts and schools. During this time, we met outstanding leaders and witnessed great success stories as districts and schools completely transformed themselves by embracing the fundamental changes in assumptions and practices that come from moving from a focus on teaching to a focus on learning. At the same time, we saw a fair number of schools that tried to restructure and reculture themselves as PLCs only to run into roadblocks and hurdles that stalled, and sometimes derailed, their efforts. As much as the inability of some schools to transform as PLCs has disheartened us, we have been curious about their struggles as well.

The PLC Knowing-Doing Gap

Our close examination of schools that have not been able to initiate or sustain PLC processes has demonstrated that the critical variable is a lack of effective leadership. What surprised and interested us about these districts and schools is that many of their leaders are hardworking and thoughtful, and they have a fairly strong understanding of the big ideas that drive the transformation into a PLC. We quickly realized during our research that while a clear understanding of the big ideas is important, it is never, ever, enough.

Consider the following descriptions of leaders we met who demonstrated an understanding of PLC concepts but had difficulty initiating and sustaining PLC practices in their schools:

- Leader A has read all the books on PLCs, attended numerous conferences, and even participated in a PLC summer institute. At the start of the school year, the leader purchased copies of a PLC book for all the teachers and declared that they would become a PLC. Much like a cheerleader or a fan at a sporting event, Leader A spent considerable time praising the work of teachers and students when good things happened in their school. Unfortunately, the school spent very little time and effort on actually doing the work necessary to become a PLC, and there was no noticeable gain in student learning. At the end of the year, however, despite the lack of progress, Leader A celebrated the fact that nearly a dozen teachers participated in the PLC book study.

- Leader B worked tirelessly day in and day out to reshape the structure and culture of his school as a PLC. Leader B had a clear understanding of the work that his school needed to do. To get started, Leader B assumed a tremendous burden by working from teacher to teacher and student to student in an effort to align curriculum; help write clear, student-friendly learning standards; develop common formative assessments; provide meaningful and relevant feedback to teachers and students; and create interventions for students when they were not learning. Through no fault of the leader or his sheer force of will and effort, the teachers still seemed confused, and the school managed to witness only slight to modest improvement in student achievement.

- Leader C worked hard to create a safe, warm, caring environment for everyone. Teachers, students, and parents liked and respected Leader C. While attending school activities, sporting contests, and cocurricular events, Leader C talked passionately about creating a PLC school. When working with teachers, however, Leader C practiced the art of "olé" leadership. Like the matador in a bullfight, Leader C would wave the cape of PLCs as the authority for change. Leader C sympathized with teachers' frustration and increased workload but explained that the district's commitment to PLCs required that they complete the work. Leader C explained that the district office issued a top-down mandate to implement PLCs across the district. Although some teachers began meeting in groups throughout the year, they initiated very few significant changes, and no noticeable gain in student achievement occurred as a result.

What we find fascinating about these leaders is that they all could articulate what a PLC is and what it should look like. There is no doubt that these leaders had a clear picture of the big ideas of PLCs. They also had a solid understanding of effective curriculum, instruction, and assessment. These leaders knew what they needed to do. So what happened? What went wrong? Why are some leaders effective and others not?

As you might imagine, *knowing* the big ideas is not enough. No matter how smart someone is, no matter how great a classroom teacher a leader once was, no matter how effective he or she may be at building relationships, an effective leader must be *doing* the work of implementing and sustaining the concepts of a PLC in the daily lives of his or her districts, schools, and teams in order for significant change to take place.

The Research

Richard DuFour, Robert Eaker, Rebecca DuFour, and others have given us a clear picture of what professional learning communities are doing to produce better results for students. As practitioners working every day in schools and as PLC associates, we both have been given the special opportunity to learn from the PLC architects and other associates. We were able to consult and work with schools on their journeys toward functioning as PLCs. And PLCs are getting results. Under the direction of effective leadership, the process of becoming a PLC works exactly as envisioned and described by the PLC architects. Some leaders, however, are more effective than others; they not only achieve improved results more quickly, but they also achieve long-term sustainability. These are the leaders we worked to identify and study for the guiding research question behind this book: *What are the practices of effective leaders (central office administration, building administration, and teacher leaders) in districts and schools that function as exemplary PLCs?*

Our plan was to spend time in successfully functioning PLCs and to pay considerable attention to what effective teacher, school, and district-level leaders were doing to initiate and sustain meaningful change. Educational researcher Janet Schofeld suggests:

> Research in education can be used not only to study *what is* and *what may be* but also to explore possible visions of *what could be.* By studying what could be, we mean locating situations that we know or expect to be ideal or exceptional on some *a priori* basis and then studying them to see what is actually going on there. (1990, p. 217)

More than anything, we wanted to explore the strategies, practices, and skills of leaders in schools functioning as exemplary PLCs to determine what those leaders were actually *doing* to help their schools succeed. To guide our curiosity and answer our questions, we visited and interviewed effective leaders in central office, building administration, and classroom teacher roles at the elementary, middle, and high school levels.

The leaders we identified had been doing the work of PLCs for more than a year and had already demonstrated clear results in student achievement. Furthermore, DuFour, Eaker, and DuFour had recognized the majority of their schools as exemplary and included many of them in the effectiveness database on the AllThingsPLC.info website. We created the protocol in table I.1 to guide our inquiry.

Table I.1: Research Protocol

Question	Purpose
1. Do you believe there is a difference between leading within a PLC and leading within a traditional system? If so, what is the difference? If not, what is the same about it?	Identify the distinctions of PLC leadership.
2. If you were to isolate the three leadership practices that *most* help you to be effective in leading PLC work, what would those three practices be, and why is each important?	Identify key leadership practices that are helpful in leading PLC work, and establish the value of each strategy.
3. How did you identify that you needed those three practices, and what did you have to do to grow them in your own leadership work? Please be specific about any strategies you used to develop these practices.	Identify the ability to recognize and develop effective leadership practices.
4. Should these three practices be encouraged at all levels of a PLC organization?	Evaluate the transferability of the leadership practices.
5. How do you grow these practices in your colleagues?	Evaluate the transferability of the leadership practices.
6. Describe some of the setbacks and mistakes that you experienced in your PLC journey before you defined or fully mastered these leadership practices. Be specific, and provide examples.	Identify the kinds of setbacks that can occur when key leadership practices are not in use.

Question	Purpose
7. Describe some of the greatest successes or triumphs you have experienced as a result of the practices you employ. Be specific with examples in your explanation.	Celebrate the practices used well.
8. Is there anything else you would like to share about leading in a PLC? Is there any question I have not asked or any important idea I might not have discovered during our time together?	Provide an open option for leaders to share any additional insights or information.

We began our research with a working hypothesis—based on our own experiences working with remarkable educational leaders and healthy PLC-based systems across North America—about the practices we thought we would find along the way:

- We believed we would find that strong PLC leaders create vision and support it with rationale.

- We believed we would find that strong PLC leaders build collaborative cultures.

- We believed we would find that strong PLC leaders articulate expectations and empower teams to meet those expectations in unique and powerful ways.

- We believed we would find that strong PLC leaders are reflective practitioners.

As we conducted our interviews, we listened to see if the practices we identified were, in fact, the practices that strong leaders employed. We listened to determine which strategies or beliefs might support the practices we anticipated finding. Finally, we listened to discover and explore any leadership practices that we might have misunderstood, missed altogether, or misrepresented in our initial hypothesis.

We found that for the most part, our hypotheses proved to be true; however, the framework that emerged from our many interviews intrigued and delighted us with a new sense of coherence and clarity. We discovered we were on track with the kinds of practices effective leaders employed, and that even though the practices aren't sequential, they definitely build on one another in significant ways. For example, using just *some* of the practices can create change, but will not suffice to sustain change. We were even more excited to find that anyone, anywhere could replicate the leadership strategies and practices we identified in effective teacher, school, and district leaders—if they were willing to try.

During the course of our research, we had the wonderful opportunity to interview many masterful leaders at the central office, building administration, and teacher levels across North America. Although they sometimes struggled to articulate what they did that worked so well, they were eventually able to do so with specific examples and strategies. They taught us so much.

In her description of effective educational research, Schofeld suggests that "research studies gain their potential for applicability to other situations by providing . . . comparability and translatability" (1990, p. 208). In order to achieve that applicability, translatability, and credibility, we have compiled the stories of these leaders into case studies and interview transcripts. Although we would have loved to recognize and celebrate the wonderful leaders we interviewed for this project in the text, ultimately we decided to keep their stories confidential so they could continue to work comfortably with their colleagues in the settings they described for us. We found these remarkable educational leaders to be what Collins describes as Level 5 leaders in *Good to Great*: "a study in duality: modest and willful, humble and fearless" (2001, p. 22). We remain grateful for the insights, expertise, and humility of these outstanding leaders. While modest about their own skills and successes, they have proven willful in their commitment to share what works and fearless in their effort to build leadership capacity in others.

A Leadership Framework—The Missing Link

Over the past fifty years, our profession has seen the development and articulation of numerous theories of curriculum, instruction, and assessment. Many of these theories have been a tremendous help, as they have contributed to an understanding of the concepts, practices, and strategies that must guide the work of classroom teachers. Given the strong literature and research base (Danielson, 2007; Jacobs & Johnson, 2009; Marzano, 2007; Stiggins, Arter, Chappuis, & Chappuis, 2011; Wiggins & McTighe, 2005, 2007; Wiliam, 2011), we seriously doubt that anyone would suggest it is not important for teachers to develop a coherent theory of effective practice to guide their daily work. Having a coherent conceptual framework and a solid understanding of effective curriculum, instruction, and assessment allows teachers to develop meaningful learning opportunities for students, provide research-based instructional strategies that promote student engagement, and formatively assess student progress over time. Of course, one can only imagine the difficulties a teacher would experience without a coherent theory to guide daily practice. It would be the teaching equivalent of going on a 180-mile road trip without a map or a compass and with no clear picture of how to get from here to there.

What surprised us in our research was that the single most important difference between leaders who are successful and those who are not is that *the work of effective leaders reflects a clear understanding and a coherent theory of leadership*. In the same way that effective teachers develop deep clarity regarding what effective classroom instruction looks like, effective leaders must develop deep clarity regarding what effective leadership looks like in their districts, schools, and teams. Effective leaders understand that leadership is more than just saying they prioritize relationship building, create a climate for learning, or give teachers what they need and then get out of the way. We have found that the missing link between ineffective and effective leaders in high-performing PLCs is that effective leaders build a framework for leadership development and then engage the entire system of educators in creating a solid understanding of leadership to guide their daily work.

Mike Schmoker eloquently states, "Clarity precedes competence" (2004, p. 85). We could not agree more. Through our experiences and research, however, we have found that having clarity—understanding the big ideas of PLCs—while necessary, is not sufficient for developing effective leadership. So we offer a corollary conclusion: clarity precedes competence, but competence demands capacity building. Prior to successfully initiating and sustaining PLC practices, leaders must have deep clarity about what work they need to do and an understanding of how the work needs to be completed; most importantly, however, they must continuously build their own capacity and the capacity of others to actually do the work of becoming a PLC. Only by learning and using proven and effective leadership strategies and practices will leaders develop the capacity to successfully lead schools as PLCs.

The practices and strategies we identified throughout our study are not altogether new. In fact, they are well supported and discussed in research-based literature on how to lead in schools that operate as PLCs. We have found that effective leaders of high-performing PLCs are deliberate in their efforts to create structure and culture in their districts, schools, and teams that support learning for everyone—community members, board members, administrators, faculty and staff, parents, and students. At the same time, we have found that the most effective leaders are curious about their own practices and are engaged in a cycle of continuous reflection on how they might be able to improve. It is our sincere hope that this project will offer new insights and specific ideas worthy of replication to readers intent on improving their ability to provide effective leadership. *Leading by Design* is our attempt to contribute to the professional dialogue, provide a point of departure for conversation, and offer a conceptual framework of leadership—relentless, passionate leadership.

Leading to Learn and Learning to Lead

> As we look ahead into the next century, leaders will be those who empower others.
>
> —Bill Gates

It should come as no surprise that the most significant place to impact student achievement is at the classroom level. This is why the work of PLCs is so powerful: teachers work collaboratively to solve complex issues in the classroom and ensure that all learners learn. There are many definitions and variations of the terms used to describe the PLC model. Richard DuFour, Robert Eaker, and Rebecca DuFour—the architects of the PLC concept—have worked tirelessly to clarify a *professional learning community* as "educators committed to working collaboratively in ongoing processes of collective inquiry and action research to achieve better results for the students they serve" (DuFour, DuFour, & Eaker, 2008, p. 14). Educators engaged in the PLC process are working collaboratively and tirelessly to lead everyone—their students and themselves—to learn at the greatest achievement levels imaginable.

Even less surprising, the most significant position to impact the work of teams at the classroom level—from monitoring achievement to ensuring quality practices in each classroom and across the organization—is the leader or leaders who work with teams (Marzano, Waters, & McNulty, 2005; Seashore Louis, Leithwood, Wahlstrom, & Anderson, 2010). In PLCs, leadership is required at all levels of the organization, from the district and building to the equally important and often overlooked teachers (DuFour et al., 2008; DuFour, DuFour, Eaker, & Many, 2010). Teaching and leading go hand in hand: great leaders are teachers first. But it is not fair to assume that anyone who can teach can naturally lead. In high-performing and self-sustaining PLC systems, effective leaders engage the entire system in learning to lead.

The Need for Organizational Leadership Development

In the past, educators and school systems have left leadership to chance, much like teaching. Of course, to minimize that chance, school systems and administrators have always tried to place the brightest and the best in leadership positions; still, each leadership position is usually left completely to the individual's level of expertise and personal beliefs regarding leadership practices and organizational change processes. In a 2008 interview, educational expert Richard Elmore states, "Americans in general have what I call attribute theories of leadership, which is when you put the right person in the right place at the right time and a miracle happens" (Crow, 2008, pp. 42–43). This hope-filled strategy is not much different from the "educational roulette" educators have played with classrooms in which the depth and breadth of student learning depended largely on the quality of skills and the educational belief systems of the teacher at the front of the class. Just as there are variances of quality in the classroom based on the individual teachers, so too are there variances in the quality of leadership provided at the grade, department, building, and even district levels based on the individual leaders of those levels. Teachers must work collaboratively in PLCs to demystify teaching, and leaders at all levels in PLC organizations must work collaboratively to demystify leading. We cannot overstate the significance of building capacity for the leadership role, which should not be left to chance or individual preference.

Educators have traditionally used professional development as the primary strategy for developing a stronger understanding of educational practice at both the classroom and leadership levels. Over time, educators have become far more strategic in tying their professional development efforts tightly to the school improvement goals and, of course, research-based practices. With the help of researchers and expert practitioners, the field of education has identified the most powerful instructional strategies, classroom management strategies, assessment design and use features, and leadership competencies; all have been fertile ground for training to increase the personal capacity of individual educators.

But relying on training as the sole, or even primary, mode of professional development does not suffice for two reasons. First, "meaning making is not a spectator sport . . . Humans don't get ideas; they make ideas" (Costa, 2007, p. 95). In other words, training sessions that rely on direct instruction as an input model fall staggeringly short of helping the participants make meaning that transfers consistently into changed practices. In the "sit and get" model, participants would still need time to discuss, digest, and ultimately make decisions about what to do with the information being shared. Second, as focused and specific as the selected professional development training opportunities might have been, leaders ultimately leave it to individual participants to self-select the content they found most interesting or desirable and to decide whether or not they will integrate any of the ideas into their daily routines. As M. Hayes Mizell notes:

> The hard truth is that, until recently, the field of professional development has been underdeveloped and immature. . . . It has tolerated a lot of sloppy thinking, practice, and results. It has not been willing to "call out" ineffective practices and ineffective policy . . . It has not devoted attention to outcomes. (as cited in Sawchuk, 2010, p. s2)

In the absence of collective agreements regarding specific, unified action steps following a professional learning event, the notes participants take are often no more powerful than "PD shopping lists." From the packaged strategies provided at any given workshop, participants choose things they find either supportive of their personal efforts or interesting enough to remember. Allowing individual choice regarding how or when to implement something proves ineffective. Such an approach comes at the cost of organizational clarity and consistency in the following ways:

- Desired changes are rarely implemented to scale.

- The chasm between what educators know and do widens.

- The lack of responsiveness in organizational capacity becomes debilitating.

In short, the implementation effort fails, and the system loses.

Like teachers, leaders need to be learning by collaboratively *doing* rather than learning by individual preference, ability, or interest. Working to create stronger leaders is as much about helping individuals intentionally select and apply the appropriate leadership practice in the immediate moment as it is about helping the organization understand quality leadership practices for the long term. Schools must do this work with current and future leaders identified by formal and informal titles throughout the organization. In sustainable, strong PLCs, leadership happens by design. Effective PLC leaders create better structures to guarantee learning: they are *leading to learn*. Simultaneously, they create opportunities to enhance understanding and inform practices regarding effective leadership; they engage themselves and their entire system in *learning to lead*.

The Study of Leadership Practices

Effective leaders are tenacious in their focus on and commitment to studying successful leadership practices, that is, to developing a "repertoire of dispositions, behaviors, and skills in specific areas of performance, such as designing instruction and measurement strategies, interacting with students, developing relationships with families, collaborating with colleagues, and implementing school-wide reforms" (York-Barr, Sommers, Ghere, & Montie, 2001, pp. 7–8).

A leadership practice is larger than an isolated skill or strategy. A *strategy* is specific to a need (for example, employing a decision-making protocol to engage staff in coming to consensus on a given issue), whereas a *practice* is a discipline with a variety of options generalizable to the overall process at hand. For example, the practice of facilitating shared responsibility requires many different strategies, such as establishing expectations for the work, requiring teams to create and adhere to team norms, offering teams protocols to use when discussing student work, supporting teams in generating and interpreting student data reports, nurturing and monitoring team success, and intervening with struggling teams.

While the number and variety of strategies used to employ them vary, effective leadership practices share these common characteristics:

- **They are applied to leverage change**—Unlike the managerial duties and rote tasks that often fill our days, leadership practices require deliberate thought and strategic application to reculture, restructure, and impact results. While a strategy or task to support change often has an ending point, a leadership practice to support change continues even after the indications appear that change is on the horizon.

- **They are systemic**—Effective leaders never apply leadership practices to single initiatives or events. A practice such as developing coherence and clarity is used with consistency *no matter the initiative at hand*. Toward that end, effective leadership practices can and ultimately should become engrained in the way they do things: the established norm or habit. When this happens, the organization learns to anticipate and appreciate these habits. When leaders apply practices with fidelity and consistency across the organization, the desired changes transform into predictable expectations; in other words, expectations move from wishes to reality.

- **They are engaged to align words with deeds**—Effective leaders use their leadership practices to mirror their message and illuminate a path toward the desired vision, mission, values, and goals of the organization. Leaders should only espouse beliefs and encourage habits they are willing to deliberately model. They know that what they say and do matters when inviting others to follow.

- **They are dynamic and responsive**—There is an old adage that when you only have a hammer, everything looks like a nail. Leadership practices must remain fluid and responsive to a given context and set of circumstances. Effective leaders use their leadership practices in equitable but not necessarily equal ways. In other words, effective leaders employ a variety of appropriate leadership practices that will accurately target the needs of individuals or individual teams; they know better than to make everyone do exactly the same thing at exactly the same time.

  Different teams and different situations require different leadership responses and levels of interaction or involvement. A strategy or tool applied as a blanket response will be overkill for some teams and inadequate for others. Leaders who work toward equity instead of equality provide a clear and consistent set of expectations and criteria for everyone, so they can remain just and impartial in a given situation while remaining responsive to each team's needs. Ultimately, the leader's ability to adapt leadership practices appropriately creates a stronger sense of fairness than employing a uniform series of strategies indifferent to the needs of individuals or teams ever could.

- **They can be replicated by current and future leaders**—Effective leaders develop leadership practices they can identify, refine, and teach to others. These practices should not be limited to those few individuals deemed to have the innate talent or mysterious skill of natural leaders. If a leadership practice is successful, the organization benefits by sharing the practice so all can learn and employ it.

In his foreword to Sharon Daloz Parks's 2005 book *Leadership Can Be Taught: A Bold Approach for a Complex World*, renowned leadership expert Warren Bennis states, "Many of the most significant shapers of history were themselves shaped gradually, not ready to make an impact on the world until time and the crucible of experience had first performed their duties" (Bennis, 2005, p. ix). Education must abandon the assumption that there are only natural-born leaders and must embrace the work of intentionally developing current and future leaders.

The most effective leaders we have met—at any level of the organization or in any field—understand that they must learn leadership by practicing leadership. Leadership is a practice that requires craft knowledge, pliable skills, and a lifelong commitment to self and organizational improvement. True leaders are learners first.

The Seven Leadership Practices of Highly Effective PLC Leaders

In our study, high-functioning PLC leaders at all levels of the organization consistently designed their efforts to support collective capacity around the core work of both collaborative teams and leadership development for the leaders supporting those teams. As we interviewed successful PLC leaders from the classroom to the boardroom about their understanding of and experience with effective leadership efforts, seven common practices emerged (see fig. 1.1, page 14):

1. Creating and sustaining collaborative relationships
2. Aligning systems
3. Facilitating shared responsibility
4. Building coherence and clarity
5. Modeling practices and expectations
6. Reflecting on leadership effectiveness of self and others
7. Developing leadership capacity in self and others

These leadership practices are not hierarchical, nor do they have finite timeframes. As the sphere suggests, they share interconnected relationships.

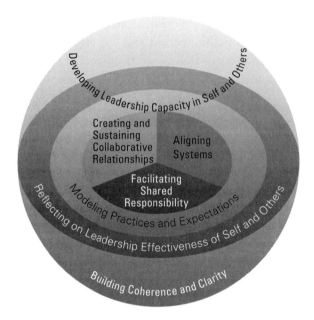

Figure 1.1: The seven leadership practices of highly effective PLC leaders.

In figure 1.1, all things radiate out from the center of the sphere. There are three core leadership practices at the epicenter, or "hub": (1) creating and sustaining collaborative relationships, (2) aligning systems, and (3) facilitating shared responsibility. Effective leaders use *each* of the three practices to facilitate immediate change. Each core practice influences the others; when leaders engage in the core work in interdependent ways, they can generate fantastic student achievement results in short order.

The foundational practice of building coherence and clarity serves as the base of figure 1.1. The deepening of the core work happens when leaders create coherence and clarity along the way. When leaders try to build coherence and clarity *without* launching the actual work, they spend time just studying the concept. Many who launched their PLC journey with a year of exploration have told us they now recognize that they were no further ahead for all the time they invested in helping people first understand conceptually. It is only when changes are *tried* that coherence and clarity can actually take form. On the opposite end of the continuum, leaders who launched their efforts with the three core practices but did not engage in the work of creating coherence and clarity felt they spent all their time repeating rationale and urging teams to move forward. Building coherence and clarity is integral to success, and it underpins all leadership work as a means to deepen understanding.

The two concentric bands of leadership practices that encircle the core work—(1) modeling practices and expectations and (2) reflecting on leadership effectiveness of self and others—serve to extend the work of the core practices as well as broaden the base of building coherence and clarity. In other words, the leadership practices of modeling and reflecting on effectiveness continue an organization's effort to lead a collaborative culture by practicing, refining, and sharing quality work overtly so everyone learns along the way.

The dome of figure 1.1, developing leadership capacity in self and others, serves as the pièce de résistance. The most effective PLC leaders we have met began their work with the understanding that change had to happen throughout the *entire* organization, and that meant beginning with themselves as leaders. Changing practice requires focus and commitment to developing new beliefs and skills. Moreover, they understood that unless they built leadership capacity en route, the changes they implemented would remain leader specific. The dome, then, like the base of the framework, must be integral to the inner workings of all the other leadership practices. It completes the full system for leading and sustaining change. Developing leadership capacity in self and others is the flagship leadership practice; it marks the difference between creating a PLC that is fleeting and creating one that is steadfast.

The seven leadership practices helped us understand how some leaders are better able to create successful, sustainable professional learning communities in their settings. No leadership practice can stand alone, and each leadership practice is interdependent with the entire framework. Since they are interdependent, it is important to have a cursory understanding of each practice before reading the chapters designated to a single practice. Toward that end, an introductory explanation of each practice follows.

Creating and Sustaining Collaborative Relationships

Figure 1.2 (page 16) identifies the most logical and predominant place to begin leading the work of PLCs: creating and sustaining collaborative teams. When effective leaders engage in this leadership practice, they attend to both structure and culture as they lead change efforts.

It is no secret that teams who collaborate can capitalize on their collective wisdom, passion, and creativity. Collaborative teams can create powerful solutions and positive outcomes while moving faster and further as they maximize efficiency and effectiveness. The synergy of collaboration, however, rarely happens with the gathering of job-alike coworkers. In fact, even though the return on investment of organizing work around teams sounds magical, many teachers state outright that they would prefer *not* to collaborate because they understand the toil of the investment. Effective leaders do not leave collaboration to chance. Our colleague Richard DuFour (2011) has often asserted that collaboration by invitation simply does not work.

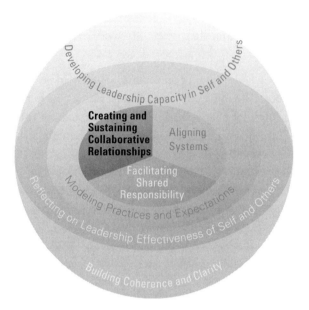

Figure 1.2: **Creating and sustaining collaborative relationships.**

Once teams are in place, leaders need to help them understand the *how* and the *what* of teamwork. Effective leaders provide resources, protocols, templates, and processes to guide team endeavors. In addition, they define their expectations of team products up front, setting parameters for outcomes but remaining flexible regarding methods. For example, some teams require agendas while others do not—teams must decide what will work best for them. An effective leader offers a template as a tool rather than a rule. If, on the other hand, team members can organize their common assessment data so they can cull the answers necessary to adjust instruction and support all of their learners, they may improve on or depart from the template. Outlining criteria in advance will set teams up for success and encourage natural improvements along the way.

Effective leaders don't just hope for a collaborative culture; instead, they establish clear expectations and criteria for quality of the required work and then monitor the conditions that promote a collaborative culture. In addition to monitoring the products of teamwork, they continually survey the culture, making sure all teams are working collaboratively. They develop strategies and tools to help teams who either avoid conflict altogether (by remaining in pseudo community or false consensus) or become embroiled in conflict. However they handle the problems, effective leaders *do* address struggling teams: "When educational leaders at the district or school level avoid confrontation because they favor keeping the peace over productive conflict, they can do tremendous damage to any improvement process" (DuFour, DuFour, Eaker, & Many, 2006, p. 172).

In anticipation of both team- and system-level hurdles, effective leaders identify how they will monitor the conditions that support collaboration and the indicators that align with a healthy, collaborative culture. Likewise, effective leaders acknowledge up front what they are willing to *do* to guarantee that the culture is collaborative. In other words, effective leaders align *actionable* strategies with their desired state. One building principal summarized the importance of this practice with a metaphor:

> I have discovered that when one team is out of alignment with collaborative processes, you can feel it; it's like a flat tire on the car. As you are driving, you can feel the flat tire, but you still have to figure out which one is flat and how you should best position the car on the side of the road so you are not in harm's way as you work to fix it. When the issues are small ones, you can pinpoint and patch the flat a lot quicker. But when the tire (or noncollaborative team) is truly flat, then something has to be done about it and you have to take the time and design some really specific steps to address the flat or that team is never going to move like you need them to move. One flat tire can create an entirely stationary car! (Principal interview, spring 2010)

Aligning Systems to Reflect Vision, Mission, Values, and Goals

Figure 1.3 highlights a leadership practice that must happen in tandem with creating and sustaining collaborative teams: aligning systems. A shift toward collaborative practice requires educational leaders to align systems to support the inherent changes.

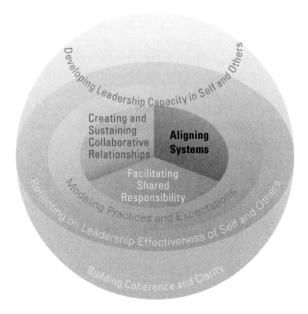

Figure 1.3: Aligning systems to reflect the vision, mission, values, and goals.

In any change process or reform effort, educators often begin by examining or rewriting their vision, mission, values, and goals. However, these exercises, while rich in conversation, stop at being nice exercises if educators do not align the systems to support the words. As DuFour and colleagues (2006) note:

> We have found no correlation between the presence of a written mission statement, or even the wording of a mission statement, and a school's effectiveness as a PLC. The words of a mission statement are not worth the paper they are written on unless people begin to do differently. (p. 19)

Conversely, sometimes educators try to *do* differently before clarifying the organization's collective purpose and direction, which is equally susceptible to failure. In the late 1980s, workshops on cooperative learning were popular. Teachers spent time in training sessions learning the *hows* and *whys* of cooperative learning but returned to schools and classrooms that maintained the misaligned policies and practices of a competitive, bell-curved grading system. The disconnect between what the school system asked teachers to do and what the system valued proved so great that the incredibly powerful instructional strategy of cooperative learning often fell to the wayside as teachers individually struggled to rectify the gap with disgruntled parents and students.

For change to happen, what educators are required to do must parallel what educational leaders know and want. A teacher leader explained the frustration he experiences from the disconnects between stated visions and hiring practices:

> We went through a leadership change to a new principal who wasn't necessarily as knowledgeable about PLCs as our previous principal was. I don't think he [the new principal] understood exactly how important mission and vision plays in our school and so the new hires that we've added to our team . . . aren't necessarily as committed to our core values and beliefs as the teachers who were here from day one. . . . It's really hurt us. I have a passionate commitment to our original mission and vision and values and goals and . . . yet the same commitments aren't there on the part of every teacher in our team and so that creates a natural tension that's hard to work with because we're never on the same page at the same time. It's hard. (Teacher leader interview, spring 2010)

Effective leaders align the organization's practices, policies, and structures to reflect its public promises (vision, mission, values, and goals) so that success is inevitable.

Facilitating Shared Responsibility

Facilitating shared responsibility, figure 1.4, is listed last of the core leadership practices, but it is by no means the third thing leaders do. Effective leaders utilize all three core leadership practices almost simultaneously. Collaborative cultures can only *truly* operate from the place of shared responsibility.

A PLC system (district, school, or individual team) is only as strong as the least committed individual. Facilitating shared responsibility is integral to an effective leader's success in empowering PLCs to act.

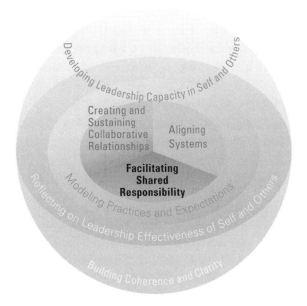

Figure 1.4: Facilitating shared responsibility.

Much of the current literature on leadership highlights the importance of empowering others, sharing responsibilities, and leading by serving. We have found that facilitating shared responsibility involves setting the context and the structures for the *right* work to happen in the *right* places by the *right* people. Since the best decisions about what needs to happen for student learning reside at the classroom level, teaching teams are integral to the decision-making process. Richard Elmore (2002) states:

> Accountability must be a reciprocal process. For every increment of perfor-
> mance I demand from you, I have an equal responsibility to provide you with
> the capacity to meet that expectation. Likewise for every investment you
> make in my skill and knowledge, I have a reciprocal responsibility to dem-
> onstrate some new increment in performance. (p. 5)

Leaders in this context cannot be the givers of answers; instead, they frame the important questions, call the appropriate stakeholders to the table, set the guidelines for the conversation, and then engage the system in finding its own right answers. Building a learning-centered school is not any one person's responsibility; it is everyone's responsibility. One of the central office administrators we interviewed said:

> I always have to ask myself, if I'm expecting them [principals] to accomplish
> a task, what am I doing to support their ability to do that work? If I want
> teachers to write and use common assessments, then what am I doing
> with the principals ahead of time to build their capacity in leading that work
> at the building level? How are we building shared knowledge with them
> so they can employ reciprocal accountability within their buildings too?
> (Assistant superintendent interview, spring 2010)

These three core practices are not new to us, nor would they be to anyone who has a solid understanding of the basic principles of professional learning communities. What did surprise us, however, was our newfound understanding that schools can still achieve great gains in student achievement with just these three practices in place. However, those gains will only last as long as the leader who is orchestrating the changes remains at that school.

Building Coherence and Clarity

Figure 1.5 offers a visual representation of how significant the leadership practice of building coherence and clarity is for the entire framework. Helping individuals understand the *why* and the *what* with consistency is critical. Building coherence and clarity underpins *each* leadership practice. Done well, it moves the work from compliance to ownership.

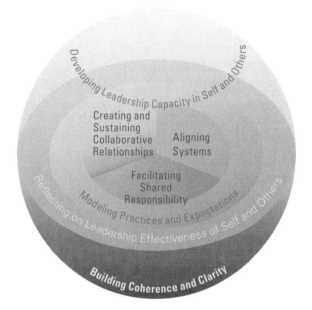

Figure 1.5: **Building coherence and clarity.**

The most effective leaders add the strategy of building coherence and clarity to all of their core practices as a means to support the cultural endeavor of implementing and sustaining the work of PLCs. In fact, the most effective leaders we interviewed repeatedly described the importance of building coherence and clarity—early and consistently—in a PLC setting. The PLC architects state:

> When teachers and administrators have worked together to consider those questions (mission, vision, values and goals) and reach consensus regarding their collective positions on each question, they have built a solid foundations for a PLC. . . . addressing these questions increases the likelihood that all subsequent work will have the benefit of firm underpinnings. If staff

> members have not considered the questions, have done so only superfi-
> cially, or are unable to establish common ground regarding their positions
> on the questions, any and all future efforts to improve the school will stand
> on shaky ground. (DuFour et al., 2010, p. 30)

Given that the PLC architects consistently state the importance of creating the compelling *why* before the *how*, a reader might wonder why it took us so long to get to the
leadership practice of building coherence and clarity. Originally, we also believed
this practice would be the most important practice, residing at the core of the framework. Logically, leaders begin with the compelling *why* before engaging teams in the
how. They understand that "employees in any organization are volunteers. We can compel their attendance and compliance, but only they can volunteer their hearts and minds"
(Reeves, 2006b, p. 52). Change cannot happen unless educators bring people along, and
people will not change without a compelling reason.

We discovered along the way, however, through our experiences as well as in our interviews, that not all leaders engage this practice early in their efforts. Schools can gain high
levels of success by rearranging schedules, aligning systems to support changes, and
encouraging shared participation and empowerment, but those schools devoid of a firm
foundation in the compelling *why* question do indeed "stand on shaky ground." When
the leader leaves or retires, the initiative follows the leader out the door.

Even in our interviews with highly effective leaders, several individuals—from all
ranges of leadership positions—commented that they believed they had built coherence and clarity for the journey by offering a rationale as they progressed along their
path. However, these same individuals realized six months to a year into the work that
they had not built coherence and clarity by simply "providing" a rationale. Each time
they met resistance—whether in a team meeting, a staff meeting, or an administrative
meeting—they realized that *providing* and *building* were two very different things. These
leaders had created their own coherence and clarity, but those with whom they worked
had not adopted the shared ideas. Fortunately, the leaders we interviewed were consum-
mate learners; they recognized their missteps and redirected their efforts to engage their
colleagues in building a personal rationale and shared understanding of their collective
work. Many felt they had lost valuable time, but all clearly achieved high levels of success
in the end. The leadership practice of creating coherence and clarity must serve as the
base to all of the PLC work.

Building coherence and clarity can begin with using clear and consistent language
with shared understanding of what the terms mean. As pedantic as that might sound, it
is a critical first step in a field filled with buzzwords. Several of the superintendents we
interviewed talked about the importance of creating a common vocabulary early in the
process. One superintendent stated:

> We've been deciding what language we are going to keep and what we're
> going to stop using. All of our teaching and learning language is confus-
> ing people. It sounds good, and we might even agree on what it means, but

> it can be confusing to our constituents. I asked everyone to do it, but we
> began by engaging people in looking at the letters I send to the parents. We
> pulled out a plethora of terms and began a long list. We stepped back to
> look at the list and realized we're going to have to decide which terms we'll
> use and which terms we're just going to forget about using for the moment
> because it's not helping bring clarity to the organization. (Superintendent
> interview, spring 2010)

Initiating and sustaining change at the systems level requires the engagement of the entire system:

> When a school functions as a PLC, staff members attempt to answer ques-
> tions and learn together. When all staff members have access to the same
> information, it increases the likelihood that they will arrive at similar conclu-
> sions. Without access to pertinent information, they resort to debating opin-
> ions or retreating to a muddied middle ground. (DuFour et al., 2006, p. 16)

In the absence of coherence and clarity, change becomes confusing, chaotic, and ulti-mately unwieldy. It is virtually impossible to overcommunicate in times of change, so strong leaders employ leadership practices that consistently create systemwide coher-ence and clarity.

The leadership practice of building coherence and clarity is foundational to building a professional learning community. It is imperative to everything educators do—in and beyond the classroom. All of the leadership practices that follow are embedded in the leader's effort to continue building coherence and clarity. Likewise, these strategies shift the focus of the leadership practices from leading to learn to learning to lead.

Modeling Practices and Expectations

Modeling practices and expectations, figure 1.6, surrounds the core of the framework. Effective leaders use modeling for both their work and their expectations regarding each of the core practices. They also engage in modeling as a means to continue to build coherence and clarity.

One of the most important things a leader can do is model for those who follow. As Kouzes and Posner (2007) note, "Exemplary leaders know that if they want to gain com-mitment and achieve the highest standards, they must be models of the behavior they expect of others. Leaders model the way" (p. 15). Modeling as a way of teaching involves clarifying expectations, committing to people and values, putting words to action, show-ing people the way, and—equally important—earning trust and respect while creating a culture of collective efficacy. People follow people—not grandiose plans.

A National Board Certified teacher leader offered the following regarding his efforts to model within and beyond his PLC:

> Even I get nervous when we sit down to look at results simply because
> I'm afraid that I'm going to be judged by my teammates . . . comfort with
> "transparency" is something that I don't think many teachers have. I think

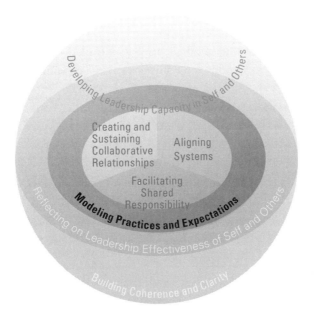

Figure 1.6: Modeling practices and expectations.

> a school leader who is willing to model transparency about [his] own work
> would be more successful at getting other teachers to embrace [the] foun-
> dational principles of PLCs. . . . I consciously try to model things when I
> know that I have to step forward and run a particular session . . . or activ-
> ity. I'm very aware of what it is that I'm doing and when the session is over
> I'm able to go back to those teachers and say, "Hey, did you notice what I
> did today? What was good about it? What was bad about it? Can you give
> me some feedback on it?" I do this so that they are reflecting about the pro-
> cess of getting something done as opposed to just the content of what it is
> that we did. (Teacher leader interview, spring 2010)

As this teacher leader suggests, effective leaders model more than just the protocols and strategies they ask their staff to employ. Leaders model curiosity, risk taking, collaboration, a focus on learning, and a focus on results. In other words, the work of modeling extends to all parts of the leadership framework, and it serves as the bridge to developing leadership capacity in others. Leaders model being teachers *and* learners (Daloz Parks, 2005; DuFour et al., 2008; Kouzes & Posner, 2007; Pfeffer & Sutton, 2006; Senge, 2006; Tichy, 2004; Tichy & Cohen, 2002). As Eaker and Keating (2009) write, "Simply put, student learning is positively affected by the quality of the professional learning of adults, and the quality of professional learning within school districts must not be left to chance" (p. 50). Modeling, a powerful form of staff development, leads to practice, and practice provides experiences that enable individuals to develop their own tacit knowledge about the work at hand.

Reflecting on Leadership Effectiveness of Self and Others

Figure 1.7 highlights our understanding that reflecting on leadership effectiveness encompasses all of the previous strategies; effective leaders reflect on all of their leadership efforts. Reflection also builds and refines continued coherence and clarity.

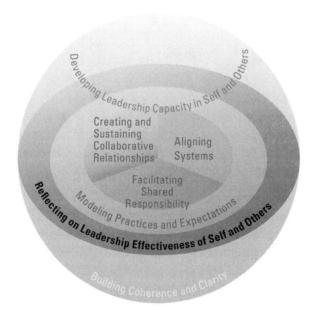

Figure 1.7: Reflecting on leadership effectiveness of self and others.

Reflection on current or new knowledge and past experiences is the only way effective leaders can develop and solidify their craft—always working to hone and refine their own effectiveness. Reflection is powerful, because masterful leaders cull through broad experiences and key learnings to find patterns, explore their own tacit knowledge, and discover insights that will strengthen and affirm future efforts to lead. As Reeves states, "Reflective leaders take time to think about the lessons learned, record their small wins and setbacks, document conflicts between values and practice, identify the difference between idiosyncratic behavior and long-term pathologies, and notice trends that emerge over time" (Reeves, 2006b, p. 49). Effective leaders lead from a place of incredible self-awareness and self-monitoring. A teacher leader we interviewed offered the following thoughts about her leadership:

> I've made so many mistakes; most often I find it's when I impose my way of doing things. I've learned I need to be more concerned about the outcome and then find ways to help the team get there. I've had to learn to let other people be in charge of their own process and learning. I've learned that if there's a specific outcome I want, then I can give the team a structure through a template, but I think we're better off when things are just open ended for the team to work through, as uncomfortable as that sometimes

might be. I've also learned that the team sometimes thinks that it can't meet my expectations. I have to be more careful about giving parameters and telling people what I'm looking for and helping them to see how their vision also fits in with that. (Teacher leader interview, spring 2010)

Reflective practitioners are lifelong learners. As Senge (2006) notes:

> People with a high level of personal mastery live in a continual learning mode. They never "arrive." . . . It is a process. It is a lifelong discipline. People with a high level of personal mastery are acutely aware of their ignorance, their incompetence, their growth areas. And they are deeply self-confident. Paradoxical? Only for those who do not see the "journey is the reward." (p. 133)

These lifelong learners are voracious readers; they read all they can get their hands on about leadership, within and outside the field of education, and they even read what they disagree with so they can better understand the alternative perspectives. They are open to feedback—in fact, they seek it as a primary source of information about their own effectiveness. They find and tap into every potential resource at their disposal to support their own learning curve. They know they are in charge of their own learning journey, and they strive to master their own leadership skills. As Collins (2005) states, there is no stopping point when striving for excellence:

> No matter how much you have achieved, *you will always be merely good relative to what you can become.* Greatness is an inherently dynamic process, not an end point. The moment you think of yourself as great, your slide toward mediocrity will have already begun. (p. 9)

Developing Leadership Capacity in Self and Others

Figure 1.8 (page 26) highlights the cap of all leadership practices, which involves developing internal leaders who can do the work of all of the previously mentioned leadership practices. It is significant for building organizationwide capacity and sustainability.

It is one thing to engage teams in the work of PLCs—from that place, they can do the work and make gains in student achievement. It is quite another, however, to develop the leadership capacity of everyone within the organization as *part of the work leaders do.* The effective leader's

> task is not only to help people throughout the organization acquire the knowledge and skills to solve the intractable challenges of today, but also to develop their capacity and confidence to tackle the unforeseen challenges that will emerge in the future. (DuFour et al., 2006, p. 185)

The distinction is significant. It will determine the difference between PLCs that survive and PLCs that thrive; between PLCs that simply manage their work and PLCs that self-mobilize in response to their ongoing, emerging concerns; between PLCs that rely on existing tool kits and PLCs that actively search for new innovations and patterns of

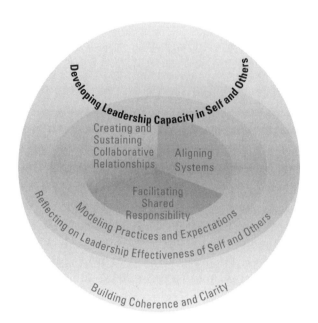

Figure 1.8: Developing leadership capacity in self and others.

behavior; and between PLCs that get results based on who's leading and those that get results despite who's leading. The former might create a newsworthy breakthrough story, but the latter creates a culture of learning and a legacy of excellence.

The notion of developing leadership capacity in PLCs is widely accepted and promoted. Yet some fear it is not happening. In his article titled "Leading Professional Learning," systems-thinking expert Michael Fullan writes:

> The spread of professional learning communities is about the proliferation of leadership. Henry Mintzberg, in his book *Managers Not MBAs*, captured this when he observed that "leadership is not about making clever decisions. . . . It is about energizing other people to make good decisions and do better things." Doing better things is all about cultures of professional learning. PLCs need to be seen explicitly in this light or they will go the way of just another innovation that captures the limelight ephemerally. (2006, p. 14)

Indeed, many schools implementing PLCs have existing leaders who make clever decisions and get results. The practice of developing leadership capacity in self and others is about energizing everyone, *including the self as leader*, to strive for mastery. During our interviews, an assistant superintendent offered her perspective on doing better:

> A leader in a professional learning community has to be very comfortable with distributing responsibility amongst staff. . . . Ultimately, the responsibility of the leader of the PLC is to develop the talent of the staff you're working with so that they are able to lead others in collaborative discussion and decisions. A principal must really shift from that whole hierarchy

approach to one where he or she is building a matrix of leadership amongst the staff. . . . Right now, as the assistant superintendent, I'm doing that same work with a group of principals. Building that matrix of leadership is really critical because as PLCs we need to have people who will be out working with teachers to facilitate the collaboration that needs to be done in a PLC. I think rather than the hierarchical, directive approach to leadership, a PLC leader has the responsibility as a leader to develop the strengths and talents of others and to facilitate the learning of a group of leaders in the building so that they can facilitate the work of their colleagues. (Assistant superintendent interview, spring 2010)

In some cases, educational leaders assume people know how to lead just as they assume teams understand how to be collaborative. Effective leaders realize they must monitor for collaboration. The remarkable leaders we interviewed, those who we would deem "a cut above" the norm, also realized they had to develop the leadership capacity in others: "widely dispersed leadership is essential in building and sustaining PLCs, and it is important that individuals *at all levels* lead effectively" (DuFour et al., 2006, p. 185, italics added). Developing leadership capacity in others is the rarely found but clearly indispensable condition of highly effective PLC teams, schools, and school systems *that last*.

The Journey

The work of transforming schools into PLCs requires systematic change. For systems change to occur on a larger scale, district and district leaders, schools and school leaders, and teams and teacher leaders must all learn from one another. Fullan (2008) calls this *lateral capacity building*, and we found it to be absolutely crucial for widespread and systematic reform. Such reform simply will not happen without thoughtful and intentional leadership by design.

The journey of leadership in districts, schools, and teams is not an easy one. It is, however, vitally important.

CHAPTER TWO

Creating and Sustaining Collaborative Relationships

> The collaborative team is the fundamental building block of the organization. A PLC is composed of collaborative teams whose members work interdependently to achieve common goals—goals linked to the purpose of learning for all—for which members are held mutually accountable.
>
> —DuFour, DuFour, and Eaker

At the heart of it all, the work of a PLC requires collaboration. Effective leaders begin the PLC journey by building the community in both structure and culture—efforts that require all three of the core leadership practices to launch simultaneously. The paradigm shift from autonomous classrooms to collaborative teams, however, places the early emphasis and focused discussion on the notion of collaboration. This leadership practice does not happen in isolation from the other practices, but it is one of the most *visible* places to signal that a change in behaviors is expected. As schedules change and leaders work to empower teams, educators can immediately see that the work of collaboration has begun.

Yet collaboration requires a set of skills and belief systems that are often assumed to be natural and readily available to any team player. Anyone who has tried to implement the work of professional learning communities quickly realizes that such is not the case. Teams not only need to be productive, they need to be *healthy*. Effective leaders must monitor for both health and productivity in their collaborative teams. Both aspects are important when teams try to accomplish tasks. One aspect can either trump or feed the success of the other aspect. In the ideal, teams would be both healthy and productive.

Engineering Success

Often, when leaders organize people into teams, they ask them to function collaboratively without much support or guidance, perhaps assuming that the process of working together will be both straightforward and intuitive. We have discovered, however, that collaboration is neither straightforward nor intuitive—in any industry. Research conducted across industries on teaming continues to highlight how desirable yet challenging true teaming really is; in fact, many leaders deem the work of creating and sustaining collaborative cultures to be their primary challenge (Wolff, Druskat, Koman, & Messer, 2006). In their ongoing quest to understand effective teaming, Wolff and colleagues (2006) find that "social interactions create emotion and that the frequency of required interactions in a group amplifies the need for emotional intelligence in a group setting" (p. 224). Teams need to understand how to navigate emotion and conflict safely.

A healthy team can create and sustain an environment that enables the individuals' knowledge, skills, and expertise to be accessed and used effectively, resulting in the collective capacity to achieve success (Druskat, Sala, & Mount, 2006). A healthy team is responsive and adaptive to both the needs of the individuals and the work of the team. If discrepancies arise between members or ideas, the team proactively and optimistically rectifies the differences while maintaining the appropriate course of action to address the tasks at hand. Healthy teams are mature, competent, and authentic in their social interactions. This is not to suggest that team members are all close friends or that they even like one another, for that matter. In healthy teams, individuals set aside personal interests and dislikes so the group can be effective. In most cases, once a healthy team has found its synergy, members develop deep levels of trust and mutual respect for one another.

Productive teams get the job done. Their common purpose and mission guide them, and they create the products or ideas required to yield formidable results. They delineate the expectations of the team and its members and then hold one another mutually accountable (Druskat et al., 2006). Productive teams are always aiming for continuous improvement, so learning is integral to how they understand and refine their craft. In the spirit of accomplishment, productive teams are always looking for the win; when they miss a target, they can readily identify the learning they gained as a result to improve for future opportunities. Productive teams are efficient with time and resources so they can maximize their potential to be generative.

Leaders dedicated to creating and sustaining a collaborative culture might find the work daunting—especially in a profession in which the historical norm is to work in isolation, which has created a strong culture of individual autonomy. Daunting though it may be, the true work of meaningful collaboration and powerful teaming is not insurmountable; however, it requires a fundamental paradigm shift in both beliefs and actions across the organization.

Collaboration is as much about beliefs and culture as it is about skills and practices. Educators don't always believe that becoming more collaborative is necessarily a good thing. Toward that end, effective leaders have learned to support the necessary beliefs with rationale while moving forward in the work rather than waiting for everyone to come on board with their beliefs. When leaders work to change behaviors first, they can help staff see the benefits through results.

Change happens more rapidly, consistently, and effectively when educators see results firsthand. Clear evidence discovered at the local level creates a far more compelling argument than the research cited from theorists elsewhere—even when the plethora of expert research is irrefutable. The *Harvard Business Review* article "The Uncompromising Leader" quotes Doug Conant, CEO of Campbell Soup, as saying, "You can't talk your way out of something you've behaved your way into. You have to behave your way out of it" (Eisenstat, Beer, Foote, Fredberg, & Norrgren, 2008, p. 54). Beliefs are foundational, and individuals will not change beliefs just because someone said they should; rather, they will change beliefs when positive results from changed behaviors offer startling awakenings into what might work better.

Striving for Team Health With Norms: A Proactive Approach

As stated earlier, collaborative teams need to be both healthy and productive. One strategy leaders use to move teams toward being healthy is to engage them in creating team norms. Developing group norms is not only a task that immediately generates a team product; it is also an early opportunity to engage team members in collaborative conversations regarding their individual hopes and fears about functioning on the team. New skills, new ways of behaving and believing regarding familiar work, especially within the context of preexisting relationships, can cause stress, worry, and an increased sense of vulnerability (Wolff et al., 2006). Teams can best develop interpersonal understanding and group awareness with specific, facilitated conversations about needs and expectations for each other in advance of the changes and challenges they will experience when teaming.

Norms are most commonly defined as a group's agreements—implied and explicit—for meeting conduct. Many teams begin developing norms by identifying conversational niceties or professional etiquette, such as *we are going to show up on time, we are all going to contribute, we commit to turning our cell phones off,* and so on. Sometimes, in a misguided attempt to create initial comfort with changes in practice, teams include norms that accidentally or intentionally preserve the status quo. For example, *we agree to disagree* might sound desirable and even respectful when, in fact, it is actually enabling a culture of independent contractors that is counterproductive to collectively ensuring quality and systematically cocreating shared understanding of the best-practice strategies for teaching and learning. When leaders who facilitate the work of setting norms have a firm understanding that quality teaming involves confronting the practices, behaviors, and beliefs that do not align with the organization's values, they have better success in helping teams shape the norms that will empower healthy team development.

The standards for professional conduct should be a given in any educational setting, and norms are much more than pleasant discussion guidelines. We suggest a different definition: *norms* are our collective, public promises to keep one another safe while working collaboratively. Leaders need to employ team norms both in and out of meetings, as collaboration is the way the team or organization does business, and *business* requires navigating through tumultuous situations and complex problem solving at all times—not just during team meetings.

When teams truly engage in using the norms they have created, they learn by doing—literally working their way into developing the interpersonal congruence needed to complete teamwork successfully. Interpersonal congruence is critical to team health:

> Another recent study found that interpersonal congruence, defined as the degree to which team members feel other members accurately know and understand them personally, was linked to high levels of social integration and group identification within the team and low levels of emotional conflict (Polzer, Milton, Swann, & William, in press). The same study also found that in teams with high levels of interpersonal congruence, team member diversity enhanced creative task performance. McAllister (1995) showed that interpersonally attentive behavior within a group helps build interpersonal trust and safety, which have been found to trigger the cooperation and knowledge sharing (Larkey, 1996; Rousseau, Sitkin, Burt, & Camerer, 1998) that increase group effectiveness (Campion, Medsker, & Higgs, 1993). (Wolff et al., 2006, p. 230)

We have discovered that teams overlook several important issues when setting norms. Norm setting must address and accomplish these things:

- Create consistency and clarity regarding nebulous or soft terms (such as *respect*).
- Secure individual, public statements of commitment to the norms.
- Develop agreements on strategies to hold one another accountable to the norms.
- Generate collective understanding of how the team will function collaboratively when an individual does not agree but the will of the group is clear and the team is moving forward.

These issues are seldom addressed, and yet they are critical to turning norms into true promises that create a sense of safety for a team. Some concepts, such as respect, offer fertile ground for a multitude of personal perceptions without detailed definition. What does respect look like in action? What does it *not* look like? Everyone has a different definition of *respect*, and if one team member's idea does not match another's, then that individual can unwittingly offend others.

Once a team has created its norms, it is fair and important to require each individual team member—in round-robin fashion and one person at a time—to respond to the question, Is there any norm on this list with which you cannot live? This is very different from asking, Do we all agree to these norms? Teams operate on false consensus when they call for agreement through choral group response and some individuals simply choose to remain silent. If a team member claims it would be difficult to abide by one or more of the norms, the entire team must discuss the matter until they have addressed the norm, the team's understanding of the norm, or the potential behavior in agreeable terms. Imagine, for example, that Paul says he can't live with the norm of being on time right now since he's responsible for getting his four-year-old son to daycare and the child has recently taken to refusing to get dressed in the mornings. He'll try, he says, but every morning seems full of unhappy surprises as he struggles with his noncompliant son. The moment Paul makes the statement, the team must discuss it and decide what will change—the team norm or the individual behavior. In this case, the team decides that being on time really is one of their expected norms. They agree, however, that if Paul ends up being late due to family complications, which they all understand from their own personal experiences, then he should plan to slide into the meeting already in progress without causing a disruption, and during a break, he should follow up with someone to get up to speed on the parts he missed. Everyone agrees to the terms, and the team moves on to the next person to ask, "Is there any norm on our list with which you cannot live?" until everyone on the team has publicly acknowledged they can live with the norms or the team has developed a strategy for managing a complication regarding a norm. This is *not* to excuse conduct unbecoming of a true team; rather, it is to acknowledge that life challenges foil a team's best plans if the team does not address the various scenarios when making commitments. Healthy teams demonstrate an interpersonal understanding of each member. Teams will only have *shared* agreements after soliciting each individual's public response and addressing it in mutually agreeable terms.

With those agreements must come the specific language, strategies, and collective permission to confront broken norms. Norms are just nice words on a page if teams are not willing to answer the question, What will we do the first time—and every time—a norm is broken? In the absence of a clear and agreed-upon plan, the team does not really have agreements; with or without intent—norms *will* be broken. A team's ability to confront and hold one another mutually responsible transforms stated agreements into true promises. If team members do not have a shared understanding of their own intervention plan, then one team member's confronting style might offend others, eroding trust and perpetuating the issues that created unhealthy habits in the first place.

Finally, effective leaders facilitate collaborative conversations regarding how the team will make agreements. Likewise, they share examples and even rehearse how healthy team members might respond if the team makes a decision that an individual did not vote to support. Passive or blatant aggressive behaviors during meetings and sabotage behaviors outside the meeting are the hallmarks of unhealthy team players, but tolerating those behaviors to avoid confrontation is the hallmark of an unhealthy team. As Wolff et al. (2006) note, "Groups that ignore inappropriate member behavior in an attempt to avoid conflict decrease their ability to solve problems that are often conspicuous. Avoiding conflict frequently results in hostility and reduced performance" (p. 230). Education has a long-standing history of leaving individuals to their fiefdoms without challenging beliefs or behaviors that are not conducive to ensuring success for all learners. Healthy teams challenge unproductive patterns.

Once norms are created and agreed upon, team leaders still need to model using the norms and enacting the agreements created to challenge broken norms. Building leaders also participate in creating healthy cultures and structures by modeling norms and holding individuals mutually responsible for team agreements. One of the principals we interviewed recognized the need to model for her teachers:

> I try to model our faculty meetings using the same idea of effective teams, so we also have norms. Because I wanted the teams to always focus on student achievement, looking at data, and determining student needs, we had norms about those things in our staff meetings. I make sure team meetings are never about field trips and other scheduling things, so I try to model our faculty meetings the same way that a team meeting should be held. (Principal interview, spring 2010)

Moving Beyond Norms

Engineering for success always involves beginning with the end in mind. Beyond simply sharing the expectation that teams collaborate in healthy and productive ways, effective leaders develop a conceptual framework of what they require their teams to know, do, and produce in their work. The PLC literature advocates developing team norms so that teams can successfully focus their energy and efforts on creating and navigating the required products. Norms alone are not enough, however; the teams and systems that thrive early are those that spend time building coherence and clarity around the desired processes and products for teams.

Since leaders are asking educators to function differently, it helps when they share a conceptual framework for what *differently* actually looks like. When we are out in the field, many teachers approach us to say, "We understand our district wants us to work collaboratively, but we're not really sure what it looks like. Do you have any schools we can visit that are doing this work or any videos of teachers engaged in a PLC conversation so we can see it in action?" Effective leaders take the time to define what healthy and productive teams look like, and they develop the tools, resources, templates, and protocols that will enable teams to quickly function in the desired manner.

Simply handing teams definitions and lists does not work, just as handing teachers a list of standards has not worked to ensure learning. Leaders make sure that teams develop a concept of quality teaming as it aligns to the organization's framework for healthy and productive teams. One of the principals we interviewed explained it this way:

> I think an effective leader has to have a vision. They must understand what success looks like within that vision, and they have to have other people understand what success looks like too. Then, if it's not happening, that's where the rubber hits the road, and we can move teams into action. (Principal interview, spring 2010)

In this manner, everyone across the organization can begin with a shared understanding of quality teaming.

Effective leaders who facilitate the important work of collaboration leave little to chance. They anticipate the needs and concerns of the teams. They proactively plan while acknowledging that a perfect pathway would be impossible. They lead from a place of learning and demonstrate a willingness to make adjustments along the way. To do so, they must create the knowledge, skills, and tools to support their success. Just like the collaborative teams they are supporting, effective leaders design for success by back mapping their way through the four corollary PLC questions (DuFour et al., 2008):

1. What is it we want our teams to know and be able to do?

2. How will we know when teams know it?

3. What will we do when teams don't know it?

4. What will we do when teams already have learned it?

When organizations engage leaders in answering the four corollary questions, they experience the very work they are requiring of their teams and teammates. This enables them to effectively model the work for others. In addition, answering the four questions requires leaders to create their own tools and resources with which to guide and support teams.

Clarifying the Knows and Dos of Collaborative Work

Strong leaders work tirelessly with their teams to help them become more effective in asking important questions such as the following:

- **What is the work of collaborative teams?** (For example, answering the four corollary questions, focusing on learning, and attending to results) What have we already done to address those kinds of questions in our current system? What resources have we generated from our past work that will support our current efforts? What do we need to add or change in our current work?

- **What are the common characteristics of healthy and productive teams?** (For example, trust, respect, rapport, and positive attitudes) Are they characteristics we can develop?

- **What are the practices or processes of healthy and productive teams?** (For example, probing ideas, pausing to listen, seeking feedback, and proactive problem solving) What are the best ways to nurture a team's capacity to practice healthy habits?

- **What are the tools and protocols that will best support meaningful conversations in short periods of time?** (For example, team norms, agendas, data dialogue protocols, role clarity, and shared facilitation) Do our existing resources support this kind of work? What are we missing? What might we need to tweak?

- **What are the successful ways that healthy and productive teams navigate conflict as it arises?** (For example, willingness to confront with a caring orientation, positive assumptions, and courteous probing)

- **Who in our system or team is best positioned to help and in what ways?** What are the various virtuosities and assets of our own staff so that we might capitalize on our strengths and grow our capacity from within?

Fortunately, many research-based frameworks and aligned tools already exist to help answer most of our questions regarding effective teams (DuFour et al., 2008; Garmston & Wellman, 2009; Wolff et al., 2006).

Identifying the desired knows and dos of teamwork leads into a natural self-assessment: *Where are our teams now?* Effective leaders engage teams in self-assessments and scan the current situation as a means of identifying immediate and long-range action steps:

- Where are we now relative to the ideal standard for our work as defined in the research?

- What are our strengths, weaknesses, opportunities, and threats as we move in this direction?

When leaders facilitate these kinds of conversations, they are able to hear the concerns of their staff, facilitate the necessary next steps, and build coherence and clarity around the expectations for their teams.

Monitoring for Success

Once leaders identify a team's knowledge and skills, they most often want to start offering training opportunities, assuming that knowledge is necessary to fill any gaps. While this approach may be common, it is rarely effective. Pfeffer and Sutton (2006) suggest that there are a number of reasons why organizations are unable to close the knowing-doing gap, not the least of which is that "training" often becomes a barrier to action. Thoughtful leaders, including the teacher leader of the team, stop to consider first, How will we know when the team has learned the new information? In other words, they create the assessment first, before aligning the curriculum or designing the lesson: the same work that an effective teacher would do to achieve targeted and meaningful classroom instruction (Wiggins & McTighe, 2005). Effective leaders begin with the end in mind; they design backward so they can provide more focused and specific support for adult learning. This support may not always entail training. When leaders design the tools and processes to monitor for successful collaboration in advance of implementation, it enables them to track what must be *done*, so that they can formatively assess what must be *known* to better support the work. This approach also helps them find the best way to offer information for a knowledge gap—often in a collaborative setting that requires learning by doing rather than learning by listening. Effective leaders make sure they have sufficiently addressed the essence of the work the team must accomplish. The clarity and focus they gain when they begin with the end in mind provides them with the framework for tight/loose structures and empowers everyone to make quality, prioritized, systemic choices along the way.

There is a well-known adage that what gets monitored, gets done. For many, the concept of monitoring strikes immediate discord, and that makes sense, given that education has so many poor examples of monitoring in high-stakes, penalty-based, obstructive systems. Sadly, we can cite case after case of such monitoring systems replicated at local levels. For example, a local union challenged the administration in one district to stop all collaborative work after one year if the district did not make a staggering gain in student achievement by that time. So the administration decided to attend *each* collaborative meeting, clipboard in hand, to evaluate whether teachers were truly using the process they were so eager to discard. No party wins in a case such as this. It is a lose-lose proposition, and it is not at all what we mean by *monitoring*.

Quality monitoring is good teaching. Master teachers are constantly on the lookout for learning in action, and they hunt for evidence of the learners' struggles and successes so they can continue to help all learners succeed at higher levels. Strong leaders are good teachers (Lieberman & Miller, 2004; Senge, 2006; Tichy & Cohen, 2002), and they begin by designing the systems and tools that will set everyone up for success along the way. Leaders who monitor well are putting formative assessment into action at the professional development level.

To support the work of monitoring, effective leaders develop plans that address the following questions:

- **The what**—What is the team process, practice, or event worth monitoring?

- **The how**—What are the tools, protocols, or processes we could use to gather evidence of the things we are monitoring?

- **The success indicators**—What evidence will we seek from each data-gathering activity?

- **The who**—Who will we charge with the task of gathering data and seeking the indicators of success from the things we are monitoring?

- **The response plan**—How will we acknowledge good work when it is happening? What are we willing to do if it is not happening?

When leaders are concerned with creating clarity regarding the work, they engage the staff in answering these questions. Engaging others in developing a simple chart or template can easily help everyone involved understand the work of monitoring collaborative cultures with data. Table 2.1 (page 38) outlines an example of the *what*, the *how*, the *success indicators*, the *who* for monitoring, and the *response plan* for times when teams struggle. Highly effective PLC leaders attend to these details as they establish their support systems for collaboration. Such planning provides leaders with focal points, tight/loose clarity, response plans, and contingency options when things don't work perfectly.

Many of the commonly identified options for monitoring (observations, interviews, round table discussions, surveys, and so on) require the direct involvement of collaborative leaders. In our travels to work with teams across North America, we have found leaders who believed it was not their place to involve themselves in the work of their teams for a variety of reasons: (1) it would send the message that they don't trust the teams, (2) it would be in direct conflict with their effort to empower others, as their presence often leads to an administrative to-do list when the meeting is done, (3) it would alter

Table 2.1: Beginning With the End in Mind for PLC Success

The What: Team process, practice, or event to monitor	The How: Tools and materials to gather evidence	The Success Indicators: Evidence (data) to seek in tools and materials	The Who: Person(s) responsible for monitoring	The Response Plan: What we are willing to do if it is or is not happening
Team product example: Team identifies the priority standards or learning expectations.	The list of expectations by semester	Learning targets are posted in a variety of locations and mediums: Curriculum maps and classroom walls Teacher web pages Parent newsletters Student portfolios	Team leaders, department chairs, or grade-level leaders Administration or site leadership (guiding coalition) team	Administration meets with department chair and maps out a facilitation plan with supporting resources. Administration brings struggling teams to a general location to facilitate supporting processes.
Team product example: Team builds common formative assessments.	The actual assessments	Learning targets align with team learning schedule and enduring understandings.	Team leaders, department chairs, or grade-level leaders Administration or site leadership (guiding coalition) team	Administration meets with department chair and maps out a facilitation plan with supporting resources. Administration sits with teams to create common formative assessments.
Team health example: Team engages in proactive problem solving.	Team self-assessment Observations Interviews	Team discussions seek solutions in anticipation of possible concerns. There is a reduction in the number of problems a team must address.	Team leaders, department chairs, or grade-level leaders Administration or site leadership (guiding coalition) team	Team leaders and/or administrators provide staff with problem-solution protocols, such as a force-field analysis or best possible outcome decision-making grid. Team leaders or administrators facilitate staffwide conversations to identify possible problems and brainstorm potential solutions.
Team health example: Team confronts with caring orientation. (Wolff et al., 2006)	Team self-assessment Observations Interviews	Agreement among team members that their conflicts are managed carefully and completely. Increase in team collegiality and shared decisions.	Team leaders, department chairs, or grade-level leaders Administration or site leadership (guiding coalition) team	Team leaders or administrators provide staff with conflict management support at staff meetings. Team leaders or administrators role-play options.

team dynamics, and so on. There is a nugget of truth in all these concerns, but we submit that these assumptions are based on an old paradigm of monitoring as evaluation, rather than monitoring as formative assessment to *support* teams in their learning.

Obviously, teacher leaders must be involved with their teams, as they are integral to the meetings. The successful teacher leaders we interviewed used quality formative assessment practices to monitor and support their team's success. Teacher leaders strive to espouse and model healthy team practices while facilitating the team's development of critical products. Moreover, they take important and calculated risks in confronting unproductive or unhealthy habits and activities, and they focus on the positive as they catch and celebrate excellence in action.

Teacher leaders create multiple opportunities for teams to self-monitor. Such monitoring will develop a deeper understanding of the work and bring issues they need to address to the surface. This strategy of "team self-evaluation encourages the surfacing and evaluation of routines or habits that may be compromising team effectiveness. Evaluating the status quo is a prerequisite for positive team development and team effectiveness" (Wolff et al., 2006, p. 230). Strong teacher leaders make self-monitoring an integral part of the team's work. They seek feedback regarding their own performance as the team facilitator and the team's performance overall using regular processes, such as team meeting exit slips, meeting evaluation forms, or group discussions around the plus/delta/more strategy (plus: What did we do well today? delta: What could we have done better today? more: What do we still need to accomplish or address moving forward?).

Sometimes the leaders we interviewed used more formal processes, such as anonymous team surveys or formal discussions on how well the team was adhering to norms or accomplishing tasks. In all cases, the effective leaders we interviewed learned to depersonalize the feedback, removing ego and aligning the information received to the work of the team and to opportunities for improvement. They also learned to honor the feedback by acknowledging it at the beginning of the next meeting and highlighting the changes that would be made as a result of the team's valuable input.

More than that, strong leaders also checked on the well-being of their team "offline," at unscheduled and informal times. They were strategic about how they handled sensitive matters as well. For example, in a 2009–2010 case study, one strong teacher leader was concerned about how her team always seemed to speak negatively about the students. She knew that if she launched the conversation about a bad team behavior, the team would not receive it well and might conceivably turn on *her*. To avoid that and still address the problem, she opted to discuss it individually with each colleague at her grade level by asking for his or her support in making a culture change, saying, for example:

> Sometimes I get stressed when I hear us speaking negatively about the children with whom we work. I know myself well enough to understand that verbalized negative thoughts might impact how I view that child too. I would like to invite you to join me in changing that practice. Together, if we avoid talking that way ourselves, and if we support each other in stopping

> it when it happens, I think we can make a big difference and help the team
> think more positively about our learners.

The team responded well to her approach, and the problem stopped almost instantly.

Building administration must also remain attuned to the health and productivity of its teams. Effective leaders find ways to formatively assess teams without the heavy hand of evaluation, or worse, the hands-off approach of empowerment by absentia. Members of one administrative team, for example, believed they should be available to all teams, so they decided to remain in their individual offices while the teams worked together during collaborative time. These administrators had the best interest of teams at heart: they wanted teams to be able to find them easily if any came seeking help. Unfortunately, their plan backfired. They accidently sent the message that collaboration was only for teachers, and tremendous resentment spread across the teams over time. Building administrators weren't present at teacher team meetings, so they did not recognize the resentment until it became a major cultural issue in the building.

Consider this contrasting example of a principal in another setting who was curious about what was happening with his teams. This principal was enthusiastic about seeking out and claiming celebrations for the whole staff so that he could both support their work and leverage continued motivation with small wins along the way. He engaged the assistant principal and the dean of students to function with him as an administrative collaborative team. He assigned each member to support several teams in the building for that year, and they rotated the teams in subsequent years so that all administration team members shared responsibility for all the teams. They agreed to conduct their work using their version of the four corollary questions regarding the teaching teams in their building (DuFour et al., 2008):

1. What is it we want our teams to know and be able to do?

2. How will we know when teams know it?

3. What will we do when teams don't know it?

4. What will we do when teams already have learned it?

Each administrator rotated to the different teams on his or her list for the year—sometimes spending entire meetings with one team and sometimes visiting a few teams in one day. The teams in the building understood that their designated support administrator would be dropping in and out of their meetings and that they could request support from that individual or any other administrator as needed.

The administrative team always scheduled its meetings to occur before and after the building collaborative team meetings so that administrators could predetermine their look-fors regarding the upcoming collaborative team meetings and their formative findings following the collaborative team meetings. The administrative team also clarified expectations for its own work. To do that, they put the staff in cross-team groupings (including themselves in the groups) and held a carousel brainstorming session during one of the buildingwide staff meetings. They posted the following questions on four posters, and then teams rotated from poster to poster and added their thoughts on each question:

1. What is the work of collaborative teams in a PLC?

2. What is *not* the work of collaborative teams in a PLC?

3. What is the work of the administrative team in a PLC?

4. What is *not* the work of the administrative team in a PLC?

Administrators discussed the results of each poster with the staff during the meeting and concluded by agreeing to bring the typed results back to the teams for final approval on their collective agreements. Figure 2.1 outlines one school's resulting information from their process for clarifying expectations of all members of the professional learning community. Such work clarifies what is meant by *empowerment* in a culture of shared responsibility and leadership.

What is the work of collaborative teams in a PLC?	What is not the work of collaborative teams in a PLC?
Work collaboratively at all times, following team norms.	Spend time navigating logistics and details that do not support our efforts to answer the four questions.
Focus on student learning in all discussions by working to answer the four corollary questions.	Worry about issues beyond our control.
Use common assessments and data or evidence for all decision making.	Make decisions that negatively impact any other team in this building.
Engage in action research to explore answers to questions about what works best for teaching and learning.	Make excuses.
Create interventions and enrichments to help move all learners forward.	
What is the work of the administrative team in a PLC?	**What is not the work of the administrative team in a PLC?**
Rotate from team to team.	Judge harshly.
Hold teams accountable for the work.	Participate in every PLC meeting.
Gather evidence about what's working and what's not working.	Do the teams' work for them.
Seek ways to support team success, helping remove hurdles and reallocate resources as needed.	Interfere or interrupt team time.
Answer questions and address concerns as needed.	Make excuses.
Help facilitate teams through times of conflict as needed.	Conduct staff meetings with information that could be shared in other ways and that otherwise distract from the focus of student learning.
Find celebrations to share throughout the building.	

Figure 2.1: Role clarification in a PLC.

The administrative team in this building served as partners on the journey. They were supports, not threats. They helped the teams self-correct, and since they had a pulse of the health and productivity of all the teams, they were able to create buildingwide opportunities for dialogue and training as needed based on their observations.

Intervening for Success

Simply monitoring or evaluating teams is not helpful. The work only matters if leaders are willing to intervene based on the results they are getting from teams in the areas of health and productivity. As with teaching and learning in the classroom, the work is situational, and strong leaders understand how to anticipate and respond contextually in the moment to the final two questions:

1. What will we do when the team doesn't know it?

2. What will we do when the team already has learned it?

Our ability—and willingness—to answer these two questions is where the rubber meets the road. If leaders are not willing to answer these questions, chances are good they are still providing only "blanket" training and hoping that something will stick and add value to the system's work. As educational change expert Michael Fullan states, "Hope is not a strategy" (2011, p. 41).

The work requires situational leadership as strong leaders monitor for both healthy and productive teams, taking care of each team based on where they are relative to where the leaders would like them to be (see fig. 2.2). The quadrants of healthy and productive teams help leaders understand intervention needs when teams struggle with collaborative work.

		Low	High
Team Health	High	Healthy but Unproductive	Healthy and Productive
	Low	Unhealthy and Unproductive	Unhealthy but Productive
		Team Productivity	

Figure 2.2: **Healthy and productive teams.**

Many leaders would prefer to shy away from this work. One principal suggested that her teams were composed of adults and they could resolve their own issues. Her job was to get out of their way and let them fight it out. But when it comes to collaboration, a team is only as strong as its most struggling member, a building is only as strong as its most frustrated team, and a district is only as healthy as its most troubled school. It is imperative that leaders get involved. Success with a single team member or an entire team can affect the culture in significant and timely ways.

One principal we interviewed described how she responded when a team invited her to help the team get unstuck. She observed multiple meetings to understand the issues involved. She said to the team members:

> I think I have it figured out—you are not challenging each other in the moment as discussions happen. You are keeping a "happy tone" to your meetings but leaving frustrated and dissatisfied with your agreements and products. We will need to work on the language and the habits of challenging each other in the moment so that we can leave satisfied with the agreements and products we create during our time together.

Her team agreed, and things began to change for the better almost instantly. Highly effective leaders learn to isolate the variables and identify the specific issues and challenges to offer appropriate support for each team's success.

Unhealthy and Unproductive

A few teams are both unhealthy and unproductive. The team members make no attempt to pretend they are in a right relationship with one another *or* the work at hand. They are prone to complaining that they would be more effective if they had better team members with whom to work—but they do not confront one another about such concerns. Likewise, they will complain that the work is meaningless and is interfering with their ability to do the work they know they must do and that they have proved over the years that they can manage quite well when accomplishing it on their own.

Teams in this quadrant can be unhealthy in a variety of ways. In the most obvious form, they are not interested in working together and might publicly assert that they don't even like one another. They would prefer to maintain their individual levels of expertise and private classrooms. In a less obvious but equally unhealthy way, teams in this situation might individually appear happy, but there are almost imperceptible issues of codependency at play, and dominant personalities are competing for power. In either case, they are not engaging in the work of a collaborative team that focuses on learning, so they are also unproductive.

The Leadership Challenge for Unhealthy and Unproductive Teams

Leaders often have the greatest concerns about teams that fall in the unhealthy and unproductive quadrant, but these teams don't necessarily require extensive leadership intervention efforts. What is needed is considerable attention to detail. The right intervention can make staggering changes for the better.

To begin, the leader should clearly articulate a set of predetermined expectations for team health and productivity that the team must meet. Doing the right work in the right ways will more quickly advance a team to health than anything else will. Most teams find their way to health through productivity.

Leaders who work with unhealthy and unproductive teams attend the team's meetings and check in on team norms so they can model adherence to the norms and engage the team in completing the work. If a team is extremely unhealthy, the leader sometimes requires multiple successful meetings in which members adhere to team norms before the leader leaves team members to their own devices. Sometimes the leader meets one on one with the team facilitator to strategize possible responses to various team behaviors and to lay out plans for tasks that the team needs to accomplish, complete with timelines. Sometimes the leader meets one on one with individual team members to clarify that their expectations are not negotiable and that they will be monitoring whether individual members live up to team norms. Leaders always check in with teams and team members by surveying facilitators and stopping in on team meetings to make sure things are going smoothly. They model quality feedback to help the team close the distance between where it is and where it would ultimately like to be. But the norms are only the beginning. The highly effective PLC leaders in our study consistently stated that while health is important, few teams will become highly productive by simply experiencing the "Kumbayah" of team building.

Unhealthy but Productive

If a team is in this quadrant, chances are good that one or two strong individuals are really doing all of the work and carrying the load for others. Under that individual's leadership or facilitation, the team can do the work of setting goals, looking at data, and so on, but team members do not necessarily buy in to the work. Should the strong leader leave, so too will the work in which the team was engaged. This quadrant is tricky in that the members doing the work may seem healthy, when in truth they might be demonstrating a need to control quality or quietly enjoying the notion that the team really needs them. Neither is a healthy orientation for the success of the team. When a team is in this quadrant, team products become compliance oriented, and dependency issues often arise.

The Leadership Challenge for Unhealthy but Productive Teams

A great place to begin with a team in this quadrant is to observe or interview the productive individuals or to engage the team in an anonymous survey about its strengths and challenges. Whether the productive individuals are keeping the work close to the chest for quality control or are simply picking up the work to make sure *something* gets done, the individuals involved will require a conversation regarding enabling versus empowering and the necessity of empowering others to develop strong teams. Likewise, the individual doing all of the team work will require support in releasing a possible need for perfection and if needed, some facilitation tips and skills to engage others in accepting teamwork.

One team leader noted that whenever her team discussed something it needed to do, all heads would typically swing in her direction in anticipation that she would take care of it. At first, she found the pattern endearing; she liked doing quality work, and she liked that the team recognized her for that work. As time wore on, however, the pattern started to appear far from cute, and she became exhausted and exasperated. She realized that her open notebook and poised pen offered a certain guarantee that she would leave with work to do. To break the habits of the team, she decided to break her own habits first: she stopped bringing note-taking materials to meetings. When the team made a decision, she simply asked who was going to take responsibility. When the team looked at her expectantly to accept the next task they needed to accomplish, she learned to look back at the team and ask directly who would be willing to do it this week. Without complaint or making an ordeal out of how overworked she felt, she offered direct questions, free from blaming and shaming tones, and sent a clear message that she would not be accepting all of the workload in the future.

It only takes a few individuals to create an unhealthy team. Sometimes one or two players are skilled at distracting an otherwise healthy team from the tasks or conversations at hand. In this case, the team needs to become skilled at redirecting and not tolerating individual rants and refusals to contribute. Culture will trump structure, and when the entire team stands up to an individual or a small group of individuals to suggest "that is not the way we operate around here," resistant members will find themselves norming to compliance. In one example from our study, an individual good at sidetracking a conversation discovered that her entire team would no longer tolerate it when each of the team members began to respond to her distractions with similar responses, such as "That's an interesting conversation for another time. Right now, we need to work on this, so we'll have to find another time to have that conversation." Eventually, in the absence of a tolerant audience, she learned to forgo her tangential interests and commit herself to the work at hand.

Healthy but Unproductive

Although healthy but unproductive teams enjoy one another's company, the truth is, they are doing little to no work (by focusing on issues beyond their control) or the wrong work (by focusing on issues that do not affect student learning). By all appearances, they still meet the majority of the criteria for emotionally intelligent teams. Such teams might appear to be high functioning with a few of the team healthy traits in place: for example, they may take perspectives, demonstrate interpersonal understanding, create a positive environment, and even proactively solve problems. However, they are not focusing on the *issues that directly affect student achievement*. If they were to do so, you might find that they merely look healthy to the casual observer. Instead, they are not comfortable confronting one another—even with a caring orientation. They do very little team self-evaluation, rarely seek feedback, and demonstrate little organizational awareness or willingness to build external relationships. Upon closer examination, it's easy to see they are not demonstrating *all* of the traits of healthy teams.

The Leadership Challenge for Healthy but Unproductive Teams

If the team is *truly* healthy, then a simple nudge could move this team to productivity; for example, leaders could strive to focus the team's work on affecting student learning by requiring key products, such as common assessments or data sets from the use of common assessments. It is entirely possible, however, that a perceptibly healthy but unproductive team is protecting its own comfort level: for example, team members may not want to risk the possibility that they would stop liking one another if they did the important and more difficult work of aligning belief systems and practices. A healthy but unproductive team may also be compensating for a seemingly insignificant but clearly missing characteristic of truly healthy teams, such as an openness to seeking and addressing feedback or a lack of organizational awareness regarding how their role influences the greater well-being for the school.

Whatever the issues are, this team needs to become productive fast. If the team is truly healthy, this is often an easy thing to address. Sometimes, however, when pushed to productivity, the team reveals it wasn't actually healthy in the first place: the early signs of health crumble under pressure or give way to a few missing characteristics of healthy teams. Leaders need to identify the issues at play—by observation, honest discussion, a team survey tool, and so on—and then address whatever is preventing true collaboration and synergy.

Healthy and Productive

Healthy and productive teams navigate differences of opinion with grace, move to consensus with consistency, and focus all of their collective efforts on improving student learning. No instructional task (data interpretation, assessment design and use, lesson planning, differentiation, curriculum alignment, classroom management, and so on) slips by without their attention to detail. They are the highfliers that leaders wish all teams could be, and the good news is that, with clarity and support, all teams really can find a pathway to high levels of success.

The Leadership Challenge for Healthy and Productive Teams

It is a mistake to assume that teams in this position do not require attention or support. Many times, leaders assume that their involvement would be distracting, and so they opt out of monitoring such teams. The leaders we interviewed discovered that these teams often feel neglected or abandoned, and the teams wonder why others don't stop by to see how they are doing. It is also a significant mistake to always call attention to teams in this quadrant as a model for others during staff meetings. Doing so creates the go-to team members as the "principal's pets," impairs their credibility, and hampers their general fit with the overall staff. A challenge for leaders is to find successes worth celebrating in all teams to avoid accidentally sacrificing one team.

So how do leaders support healthy and productive teams? They check in, sustain momentum, encourage mastery in individual classrooms, find ways to empower individuals with new challenges and opportunities, and nurture future leaders from within the team by increasing their organizational awareness and building relationships with them outside the team.

In a PLC system, leaders from each role must approach the practice of creating and sustaining collaborative relationships from both a systemic approach—designing systems around the teams to address their culture and sustain long-term work—and a practical approach—giving teams skills, protocols, and templates for the immediate conversations and current work. When leaders engage in the first core leadership practice of creating and sustaining collaborative relationships, they attend to the details and frame the characteristics and expectations for success. This work involves so much more than finding time to collaborate or simply asking teams to cocreate a product. It takes effort and focus to behave our way into new healthy and productive habits of working. Our strongest leaders monitor for success, watching for both health and productivity along the way.

CHAPTER THREE

Aligning Systems

Have a simple, clear purpose which gives
rise to complex, intelligent behavior, rather
than complex rules and regulations that
give rise to simplistic thinking and stupid
behavior.

—Dee Hock, founder of VISA

Effective leaders know they must help align all systems to support the work of its vision, mission, values, and goals, or the work of PLCs cannot succeed. If any internal system is not aligned to these key focal points, then the overall work might be impossible to start, slow to proceed, or unlikely to maintain early changes along the way. Moreover, when leaders align systems to enact the organization's vision, mission, values, and goals, they send the clear message that the organization's guiding statements are more than words on a page; instead, they are actionable agreements.

The leadership practice of aligning systems is most certainly recursive (it is addressed repeatedly) and iterative (each effort builds on and refines previous efforts). It might seem that once an organization's or team's internal systems are aligned, the work could be considered done. Systems are dynamic, however, so there is no such thing as "done," as leaders interact with and improve them.

A system is, by nature, complex; it is a compilation of many interdependent parts that create a working, integrated whole. Systems-thinking expert Peter Senge (2006) suggests that the best way to understand a system, and any problems that might be occurring within it, is to understand the individual parts in their relationship to the working whole. Classrooms, schools, and districts are filled with systems—such as attendance, instruction, assessment, grading, scheduling, reporting, policy development, new teacher induction, mentoring, and curriculum review, to name a few—that impact daily work across the organization.

Each system has its own subparts and, at the same time, each entire system might be a subpart of another greater system. At the classroom level, grading is its own system with many interacting subparts such as a grading policy, teacher scoring and feedback practices, student learning artifacts, rubrics or scoring criteria to evaluate the evidence, gradebook notation systems, and the like. But classroom grading as a whole system is in and of itself a subpart of a larger building system that involves recording and reporting student achievement. Inside that recording and reporting system, other systems operate as subparts to the larger system, like technology-based parent portals, quarterly parent communications, parent teacher conferences, and so on. And the reporting systems, whole as they are, serve as subparts to the larger systems of intervention and enrichment responses, course selection options, and the list goes on. Notably, a system requires parts that interact internally and externally with other systems.

When creating a collaborative culture, leaders align systems to create collaborative structures that accommodate the work of teams. At the start of the PLC process, teams make time for both team collaboration and, more importantly, to extend learning opportunities for struggling learners. A simple change in time allocations can affect many other systems besides the obvious ones of bus schedules, start and end times, and teacher assignments for the various hours of the day. Even after the dust settles on changes to the schedule, unforeseen complications may emerge. Systems less obvious in the immediate moment—like extracurriculars, teacher contracts, staff meetings, professional development resources and events—may also be affected in unanticipated ways. Effective leaders realize that aligning any system requires change, and in the early stages, a systems change is only representative of the leaders' best initial thinking about what will work.

The Aligned System

In an aligned organization, "everything the school does—hiring, evaluation, professional development, scheduling, rewards, and recognition—is designed to support the message that helping all students learn at high levels requires a collaborative and collective effort" (DuFour & DuFour, 2010, p. 89). When systems are aligned, everything is integrated or scaffolded and points true north in such a way that a district, school, or team can work its way toward success on its vision, mission, values, and goals.

Aligned systems are valued because they run seamlessly in the background and provide the support educators require to accomplish their day-to-day jobs. They are "noiseless," so it is hard to know whether they are functioning in the background. A few key indicators will reveal whether systems are in alignment:

- All initiatives, directives, or efforts are directly linked to evaluation criteria that support the vision, mission, values, and goals, and all such activities are monitored on an ongoing basis using those predetermined criteria.

- There is a common vocabulary; everyone uses the same terms with the same meanings to describe core processes.

- All individuals in the organization can clearly state how their current work or engagement in a particular task directly supports the organization's direction.

- No one system competes with or accidently hijacks the work of another system.

- Continuous learning systems are in place to promote coherence and clarity for new and existing staff.

Since systems alignment is challenging work, it's understandable, albeit unfortunate, that many systems are misaligned. Programs and initiatives are added with good intentions, but often without an explanation regarding how that program or initiative ties to all other existing efforts. In the absence of such intentionality, alignment efforts become overwhelmed early and confusion and conflict reign—organizational chaos at its worst. Leaders gain momentum when they introduce new efforts by using verbal descriptions and graphic representations of the relationships between one effort and the next—coherence and clarity at its best.

Many of the current systems in traditional schools are counterproductive to the work of collaborative teams. A leader's work is to find the large and small systems that are blocking change and to remove the barriers. It is challenging to isolate, modify, remove, or add a system, and it's also challenging to attend to the success or failure of those changes later. The strong leaders we interviewed gave great attention to details when aligning systems—before, during, and after they made changes. For example, leaders from each of the levels we interviewed offered these insights:

- I began encouraging my team to separate [student] work behaviors from academics in our reporting and intervention efforts. The team began to embrace it, so we developed a system of reporting work behaviors. It was developmentally appropriate for students, and it aligned with our mission statement. (Teacher leader interview, spring 2011)

- One of the systems that [my school] did not have in place was tracking the data. I asked them to use the data collection sheet on which they had to break down . . . districtwide assessments throughout the entire year. I required them to establish proficiency benchmarks, and then using the data collection sheet, they were to break the results down by subgroups for targeted interventions. Can you imagine the teacher growth with just that one system that we implemented? It was huge. (Principal interview, spring 2010)

- I think the biggest thing for me was to use formative assessments in my role as a leader. Most people think of formative assessments in a classroom with a teacher, but I really had to put a system of formative assessment in place. I was constantly listening. I was watching. I was looking at whether it was data or the work that they were doing, and that really drove me to what I needed to do to help. . . . It was that formative assessment opportunity. In the old paradigm, we'd say, "We're going to do things and we're going to check them off the list," and we kept doing that. But now I think every single day that my role is gathering and responding to constant formative assessment data so we can adjust what we're doing and know what needs redoing, and know where we can celebrate, and so on. (Assistant superintendent interview, spring 2010)

A change in one system, even a minor change, can have unforeseen ramifications for another system. Failing to make corresponding adjustments in other systems as needed or failing to notice that an undesired response occurred in a subsystem can sabotage the primary change effort. As Reeves (2002) points out, "Understanding systems is not merely repetition of organizational structure, as is commonly assumed. It is a way of recognizing the relationships in all the work and results of the organization" (p. 164). Ripple effects can be hard to anticipate and identify; for leaders, it can be even more challenging to carefully sort through personal or organizational assumptions. Effective leaders strive to check their own mental models for accuracy and currency.

Quality teaching and learning requires systems at the classroom level that are mirrored at the school and district levels. After all, leading change demands teaching and learning for adults. At the systems level, effective leaders work to clarify the system standards, mastery expectations, assessments for monitoring growth, instruction to support adult learning, results to review for planning modifications, and support methods to intervene or enrich as needed in order to help the system function optimally. In other words, effective leaders from all levels of the organization must keep a watchful eye on aligning systems at the classroom level as well as at the organizational level.

Figure 3.1 shows the consequences of unaligned or missing components at the systems level. All of the components need to be in place in order for the proper teacher input and desired student outcomes to occur. The subtraction or marginalization of a single component will logically alter the outcome. If, for example, a teacher does not use accurate assessments effectively, he is teaching in a linear manner that results in unaccountable learning for students. The components in this figure apply to classroom learning as well as to organizational learning: the same concepts apply whether the learning described is for students (pedagogy) or staff (andragogy).

Optimum Teaching	Discrete Teaching	Linear Teaching	Prescriptive Teaching	Misaligned Teaching	Survival Teaching
Standards and Curriculum	~~Standards and Curriculum~~	Standards and Curriculum	Standards and Curriculum	Standards and Curriculum	Standards and Curriculum
Assessment	Assessment	~~Assessment~~	Assessment	Assessment	Assessment
Instruction	Instruction	Instruction	~~Instruction~~	Instruction	Instruction
Results	Results	Results	Results	~~Results~~	Results
Support Systems	Support Systems	Support Systems	Support Systems	Support Systems	~~Support Systems~~
Optimal Learning	Contingent Learning	Unaccountable Learning	Self-Driven Learning	Mystery Learning	Capped Learning

Figure 3.1: Components for aligning systems in teaching and learning.

Table 3.1 provides clarifying details of figure 3.1 regarding the labeled systems as we have defined them.

Table 3.1: Definitions of the Aligned Systems in Teaching and Learning

Term	Definitions as Referenced in the Chart of Aligned Systems
Standards and Curriculum	The organization has identified curriculum and student learning needs and has prioritized and aligned its standards accordingly. The curriculum is used to teach the standards and includes the subject-specific instruction, assessment materials, and resources that teachers and students employ in class to meet required expectations. The curriculum is readily accessible and "unpacked" to meet the criteria of guaranteed, viable, and visible learning expectations. Educators use the aligned standards and curriculum to ensure that they address all necessary academic learning requirements.
Assessment	Educators employ a balanced system of summative and formative classroom assessments to both monitor and promote student learning. Teachers design assessments to align with specific learning expectations, and the assessments accurately measure what students know and are able to do. Teachers reference assessment results for targeted, responsive instruction. They use assessment to help students grow, and they align their assessment and reporting practices to support such growth and engage learners in mastering the learning expectations.
Instruction	During quality instruction, decisions and activities are responsive to student learning needs. Teachers deliver knowledge, concepts, and skills in a manner that students can readily understand and integrate. Delivering new information through instructional activities involves the following: (1) providing a clear and comprehensive message describing the new content or skills, (2) facilitating activities that engage learners in cocreating and assimilating the new knowledge, and (3) checking for understanding with formal and informal assessments.
Results	Results of valid internal and external assessments are monitored and compared to ensure program alignment, rigor, and effectiveness and to identify potential improvements. Results include specific indicators that measure intended targets. While data for monitoring for student achievement are most important, results extend beyond quantitative data; qualitative data on how stakeholders feel about the current conditions are equally important to future decision making for sustainability.
Support Systems	All the necessary components to support fluid and responsive systems have been developed and provided. The components answer questions such as, What do we do when instruction works? What do we do when it does not work? To support learners, staff, and students alike, the following must be in place: clear expectations; evaluation measures; accountability and celebration practices; time to collaborate; opportunities to alter schedules, calendars, and processes (conferences when, with whom, about what); and support to try innovative approaches, evaluate effectiveness, and document findings.

In addition to understanding the systems outlined in figure 3.1, it is important to understand the terms of the potential teaching and learning outcomes. Both learners and teachers alike experience the effects of misaligned systems. Table 3.2 (page 54) provides clarifying details regarding teacher inputs and student outcomes in aligned and misaligned systems.

Table 3.2: Definitions of the Teaching and Learning Outcomes of Aligned and Misaligned Systems

Outcome	Definitions as Referenced in the Chart of Aligned Systems
Optimum Teaching **Optimal Learning**	Optimum teaching can occur when everything is in place: when teachers focus on rigorous, targeted, and shared learning requirements; respond daily and systemically to results; draw on research-based instructional strategies to instruct and intervene; and require learning of themselves and for their learners. The system can then expect optimal learning: *all* students achieving mastery at rigorous levels.
Discrete Teaching **Contingent Learning**	When the framework of aligned standards and curriculum is missing, teaching is confined to the understandings, values, and preferences of the instructor. Learning will be contingent on each teacher's biases and breadth of knowledge and expertise.
Linear Teaching **Unaccountable Learning**	When high-quality formative and summative assessments are not employed or their results are not addressed, the teacher relies on the sequence of pages and units in a curriculum to drive instruction. Faced with linear teaching, students are not held accountable to mastery of standards; rather, they are accountable to what they could glean from *exposure* to content.
Prescriptive Teaching **Self-Driven Learning**	If the teacher is not skilled in designing instructional strategies that engage learners and make content accessible, he or she will "deliver" information with straight lecture or scripted strategies—the purposes, logic, and intended outcomes of which may not be clear to the instructor. In that case, learners must unpack the instruction and extract their own understandings and applications of the material.
Misaligned Teaching **Mystery Learning**	When curriculum, instruction, and assessment choices are left to individual teacher preference, and teams and schools are not monitoring the effectiveness of their collective efforts against standards, SMART goals, and benchmark (internal and external) assessments, teaching efforts will not be accountable or aligned to any particular set of shared outcomes. Staff impact on student learning is unclear, and "curricular chaos" is hard to measure with consistency or accuracy, so results remain a mystery.
Survival Teaching **Capped Learning**	When schools leave teachers to their own devices and limitations—without building collective commitment; sharing knowledge, skills, and expertise; and collaboratively planning to close achievement gaps or extend and refine learning—interventions and enrichments fall to the wayside and are considered luxuries for another time and place. Operating from a place of survival, most teachers teach to the "average" in their classrooms. From the place of being limited in learning based on the depth and breadth of exposure, students experience "capped" learning. The system limits the capacity of all its learners since learning will only advance as far as the median for teachers *and* students.

Commitment to the three big ideas of a professional learning community—focusing on learning, working collaboratively, and attending to results (DuFour et al., 2008)—is necessary to align systems well. Commitment to the characteristics of PLCs—especially action orientation, continuous improvement, and collective inquiry—is also particularly helpful when aligning even the simplest of systems. For example, when leaders are in the throes of employing their new "best schedule" (action orientation), they discover what works and what doesn't (collective inquiry), and they begin to make plans for the next variation or "schedule 2.0" (continuous improvement).

Aligning systems requires careful thought and planning because system behaviors are emergent phenomena. Effective leaders design with the best in mind and acknowledge that it is not possible to achieve immediate perfection. They expect to learn by doing, and more importantly, they ensure that processes are in place to *guarantee* learning and to gradually align the system with new findings.

Leading Change

Aligning systems requires change, and "school leaders cannot passively wait for substantive change to 'bubble up.' They must understand that deep reform will require support and pressure" (DuFour et al., 2006, p. 191). Effective change leaders not only understand change, they develop a *shared* understanding of how change occurs. Wiliam and Thompson (2008) state:

> Not only must the developers understand their own theory of action and the empirical basis on which it rests, the end users—the teachers and even the students—must have a reasonably good idea of the why as well. Otherwise, we believe there is little chance of maintaining quality at scale. (p. 3)

Again, one key understanding is that even the most effective leaders will not get it right the first time around. "Leaders should," according to DuFour et al. (2006), "approach change honestly and advise staff that it is unrealistic to expect flawless execution in initial efforts to implement complex concepts. The best-laid plans and noblest of efforts will typically fall short of the desired results, at least initially" (p. 197).

Many experts have expressed opinions about the best ways to approach change and the aspects to consider. These poignant ideas from renowned experts help shape an effective leader's understanding of how to proceed when aligning systems:

- Change is a leader's friend, but it has a split personality: its nonlinear messiness gets us into trouble. But the experience of this messiness is necessary in order to discover the hidden benefits—creative ideas and novel solutions are often generated when the status quo is disrupted. (Fullan, 2001, p. 107)

- But changes in behavior do not follow the creation of a personal belief system; they precede it. Behavior does not stem from a rational consideration of evidence, but from an emotional attachment to a trusted colleague. (Reeves, 2006a, p. 33)

- When it comes to creating change, you no longer have to worry about influencing everyone at once. . . . Your job is to find the . . . opinion leaders who are the key to everyone else. Spend disproportionate time with them. Listen to their concerns. Build trust with them. Be open to their ideas. Rely on them to share your ideas, and you'll gain a source of influence unlike any other. (Patterson, Grenny, Maxfield, McMillan, & Switzler, 2008, p. 151)

- To create organizations that get smarter and more aligned every day requires an interactive teaching/learning process. It isn't hierarchical teaching. You teach me, and then I teach the people below me. It isn't about alternating roles. You teach me something and then I'll teach you something. Rather, it is a process of mutual exploration and exchange during which both the "teacher" and the "learner" become smarter. It is synergy. 1 + 1 = 3. (Tichy, 2004, p. 10)

- Leaders know well that innovation and change all involve experimentation, risk and failure. They proceed anyway. One way of dealing with the potential risks and failures of experimentation is to approach change through incremental steps and small wins. Little victories, when piled on top of each other, build confidence that even the biggest challenges can be met. In so doing, they strengthen commitment to the long-term future. Yet not everyone is equally comfortable with risk and uncertainty. Leaders also pay attention to the capacity of their constituents to take control of challenging situations and become fully committed to change. You can't exhort people to take risks if they don't also feel safe. (Kouzes & Posner, 2007, p. 19)

- New social movements do not come from those in the centers of power. The same will hold true for much of the leadership required to create a regenerative society. Look to the periphery, to people and places where commitment to the status quo is low and where hearts and minds are most open to the new. . . . Within society, it means leadership from new companies, new social entrepreneurs, new geographic areas, and in all likelihood people and places no one is expecting. . . . Unleashing the power of organizations and networks of all sorts to create the changes needed in the coming years will require millions of gifted and dedicated leaders of all sorts, many of whom will not come from obvious positions of power or have gotten permission for their efforts. This does not imply that leadership from those in positions of authority is unimportant, only that it is insufficient. (Senge, Smith, Kruschwitz, Laur, & Schley, 2008, pp. 364–365)

In sum, effective leaders understand how best to lead change. They create a theory of action that allows for complexities but ensures success despite them, and they realize that their attitudes toward change matter. The most effective leaders we interviewed were careful to begin their change efforts from a place of positive predisposition. We can find parallel examples at every level in which one leader began the work from a positive note and the other from a negative note. It almost goes without saying that those who begin with a positive predisposition will get further in their work, time and time again. Effective leaders begin from the place of what's right, even in the most difficult situations.

In the following case study from our 2010–2011 work in a school, lessons about leading change became clear in regard to the perspective adopted by the teacher leaders involved.

A building leadership team consisting of administration and teacher leaders decided that the next logical step in functioning as a PLC was to become more consistent and thorough in their work with common assessments. At the next staff meeting, the building leadership team offered their rationale and ideas to support the practice of developing, employing, and responding to the results of common assessments for all their priority standards—and not just a few times during the year. The decision to focus on common assessments was unanimous, and all of the teacher leaders left the meeting with a commitment to begin creating, immediately, a series of formative and summative common assessments to ensure student mastery of the priority standards by the end of the year.

After the building leadership meeting, Jazz, one of the teacher leaders, returned to her teacher team. Although she had publicly agreed to the terms during the meeting, she told her team:

> I'm not really sure how we're going to do this new work, guys, but the administration just announced at our leadership team meeting that we're going to need to create a series of common assessments to assess all of our priority standards by the end of the year. I just don't see how we can get that all done, and I got the sense that they are not going to be flexible on our timeline. I tried to go to bat for you, but they weren't listening. It's clear to me that they really don't understand how hard we are all working here. Our team meetings will not be enough time, so we're going to have to work above and beyond the time we've been given.

Jazz's team was overwhelmed and frustrated from the very beginning, and at the end of the year, they were the only team not done with their work. Jazz spent her time in the leadership team meetings complaining about the team's stress levels and repeating her mantra that more time would be required. The leadership team learned to anticipate her comments with each discussion. It was not a pleasant experience for anyone involved.

Another teacher leader, Hope, operated with a positive predisposition, and she returned to her team to share a completely different message: "We've had such tremendous success with our current efforts with common assessments," Hope said. "We've got evidence that proves we can close gaps quickly. But we've only done it a few times in the year. Would you agree with me that if we know it works, we have an obligation to help our struggling learners with more frequency and consistency?" The team agreed wholeheartedly and with minimal discussion. They had enjoyed closing difficult achievement gaps. Hope continued:

> We're already assessing on an ongoing basis, so how about we move those assessments that tie to our priority standards into the common assessment process? I'll help. To get started, let's map out which priority standards we've already covered and which we haven't. Then, let's identify the remaining priority standards and divvy them up. Each of us will take a few priority standards and then search for any assessment we already use to assess those standards.

The team left that meeting with assigned standards, and each member worked between meetings to gather any existing assessment materials without evaluating the quality of those materials in the initial phase. At the next meeting, Hope asked team members to lay their materials on the table and begin discussing the best way to make the next phase natural and manageable. The team decided to select the priority standards contained in the immediate curricular units and to work in pairs to frame initial assessment tools to bring back to the entire team for discussion and approval. Hope's team finished their assigned task of creating common assessments two months early. Still, they knew they would have to improve their own assessments over time and that their work was never really done. They left that year feeling as if they had a much clearer and more comprehensive assessment system for the following year.

As the case study shows, an effective leader's delivery—positive or negative—makes as much of a difference in the outcome as the skills and strategies he or she employs along the way. Effective leaders have good cause to be optimistic because they understand that resistance—no matter its origin—serves as both teacher and opportunity during the work of change. If they embrace resistance—and the learning that results from it—as a powerful learning tool, it can serve as a potential lever to help the organization move forward. Likewise, making mistakes in the process is a both a given and an opportunity to grow: "The only way to develop expertise in the concept is to learn by doing, which, to a large extent, is learning through mistakes" (DuFour & DuFour, 2010, p. 90). Leaders who maintain a positive attitude always seem to approach situations with a learning orientation: *it's almost a guarantee we'll make mistakes*, they seem to say to themselves, *but we will learn our way through it and be better in the end as a result*. The best way to maintain optimism in the face of uncertain outcomes and untried strategies is to trust that one has the knowledge and skills to survive anything and, at a minimum, become a stronger leader because of it.

Paying Attention to Context and Culture

Aligning systems is far more than just making the components integrate smoothly and accurately. The effective leaders we interviewed understand that changing culture is necessary. The PLC architects have said, "Unlike most educational reforms, which have focused on structure, the specific intent of the PLC concept is to change the context and culture of the school and district" (DuFour & DuFour, 2010, p. 91). Effective leaders begin the work of becoming a PLC in their current culture with the full intent of creating structures and practices to change that culture. Fullan (2006) notes:

> We also can see immediately why this is so difficult to accomplish on a large scale. It is a cultural change that is both deep and necessary, and one that needs to occur, not in this or that school, but in all schools and the infrastructures within which they operate. It is a system change that permanently de-privatizes teaching in order to build in continuous improvement. Professional learning communities must be seen in this light, i.e., they must be judged on their effectiveness at creating cultures of professional learning on a system scale.

Effective leaders must understand both what the current culture is and what it needs to become.

Experts do suggest, however, that working to address culture before changing practice is a mistake (DuFour & DuFour, 2010; DuFour et al., 2008; Elmore, 2004; Pfeffer & Sutton, 2006; Reeves, 2006a, 2006b). They suggest leaders begin by changing behavior across the organization. Leaders then help the organization see, understand, and even celebrate its results from the behavioral changes. Only after the results show gains in student achievement can new beliefs form and culture begin to change.

Still, effective leaders cannot ignore context and culture along the way. Doing so undermines their own change efforts. Change must be embedded in the organization's level of readiness, and readiness is best assessed through acknowledging the context and culture. *Context*, or current reality and readiness levels, encompasses the organization's history, current reality, vision, and strengths—which includes internal trusted change agents, barriers, needs, and even politics. *Culture* is found in the unspoken assumptions, beliefs, expectations, and habits that constitute the norms of behavior (DuFour et al., 2008). Context and culture can overpower a leader's best efforts to create change.

As effective leaders drive toward change, they must attend to the organization's health as well as its strategic levers for change. Fullan (2001) suggests that something as simple as sending individuals to an external training must be considered in light of context and culture—otherwise, strategic decisions become aimless arrows that miss their intended target. "Leading in a culture of change does not mean placing changed individuals into unchanged environments," Fullan warns. "Rather, change leaders work on changing the context, helping create new settings conducive to learning and sharing that learning" (p. 79).

Analyzing for System Alignment

When making changes in a system, it is important to study all of the direct and indirect components carefully and to attempt to dot all of the Is (*information, impact, integration,* and *implications*) in advance by asking strategic questions:

1. **Information**—Do we have all of the necessary information? Have we considered the explicit and implicit parts to the system we are addressing? Have we explored what research has found and what the experts advise regarding the best practice for the systems in question? Will we make an informed set of decisions regarding the changes we are pursuing?

2. **Impact**—Will the decisions or choices we are about to make create the impact we are seeking? Are there any possible unforeseen variables that might water down our efforts? Are there any possible unintended impacts? How and what will we monitor for our impact? Will we create the right changes in the places we most wish to impact?

3. **Integration**—Will we be able to easily integrate our changes into the other systems involved, or can we readily incorporate them into our practices? What will it take to integrate the system changes we are trying to add, merge, or delete? Will we properly integrate our system changes with all the other systems that this system is, or should be, connected to?

4. **Implications**—Down the road, after we have implemented our changes, what ramifications or long-term complications should we expect? What new problems might emerge from today's actions or decisions? How might we prepare for the possible scenarios we anticipate?

Effective leaders work to anticipate potential problems before making significant changes. No path to change is ever going to be perfectly smooth, even with the best-laid plans. But effective leaders still try to minimize error and maximize potential whenever possible by anticipating possible complications and creating alternatives or options for the various scenarios. Effective leaders go through the process of asking strategic questions in any systems change they are considering.

Consider, for example, the need to dot the four Is when aligning grading policies and practices—a potentially volatile change. First, there is an immediate impact internally—people will feel uncomfortable and possibly even threatened by the change. Equally important, there is an immediate impact with stakeholders, who do not personally have to change practice but who may or may not appreciate the implications for their own learners in the process. If schools and districts do not dot the four Is carefully in their considerations for change to the grading system, students, teachers, and the community at large can experience tremendous frustration and even harm. Effective leaders do not make policy and practice changes without first helping teachers understand how to apply them. People cannot support what they do not understand.

Information

There are many excellent sources with new practice and policy recommendations in grading (Guskey, 2009; Marzano, 2010; O'Connor, 2010; Reeves, 2010). The experts clearly disagree on some points, however. Some experts, for example, state that teachers can grade formative assessments, whereas others vehemently disagree and argue that teachers can only use formative assessments to receive and provide feedback.

Effective leaders help teams understand the issues and then shape an organizational response that both aligns with the organization's values and belief systems and removes the barriers to teacher practice and understanding. It would be a mistake to launch a revision to grading practices and policies without helping teams understand the benefits and rationale. Effective leaders ask, How does our local research inform our understanding of grading practices? Have we engaged in our own action research and collective inquiry? Do we have local research-based examples of how and why to make changes to our policies, or will we be launching changes without internal examples and clear rationale to lead the efforts? If, for example, we can't assign zeroes as grades in the absence of student work, then what do we do instead? Is there ever an end point? If we come to the end of a marking period, and there is no student work to base an accurate score on, and we can't assign zeroes to missing work, then what?

Impact

Effective leaders consider questions such as: If we change grading practices and policies, what will be the impact on all of our stakeholders (students, teachers, parents, and central office data processing officials)? More importantly, they ask, what is the desired impact on student achievement? Will the recommended change lead to and support the idea that learning is required? What are plausible, though not desirable, impact options?

Effective leaders help teams identify and clarify the criteria for quality that they will use to monitor the impact along the way. When evaluation criteria are created in advance, everyone can monitor for success. Teams can know, before it's too late, what the actual impact of any given change is and what stopgap measures to put in place. Leaders should never allow change efforts to proceed like runaway trains on a guaranteed crash course.

Integration

Changing a grading policy will invariably affect grading practices; changing grading practices will invariably affect student–teacher communications; changing student–teacher communications will affect recording and reporting systems, which will affect parent communications, online reporting, grade point averages, and valedictorian selection criteria. The ripple effect continues from there; a simple change to one policy is rarely the final change.

Ideally, a change in grading policy is aligned to other changes: for example, in designing accurate assessments that generate meaningful data that teachers then use to promote continued learning for students. The work is so much more complex than simply stating, "Failure is not an option, so we will do all we can to require learning." Effective leaders help their teachers—and all of their stakeholders, including the students—see their way through *all* of the changes.

Implications

Every grading decision that a school makes as a systems change will have long-term implications. For example, the experts agree that using zero in grading distorts data because it assigns an inaccurate value in the absence of a representative value: for example, if a nurse placed a zero on the medical chart every time the thermometer didn't work, and then tried to average the patient's temperature over the course of a week so key decisions could be made about whether or not to release a patient from the hospital, medical experts would be basing their decisions on flawed data (Guskey, 2009; Marzano, 2010; O'Connor, 2010; Reeves, 2010). In addition, experts agree that on a 100-point scale, the 60-point range between zero and a minimally passing score of sixty, or in many cases a grade of D–, is so significant that a gap on this lower end of the 100-point continuum is nearly impossible to overcome. If grades are to be accurate, then the spread between grades needs to be equidistant so that a single failing score of a zero cannot overpower and wipe out the evidence of success when averaged with a passing score of 80, or a B–; averaged with a zero, the B score loses any impact and becomes a failing score.

Experts also agree that averaging scores in a grading period is antithetical to honoring learning (Guskey, 2009; Marzano, 2010; O'Connor, 2010; Reeves, 2010). The practice of averaging clearly demonstrates the *middle* of where a learner was and fails to acknowledge that while mistakes may have been made during the learning process, the learner worked through it and achieved *at the end*. Many leaders, for example, would agree that they make a lot of mistakes initially when learning in their new roles. But it would be an inaccurate reflection of their current leadership skills in their performance evaluations if they were held accountable for the mistakes they learned through and fixed early in their journeys.

Unfortunately, many systems have reacted to the research by creating policy that states no learner can earn a score lower than fifty. The argument is based on the notion that educators create an equidistant scale of 10-point spreads between each grading option (50–59 = F, 60–69 = D, and so on). In this case, a score of fifty is the lowest mark a student can achieve, so the equidistant ten-point spread might be manageable, and the learners can overcome an early error and still make a good grade in the averaging process. While that might seem a rational conclusion (should one decide averaging is, in fact, still viable where grading is concerned), effective leaders engage the system in what-if thinking and scenario planning. What, for example, are the long-term and potentially serious implications of giving students a guaranteed fifty points with no evidence of achievement? Might this practice actually do more harm when learners realize they can get fifty points for nothing? Does the potential (and even likely) sense of entitlement that emerges cause unforeseen complications in classroom management, in student–teacher discussions, in student efficacy, and in teacher hope? Using fifty points as the floor might serve as a solution today and a problem tomorrow.

Effective leaders address the four Is of systems change: information, impact, integration, and implications. To do so, they build in processes, tools, and checkpoints and even designate individuals to monitor for success. Likewise, they build in opportunities for organizational reflection and redirection efforts. It works best to identify and design these components in advance of altering any system. Before leaders *do*, they have to *know* how they will monitor for success along the way.

Establishing Success Indicators and Monitoring Criteria

When system changes are about to be enacted for alignment, effective leaders engage stakeholders by starting with the end in mind. DuFour (2007) writes:

> One of the most essential responsibilities of leadership is clarity—clarity regarding the fundamental purpose of the organization, the future it must create to better fulfill that purpose, the most high-leverage strategies for

> creating that future, the indicators of progress it will monitor and the specific ways each member of the organization can contribute both to its long-term purpose and short-term goals. (p. 41)

Effective leaders build monitoring systems by selecting indicators of progress. Without such qualifiers, how will anyone know if they have made progress?

Effective leaders help others understand what expertise is before requiring it of them; they begin with the end in mind. Sadly, "few have identified the characteristics of expert performance. The challenge, therefore, is to first develop a viable tool for fostering expertise in teaching and to classify it in a way that identifies the context or situations in which specific strategies should be used" (Marzano, 2010, p. 5).

Effective leaders build a sense of understanding regarding the overall initiative and engage teams in answering the question, What signs or indicators will we monitor so we know whether we are making progress? For example, after one district in our study spent two years studying formative assessment across the organization, the administrators decided it would be important to begin searching for formative assessment in action at the classroom level to see if what they had been learning and discussing was being implemented in their buildings. To support that work, the central office staff engaged the building leaders in discussing formative assessment in action. Teams of principals gathered to discuss a series of scenarios:

- When you meet with a team that is planning an upcoming unit
- When you walk into a classroom where instruction is happening
- When you meet with a team interpreting assessment data
- When you explore the online gradebooks where teachers post grades and reports for parents
- As you monitor the effectiveness of your response to intervention (RTI) pyramid
- When you talk to a student informally regarding his or her learning

For each of those scenarios, teams of principals answered the following questions:

- What evidence or indicators will you monitor to know teachers are using formative assessments well?
- What do you need to think about in advance of entering the conversation?
- What will you look for?
- What will you listen for?
- What questions or prompts will you pose to move teachers toward understanding their current practice and use of formative assessments?
- What strategies and actions will you use to help teachers make the leap to improved practice?

Leaders were thus able to build an assessment system that all could use to monitor progress, and by doing so, they communicated to staff that the learning from professional development experiences was expected to result in specific changes to classroom practice.

Engaging everyone in conversations about indicators of success builds consistency in understanding and empowers all to look for examples of excellence in action during the implementation and sustaining stages. This strategy of clarifying the criteria of quality for staff performance is similar to the work teachers do in classrooms to help students understand learning expectations and standards of quality in student work. In her 2009 book *Seven Strategies of Assessment for Learning*, Jan Chappuis suggests that this strategy answers the question, Where am I going?

There are quality standards for effective criteria of quality. Chappuis (2009) states that the criteria need to be generalizable, rather than task specific, so that they can be applied to judge quality across diverse situations. Effective criteria are also descriptive rather than evaluative or quantitative. When criteria are evaluative, the language of judgment and interpretation is involved ("You need better examples in your writing. These are too confusing."); when they are quantitative, the language of numbers is involved ("The essay needed to be five paragraphs in length, and each paragraph needed a minimum of four sentences."). Both options diminish potential impact for the learner and may even prohibit motivation and continued learning. On the other hand, descriptive criteria help learners understand what they are doing well and what needs improvement ("I found three significant ideas in your writing, and I had trouble deciding which was your main idea for this topic. Strong writers make the main idea stand out and use additional key ideas to strengthen the main idea. Show how your ideas link to and support the main idea."). In this case, the criteria lead to quality data that will ultimately help those engaged in learning apply the information to future learning experiences (Chappuis, 2009).

What does creating this platform for success look like in action? The leadership team begins by asking, What indicators of success could we monitor to know whether our collaborative teams are becoming more effective in their critical work? What is it that we want healthy teams to produce, and what products would we monitor? Here are a few ideas:

- Teams identify priority standards.
- Teams create SMART goals to guide their work.
- Teams use common formative and summative assessments.

The list could easily continue and has been well documented in the PLC literature. While the indicators might seem clear as they are, there will still be questions about the expectations. Staff will better understand the indicators when they are aligned to descriptive criteria. Staff may already know, for example, that they need to develop and employ common assessments, but wonder to what extent. Evaluative criteria—such as "outstanding use of assessment data" or "excellent assessment tools"—do little to clarify quality. What do *outstanding* and *excellent* mean? Who defines them? Quantitative criteria—such as "all teams will use one common formative and one common summative assessment per term"—are likewise unhelpful, though commonly used regarding common assessments. In fact, giving specific numbers will likely (and accidentally) create a situation in which teams meet the standard but do not exceed it. And, in truth, the use of numbers in this case promotes the notion that there is a formula for success. There is no such thing. Teaching and learning are complex processes, and in no way can a set number of activities guarantee learning, much less *high* levels of learning. If the success indicator states, "Teams use common formative and common summative assessments," the descriptive criteria might read:

- Common assessments, whether summative or formative in nature, are collaboratively designed in advance of instruction by *all* of the teachers who will use them.

- Common assessments generate accurate data that are used to improve student learning.

- The quantity and the strategic placement of small, frequent, common formative assessments help teams identify what their learners have mastered and what they have not regarding specific learning targets so that teachers can make timely, targeted, and sufficient changes before the common summative assessment.

- Common summative assessments are used at the conclusion of teaching all essential standards so that teams can certify *learning* of all essential standards.

Again, the list could continue. Far too often, teachers lack clarity on rationale, purpose, and hallmarks of quality regarding what they are supposed to be doing—and as result, even the *best* classroom strategy can fall seriously short of supporting learning. It might even hamper learning. What is important is that all educators understand the expectations and hallmarks of quality so they can self-assess, set goals, and adjust along the way. Formative monitoring systems at the staff level are unbelievably powerful. When educational leaders use descriptive criteria, they encourage feedback, questions, dialogue, and many other learning-oriented conversations among *all* staff at the district, school, and teaching team levels.

Establishing Tight/Loose Decision Making

When leaders take the time to articulate their success indicators and descriptive criteria, they also advance their own capacity to manage tight/loose decision making. An aligned system identifies everything the system values and monitors everything the leaders do against those things the system values. The framework that leaders develop at the organizational level empowers everyone to act in good conscience and to make quality decisions that align with the given direction. As DuFour (2007) notes:

> Leaders who create schools and districts capable of sustained substantive improvement are not laissez-faire in their approach to education but rather are skillful in implementing the concept of simultaneous loose and tight leadership. . . . This leadership approach fosters autonomy and creativity (loose) within a systematic framework that stipulates clear, non-discretionary priorities and parameters (tight). (p. 39)

Effective leaders create opportunities for creativity and empowerment within a framework of non-negotiables. One superintendent we interviewed stated it as follows:

> In our schools, we will provide support for all students, specifically the language learners who are our under-represented learners. We will provide interventions that will support the needs of all kids. We will use explicit instruction. We will use formative assessment to support our learners along the pathway to success. These things are non-negotiable. How you manage them will be up to your teams.

He was quick to add that edicts disempower staff and fuel blame games. Empowerment creates a culture conducive to shared learning and continuous improvement:

> If you empower [teams] to build the structures themselves, they own them and they embrace and support and sustain them. [Teachers] are the ones who are constantly seeking system improvements at their site and it is a powerful thing for that to happen. (Superintendent interview, spring 2010)

Rather than being "tight" about having teams fill in forms, for example, effective leaders are tight about the *criteria* for quality teamwork. Instead of saying, "All teams will use this form to manage their data," a strong leader might say:

> I have a template that might help you organize your data, but you don't have to use it. What I will require of your common assessment data is that it is displayed in a manner that allows you to easily find answers to these four questions:
>
> 1. As a team, which targets from the assessment require more attention?
>
> 2. As a team, which students did not master which targets?
>
> 3. As a team, which classrooms require additional support?
>
> 4. As an individual teacher, which area was my lowest, and how can I improve?
>
> The template I have provided is a resource. It helps you answer the four questions, but I already know you will find ways to make it even better, clearer, and more efficient.

In the absence of a clear framework for decision making that includes the organization's identified values, goals, success indicators, and criteria for quality, the concept of tight/loose decision making can be hard to grasp. The idea itself seems loose if leaders are nebulous about where and how to be tight. Effective leaders define all of the aspects and guidelines that will create shared responsibility in the decision making at hand.

Case Studies: Putting It Together

Doug Reeves (2007) suggests that aligning systems is not for the faint of heart. Aligning systems often involves change, and leading change requires courage:

> Those who implement changes in assessment, grading, and professional practices and policies risk not only confrontation, but also unpopularity, social isolation, public humiliation, and ultimately, even their livelihoods. . . . Visiting senior leaders . . . have said, "But we could never do that in our system. The culture just won't allow it." The problem goes beyond culture, however. Such statements reveal an all-too-common lack of courage in the leaders, board members, and citizens who decide every day if they will give primacy to the interests of adults or to the children they serve. (p. 9)

To become a PLC, districts, schools, and even individual teams must align the systems in which they operate. Aligning systems is not impossible and need not be overwhelming. It does require patience, understanding, and a watchful eye. Effective leaders know they will never get it right the first time—systems, as complex, interactive, and dynamic as they are, require the long view. They also require organizationally sensitive responses as new discoveries are made over time.

Effective leaders at all levels of the organization commit to align systems because alignment is critical to success. Leaders launch their best efforts with the full knowledge that the *learning* in *professional learning communities* describes discoveries and changes they will need to make along the way. A principal we interviewed summed it up best:

> I look back over mistakes we've made and say to myself, "Oh, well, I could have rolled this out differently. I could have framed it differently. I could've had these people involved in the process and I didn't." I find myself sometimes second-guessing after I've enacted a process and I can see how it's unfolding. But *doing* the work is *learning* the work on new and deeper levels. Learning is never perfect. Efficacious learners learn from their mistakes and readjust. I just try to readjust, and then of course, new learning comes from that too. Learning is truly a lifelong process. I think becoming a professional learning community might be too. I don't believe we'll ever *arrive* but we will most definitely keep trying! (Principal interview, spring 2010)

In addition to the interviews we conducted, we have learned much about systems change at all levels of leadership through several case studies from real experiences in professional learning community settings. As mentioned, we have altered the names and a few of the details to protect those who shared their experiences and who are continuously striving to build a truly collaborative culture. There are examples of brilliance in aligning systems for leaders of all educational levels. Their stories and examples motivate and inspire us.

A Teacher's Story

Brandon wanted his team to be successful with the work of PLCs, but he knew the team had a lot of room to grow. The team members—himself included—had a history of teaching the textbook, and he now realized they were missing key standards and were providing instruction for content that was not in their standards. Moreover, the assessments they used did not provide accurate or sufficient information about student learning as it related to their standards. He felt the team was engaged in discrete, linear teaching, which trapped students in a system of contingent and unaccountable learning. Brandon could see that they had not aligned their textbook and classroom assessments with their state standards. The district had allocated days in the summer to do some alignment work, but Brandon felt the team could not wait since they had learners in their classrooms *today*.

Brandon knew he could easily overwhelm his already fast-paced team by adding "one more thing," so he decided to embed the work into the team's current efforts to design common assessments. Team members began by using the district's expectations for common assessments, then added their own quality criteria for assessment design and use. Brandon knew that developing these criteria would help the team better understand the district's expectations as well as provide him with the framework to align the systems as they went along. He recognized, for example, that if "accurate assessment" was one of their criteria—he was sure it would be and was prepared to bring it up if no one else did—then he could help the team focus on identifying and evaluating the student learning targets in their standards and whether the curriculum and its assessment materials were meeting those targets. That step would be essential to the team's overall success; it would align their currently misaligned classroom systems, and more importantly, it would empower the team to make critical decisions as they created new alternatives.

Brandon believed that working on one common assessment at a time would help the team create a long-term, big picture of the overall curriculum. His team would have a strong foundation on which to advance its efforts during any summer curriculum-alignment activities and perhaps could forgo the summer work altogether. He was confident that his team could accomplish the task of aligning standards, curriculum, and assessments in small doses and that he could help the team manage the alignment effectively and efficiently. Brandon's greatest challenge, he knew, was going to be aligning team members' instruction to their new assessments and their instructional responses to their assessment results. To keep from being overwhelmed by what lay ahead, he tried to focus on clear, manageable starting points. Besides, Brandon's team was amazing, and he trusted that if he could align the first critical components, the others might easily fall into place.

Brandon walked into his first team meeting to develop a common assessment for the upcoming unit prepared with all of the necessary materials: copies of the team's standards for that unit, the curriculum, current assessments, rubrics, a blank assessment template, and blank chart paper for big-picture thinking. The team members had few and precious minutes together, and he wanted to maximize their focus and energy. He distributed copies of the standards and curriculum, and then he walked to the front of the room and drew a large table with blank rows and columns on the chart paper. He asked the team to isolate the student learning targets from the standards, and he listed their targets down the left-hand column of the table. Then he asked them to identify the objectives in their curriculum materials, and he listed them across the top row. "The trick," Brandon said, "is to find the gaps between our standards and the curriculum, the natural intersections between them, and any unnecessary content in the curriculum that we can *stop* doing."

At first, the team was puzzled. "Aren't we just supposed to write an assessment?" someone said.

"Absolutely," Brandon replied, "and we're getting there. But in our criteria for quality, we said we wanted accurate assessments, so we know they must align to our standards, and our curriculum may or may not do that. We have to figure that out first. And we said we were overwhelmed with content, so I'm thinking this process might help us figure out what content we can drop if our standards don't require it. Of course, the team might want to keep content we consider essential and important, even if our standards don't include it, but we can't have that discussion if we don't first find the intersections. Plus, I'm thinking that the map we are creating will help us align future units and remember next year all that we did this year. Your thoughts?"

The team did not disagree. As team leader, Brandon was already addressing their criteria, their greatest hopes, and their desire to feel they wouldn't always be recreating the wheel. The team created their common assessment before they began teaching the unit, and to Brandon's delight and relief, conversations around changing instruction happened almost instantaneously.

A Principal's Story

Janelle wanted her teams to function as a learning community, but her first big hurdle was managing the master schedule. In its current form, it didn't allow for team time, and more importantly, it wouldn't help them achieve their mission of creating success for all learners. Changing the master schedule involved so much more than changing times. They would need to consider many systems, through questions such as:

- Does our daily schedule support time for student learning interventions?
- Are there any current practices or policies in the building that unintentionally inhibit us from intervening with students who need extra support?
- Is there a location in the building where those interventions will take place?
- Is there time for collaborative teams to meet?
- Where are team members' classrooms in proximity to one another? Do they have shared space, and if not, can we create some readily accessible team space?

- If we make schedule changes, what will be the frequency of our intervention times with students or our meeting times to explore our data and results? Daily? Twice a week? Weekly?

- Are there any district policy issues or concerns around changing how we operate or do the work of professional development?

Janelle realized she couldn't change the master schedule overnight, so at the beginning of the year she began by finding time to meet with teachers who already shared a specific curriculum or grade level of students and who had expressed interest in being more collaborative. If they opted to participate in PLC meetings, she told them, she would require them to do two things: (1) remain true to the process and engage in the work of creating common assessments and interventions for students and (2) help her identify the research on what works and their recommendations on how to make it work better. Not all of the teams in her building were interested in doing the work of PLCs in this early stage. By November, three "action teams" engaged in the work of PLCs while she searched for ways to change the master schedule.

By December, Janelle developed a guiding coalition of representatives from the collaborative teams and other key individuals such as the guidance counselor; representatives from the specialists groups like art, physical education, and special education; and a few additional teacher leaders from other teams who were beginning to express interest, for the specific task of designing a schedule that would accommodate teacher meeting time and intervention support times for struggling learners. The guiding coalition members already understood the master schedule would need to change, but she began their discussions by outlining her non-negotiables about what quality might look like:

- They must find time for interventions for learners, and that time must be *during* the school day.

- They must find time for teams to collaborate within the contract day.

- They must ensure that the time would be sufficient to accomplish the work required.

The guiding coalition then launched into researching current literature and finding specific examples of what scheduling and intervention options might be available. They also defined their criteria for quality in their preferred schedule and in their ideal intervention plans. They identified some of their criteria from best practices literature in school schedules and interventions. They also identified some of their criteria for quality by investigating their current options and their desired options for schedules and interventions. Starting in January, Janelle and the guiding coalition engaged the whole staff in clarifying the building's vision and mission statements. These statements, Janelle knew, would help make the guiding coalition's intervention plans and schedules meaningful to everyone on the staff.

As the year progressed, collaborative teams tried to focus their team conversations on student-learning data. They also tried to respond to the data by putting into practice some intervention times and strategies to help struggling learners.

In the spring, Janelle asked the action teams to share their findings, their processes, and their experiences taking part in typical PLC meetings. One team videotaped its last meeting, in which team members examined the results of their common assessment and designed corresponding interventions. The next team followed the video with a discussion of team members' overall impression of the meetings and their collective data on student achievement as a result of their efforts. The final team closed the meeting by reviewing meeting structures, templates, recommendations, and norms. All three teams then answered questions from the staff.

When the guiding coalition was finished, Janelle took the floor and highlighted not only their local findings but also the ties to the broad research she had been strategically sharing with the staff throughout their discussions during the year. She then proposed two schedules, developed by the guiding coalition with action team input, for the staff's consideration. The staff talked in depth about the benefits and challenges of what soon became known as plans A and B. Unfortunately, something didn't feel right, and people could not come to consensus on accepting either plan. Janelle agreed to take time between staff meetings to reflect and consider options.

While reflecting during her drive to work a week later, she found a way to merge plans A and B into plan C, and she believed it just might make everyone happy. When she arrived at work, she stopped to talk to every member of the guiding coalition, and to her delight, they all agreed the plan might work. Janelle was so confident that plan C addressed all of the staff's earlier concerns that she did not even wait for a meeting—she sent the plan out via email to all staff and suggested they gather to talk about it the next morning, even though it was not a scheduled staff meeting time. She knew that everyone was anxious to resolve the scheduling issue, so she was sure staff would show up for the discussion. So many staff members stopped to talk to her about their appreciation for plan C before the end of the day that it was already clear before the next morning they would likely adopt plan C.

Plan C was indeed adopted, and Janelle made public commitments to staff to (1) support their efforts in PLC team meetings, (2) continue to refine or tweak anything they discovered was not working along the way, and (3) remain open to their feedback and input for future schedule changes.

While Janelle had done a lot of work, she knew she had only just begun. Her school could have all the structure in the world, but that would not mean the right things were happening. The journey to success for all students had only just begun, and she would need to align more systems along the way.

A Superintendent's Story

Allen was the superintendent of a large district that had been trying to function as a professional learning community for three years. He was frustrated that the staff didn't seem to completely embrace the idea, and much time and energy by leaders at every level across the organization was being put into supporting team collaboration efforts and resources. Leaders felt like they were spinning their wheels, to no avail. He wasn't sure what the missing ingredient was, but he knew he needed to find it. The PLC work was too important.

Allen formed a partnership with Nancy, the superintendent of a neighboring district that was also trying to become PLC oriented. Allen offered his brightest and best leaders at the building, district, and teacher levels to serve as a review team to help Nancy's district, and he asked Nancy to also put together a team of colleagues who were strong leaders and who understood the work of PLCs to review his district. Together, he and Nancy selected the tools, criteria, and visiting processes they wanted to use to explore the health and productivity of their schools in a PLC audit. Happily, they found they could use many already-existing and published materials to frame the audit.

When they were ready, Allen and Nancy gathered two teams of eight at a common location where they explained the expectations, tools, and protocols the review teams would use. They concluded the meeting by finding strategic times when the teams could visit each other's districts to conduct the audit.

Each team visited all of the buildings in the district over the course of three days. They observed classroom instruction and team meetings, conducted interviews, and administered a survey. When the work was complete, the two district teams reconvened to share their overall findings. As anticipated, both districts discovered gaps and areas for growth; both districts also discovered their staff evaluation systems did not align with the stated expectations for staff working in professional learning communities.

Allen immediately began revamping district teacher and administrator evaluation systems. He wanted evaluations to align tightly to the work of PLCs—to be embedded in a comprehensive learning system. He formed a district guiding coalition, which included several of the leaders who were also engaged in the PLC audit. The guiding coalition consulted local data, key stakeholder groups, and expert published materials. It took six months before the guiding coalition developed a framework it could share, discuss, and refine with schools across the district.

The changes in the evaluation system involved not only *what* would be evaluated but *how*. Teams would have to become integral to the self-assessment process. In addition, the central office took a more active role. After implementing these changes, the superintendent is now in every classroom in the district no less than twice a year, as is his assistant superintendent and other central office administrators. In one year, they collectively make thousands of classroom visits—the superintendent making over one thousand of his own annually. In Allen's view, his focus as superintendent must be on learning, just as he requires his staff to focus on learning.

When any observation team in Allen's district—whether composed of administrators or peers—walks into a school, the team always has the list of agreed-upon success indicators, which focus on student and staff engagement and learning. The evaluators strive to gather evidence showing that schools are addressing those items they agreed should be tight.

Following observations of team meetings, staff meetings, and student learning opportunities, all of the building staff gather in the media center for the report. Those who participated in the observations sit in panel formation and follow a strict protocol:

- Evaluators must tightly tie all comments to success indicators. This includes aiming comments at the work of teams rather than individuals.

- Each person can only have three minutes total to speak. A timer is placed in front of the speaker, and when the timer goes off, the speaker is done, even if he or she is in the middle of a sentence. The timer passes to the next person.

- During the three minutes, the speaker must begin with celebrations, offer constructive feedback, and end with celebrations.

- Speakers must never directly point constructive feedback at or address egregious issues to individuals. Anything that requires a personal response or a disciplinary action must be handled privately.

- The session ends with no more than fifteen minutes of discussion for staff to ask clarifying questions or seek counsel on the panel's recommendations.

The staff in Allen's district quickly learned to welcome building visits from district leaders. In the past, when the superintendent and other central office staff walked through classrooms or sat in on team meetings, building staff members were nervous and hesitant. Under the old cultural and operational norm, district leaders only visited campus when someone was in trouble. Fortunately, it only took a few observation cycles to change the norm and the dynamic. Today, all staff in the district understand they are on the same team, pursuing the same vision, mission, values, and goals. More than that, building-level staff members understand that the central office has a pulse on their collective strengths, and armed with data, the central office can better support them.

The central office in Allen's district is now positioned to validate, value, and celebrate the work of PLCs. What gets monitored is what gets done. Allen's supportive and aligned system of staff evaluation has closed the gap between PLCs who function in name only and those who deeply own, understand, and engage in the work.

CHAPTER FOUR

Facilitating Shared Responsibility

A nation is formed by the willingness of
each of us to share in the responsibility for
upholding the common good.

—Barbara Jordan

It never ceases to amaze us how many insightful leadership lessons come from the
most unlikely sources. Consider the following excerpt from the classic children's book
Stuart Little:

> Just as the sun was coming up, Stuart saw a man seated in thought by
> the side of the road. Stuart steered his car alongside, stopped, and put his
> head out.
>
> "You're worried about something aren't you?" asked Stuart.
>
> "Yes, I am," said the man, who was tall and mild.
>
> "Can I help you in any way?" asked Stuart in a friendly voice.
>
> The man shook his head. "It's an impossible situation, I guess." he replied.
> "You see, I'm the Superintendent of Schools in this town."
>
> "That's not an impossible situation," said Stuart. "It's bad, but it's not
> impossible."
>
> "Well," continued the man, "I've always got problems that I can't solve.
> Today, for instance, one of my teachers is sick—Miss Gunderson her name
> is. She teachers Number Seven school. I've got to find a substitute for her,
> a teacher who will take her place,"
>
> "Can't you find another teacher?" asked Stuart.
>
> "No, that's the trouble. There's nobody in this town who knows anything; no
> spare teachers, no anything. School is supposed to begin in an hour."
>
> "I will be glad to take Miss Gunderson's place for a day if you like," sug-
> gested Stuart agreeably.

The Superintendent of Schools looked up. "Really?"

"Do you think that you can maintain discipline?" asked the Superintendent.

"Of course, I can," replied Stuart. "I'll make the work so interesting that the discipline will take care of itself." (White, 1945, p. 84–87)

Although it is safe to assume that Stuart Little had never stepped into a school or classroom, he seemed to intuitively know that one of the essential practices of successful teacher leaders is the *facilitation of shared responsibility*.

The superintendent of schools was making assumptions and prioritizing based on a deficit model in which administrators and teachers function more as managers than leaders—a model that is all too common in schools—whereas Stuart Little understood that successful teaching and leading is not about creating a culture of discipline and compliance. Instead, Stuart was quick to acknowledge that he shared in the responsibility of creating a learning-focused school culture for students; he needed to design a meaningful, engaging, dynamic lesson that nurtured learning naturally. The question of student discipline would then take care of itself. Stuart understood that effective teaching—like leading—is a reciprocal relationship that rests on shared commitment and shared responsibility.

The superintendent, meanwhile, seemed more concerned with maintaining discipline and control in Miss Gunderson's absence than with ensuring that the students under his stewardship would experience high-quality instruction. His response stresses compliance and accountability for discipline over collective commitment and shared responsibility for learning.

Sadly, in our work with districts, schools, and teams, we have found that a strong focus on accountability at the expense of shared responsibility is not uncommon. In fact, a culture of compliance and accountability is evident in the questions and comments we often hear from district, school, and teacher leaders. For example:

- Once we identify the shared mission and vision, how do I keep everyone focused on doing the work?

- We are creating forms that all teams will use as they develop their common assessments.

- I have been providing my teaching teams with the topics for their meetings; do you have any ideas for what I should tell our teams to do after they create common assessments?

- How many SMART goals should we identify each year?

- The district improvement plan calls for the development of common formative assessments; what kind of assessments do they need to be?

- The principal has required us to develop learning targets by the end of the year; how many do we need to have for each unit?

These district, school, and teacher leaders clearly have been attempting to engage their colleagues in creating professional learning communities. On closer examination, however, it becomes obvious that although the questions and the requests for products and information are accurately focused, those involved may be doing the right work for the wrong reasons.

Facilitating shared responsibility is the third of the three core practices that leaders employ simultaneously and continuously. Facilitating shared responsibility requires more than calling for a change in structure; it requires changing the culture and the fundamental belief systems behind why and how educators work together.

District, school, and teacher leaders often make a strong push to begin the PLC journey by actually digging in and doing PLC work. There is no question that the effective leaders we interviewed were inclined to learn by doing. However, we know that if leaders jump to the *doing* without creating a proper conceptual understanding of the individual and collective work, they may not be able to create individual and collective responsibility.

When leaders fail to facilitate shared responsibility, they create systems that streamline the work of PLCs at the expense of individual and collective efficacy: teachers may generate team products, but they feel as if they are simply jumping through hoops to fulfill yet another administrative mandate. In contrast, the effective leaders we interviewed made certain that their colleagues not only engaged in the right work of creating and sustaining a collaborative culture and aligning systems, but that they did so for the right reasons.

Accountability Versus Shared Responsibility

Without developing shared responsibility for the collective work of becoming a PLC, specific efforts—such as effectively using collaboration time, creating common formative assessments, and developing SMART goals—quickly become simple exercises in task completion. When we talk to teachers in schools in which leaders have not made an intentional effort to facilitate shared responsibility for their collective work, we hear vernacular that focuses on individual and collective accountability rather than an emphasis on shared responsibility. Consider the conversations we had with leaders in traditional schools.

A teacher leader:

> I gave the fourth-grade team our next common assessment. I still need to develop the fourth-grade interventions with a possible schedule for the team's consideration. Once I have that in place, I can begin developing digital drop folders with intervention and enrichment ideas for future use. I think I can even create shared files for posting our data so I don't have to keep doing all of that work on my own. I'm excited because I should have everything wrapped up before the end of school year.

A building leader:

> One of the things that I feel has been very influential is that as the assistant principal I set teachers' schedules. I have every PLC team meet every day, and I set the focus for their meetings across the school. For example, I tell them that on Wednesdays, when you meet in your teams, all you are to do is talk about assessment results. I keep us all in the media center for team meetings so I can make sure that everyone is on task and I can hear what the group needs next. It helps me to plan and them to stay focused.

A central office leader:

> I have been able to get the principals and their teachers to develop SMART goals and use common formative assessments. Now I just need to get them to care. I learned that I should change behavior first and beliefs will follow. I think they'll get there—it's just a matter of time. It is taking a long time, however. That part is frustrating.

As a noun, *accountability* has its origin in the Latin *accomptare*, meaning *to account for*. Various definitions of *accountability* identify a common theme of being required to, expected to, and subjected to. Effective leaders are very careful about the words they use, and they clearly understand that words and language frame the values, beliefs, and habits that define the culture of their schools. At its best, a culture of accountability can lead to greater levels of efficiency and high productivity. At its worst, however, a culture of accountability can create feelings of victimization and isolation. One of the leaders we interviewed described the difference:

> I think the best way to change schools is through a culture of commitment, not compliance. If you try to make changes through compliance alone you do not get to empowerment. In this case, people may do things to appease you, but they will never have the kind of dedication and understanding that it takes to truly change the way we do things. (District leader interview, fall 2009)

Without an intentional effort to build mutual understanding and shared commitment, administrators and teachers will quickly become resentful of the changes to their daily practices and routines. Effective leaders communicate that changes and improvements are considered not for their own sake, but rather to serve the shared responsibility educators have to help all students achieve high levels of learning. From the very early phases of the PLC journey, effective leaders commit to helping colleagues shift their individual perspectives and to helping organizational culture shift from a focus on accountability to a commitment of shared responsibility.

The difference between accountability and shared responsibility is significant. In a general way, the difference lies in how leaders frame the work to be done and their expectations of teams and teachers. If leaders expect their colleagues to engage in a checklist of activities to simply get tasks completed, they might unintentionally stifle creativity, innovation, and empowerment. On the other hand, if leaders expect teachers to innovate, develop new ideas and work collaboratively to solve complex problems with expertise and creativity, they must empower teams by promoting interdependence and focused commitment toward meeting the district, school, and team collective vision, mission, values, and goals. Effective leaders shift perspectives from accountability to shared responsibility (see table 4.1).

Table 4.1: Shifting Perspectives From Accountability to Shared Responsibility

Accountability	Shared Responsibility
Places priority on getting things done	Places priority on doing the right things
Focuses on answering for decisions and choices made when desired outcomes are not met (responding)	Focuses on creating new or alternative responses when desired outcomes are not met (learning)
Increases desire to blame while simultaneously decreasing motivation	Increases ownership while simultaneously decreasing stress
Emphasizes external motivation	Emphasizes internal motivation
Perpetuates micromanagement	Inspires empowerment

When educators speak the business language of assurances, metrics, and compliance, they run the risk of creating a school culture that emphasizes task completion rather than shared responsibility. We have met many school leaders who take no small amount of pride in their self-proclaimed leadership mantra of "Get 'er done." While we would agree that it is important to actually get things done, we also know that the right work must get done for the right reasons. Doing the work of becoming a PLC just so the district can check it off the list of school improvement plans falls short of the educational leader's higher calling, which is to create a professional culture of interdependent working relationships and collective inquiry for adults and high levels of learning for all.

We have seen many leaders use the "Get 'er done" approach with the best of intentions. "At least by stating my expectations," one leader shared with us, "I am getting people to act." In this approach, mandates are issued ("You must remain pure to the district pacing guides and curriculum" or "You must use one formative and one summative assessment per term"), and policies or programs are required to change. Leaders typically issue directives with the intention of getting people to behave their way into accepting and believing in the new way of doing business. Experts agree that actions precede beliefs, but only when results indicate the actions were worth the investment (Elmore, 2004; Fullan, 2008; Patterson et al., 2008). When administrators and teachers are confused or frustrated as they deploy new practices and protocols, they seldom generate the right results to influence the desired change in beliefs.

Consider the example of a district that recently began to change the grading practices and policies of teachers. One of the many related directives required that "Homework may only count as 20 percent of the overall grade for the semester. The remaining 80 percent of the grade will be based on the summative assessments." District officials believed they were helping teachers move away from heavily weighting grades on practice work and toward creating more reliable achievement data based on results. Teachers, however, interpreted the new policy to mean they had to turn classroom assessments into high-stakes situations. Teachers also worried about how students who don't do well on tests would perform and whether parents would be angry. Meanwhile, students were frustrated that the hard work they put into doing homework would no longer count as much toward the final grade. Whether the new grading policy made sense was irrelevant once teachers and students felt as if the new changes were being done *to* them rather than *with* and *for* them.

While the "Get 'er done" approach may be efficient, it is clearly not effective. A better approach is to engage administrators, faculty, and students in the shared work of answering challenging questions. Consider how one of the effective leaders in our research framed a similar conversation regarding grading and reporting:

> Given everything we know about the research in our profession and best practices regarding grading and reporting, next year we are going to change our grading policy. To get ready, we are asking teams to engage in action research around the best practices in grading and reporting. In order to effectively change the policy, we need your help and expertise. We have some parameters to guide our work so that we are consistent and aligned with best practices:
>
> - All teams must engage in exploring how to change grading practices so that we arrive at accurate grades that reflect the results of learning at the end of the learning experience.
>
> - All efforts must be tied to best practices in the work of grading according to the experts in the field. Teams must be able to articulate how they made their decisions and which research experts they were referencing as they made changes.
>
> - Teams must generate both data regarding how the change effort worked and artifacts that were used along the way (i.e. Student reflection forms, student tracking forms, grading forms for formative assessment observations, etc.).
>
> - Teams must prepare and present their results to the building at the end of this year. Presentations will need to include the data and artifacts, as well as the team's proposed recommendations for district consideration on how best to move forward.
>
> - Buildings must find ways to communicate a consistent, shared message regarding this work with their parents and students.
>
> Although we have identified the general parameters for this effort, we looking forward to the creativity and insights you bring to the process. There is quite a bit of room for your expertise and professionalism to guide our collective learning. We are here to support your efforts. We will share research with you and work to answer your questions or problem solve as

appropriate along the way. We want to hear from you and we want to sit with you so we can identify the struggles and barriers and work to remove as many of them as possible. We will work with the board of education, higher education, and the community to communicate our message and gather key data regarding our efforts. We are hoping that you will be willing to share some of your work at board meetings. We believe that it is *your* hard work that will best inform our next steps so we can continue to support that which is best for our learners. Our work together in this effort is critical to our direction of achieving success for all. (Central office case study, 2009–2010 school year)

This approach calls everyone to action and facilitates shared responsibility toward a common understanding of the collective work. Approaching initiatives with the intention of facilitating shared responsibility significantly increases the likelihood of success for both adults and students alike. Sadly, far too many districts and schools have followed the accountability approach to leadership and management. In such schools, we regularly see an unhealthy emphasis on command and control in the way educators manage curriculum, instruction, and assessment and the daily work of teachers. This approach wipes out individual innovation and creativity in exchange for rigid task completion and strict accountability systems.

Since so many traditional schools have developed structures, systems, and protocols that create a culture of accountability similar to those seen on the factory floor and the assembly line, it should not be surprising that fifty percent of new teachers move to other professions within their first five years, and the remaining staff feel more beleaguered, disgruntled, and misunderstood over time (National Commission on Teaching and America's Future, 2003). It is hard to create a culture of engagement and shared responsibility when the focus is on getting things done, rather than doing the right things (Bennis & Nanus, 2007). The former necessitates systems and controls; the latter generates passion and commitment.

Fortunately, we have had the opportunity to learn from many outstanding school leaders who are moving their districts, schools, and teams out of structures of accountability and into cultures of shared responsibility. In districts and schools developing as PLCs, effective leaders place the priorities and focus on collaboration, intrinsic motivation, and empowerment. In *Drive: The Surprising Truth About What Motivates Us*, Daniel Pink (2009) describes this profound shift:

The scientists who study human motivation . . . offer us a sharper and more accurate account of both human performance and the human condition. . . . The science shows that those typical twentieth-century carrot and stick motivators . . . can crush the high-level creative, conceptual abilities that are central to current and future economic and social progress. The science shows that the secret to high performance isn't our biological drive or our reward-and-punishment drive, but our third drive—our deep-seated desire to direct our own lives, to extend and expand our abilities, and to live a life of purpose. (p. 145)

Engaging this third drive is critical to facilitating shared responsibility. It is our individual and collective drive that makes doing the right work for the right reasons the right answer.

We consistently hear from educators working in high-performing PLCs that they feel as if they are making a difference and that their work with colleagues in pursuit of their vision, mission, values, and goals has renewed their sense of purpose in their work. The transformation is always inspiring. One of the leaders we met described the feeling of working in a culture of shared responsibility in the following manner: "We are all far more empowered and actively engaged than we were before. We are accomplishing meaningful work that is having a positive impact on students and their achievement. It's exciting" (Personal communication with a principal, fall 2011). Pink (2009) also speaks to the transformation that occurs in individuals and the importance of moving away from a culture of accountability toward a culture of responsibility:

> While complying can be an effective strategy for physical survival, it's a lousy one for personal fulfillment. Living a satisfying life requires more than simply meeting the demands of those in control. Yet in our offices and our classrooms we have way too much compliance and way too little engagement. The former might get you through the day, but the latter will get you through the night. (p. 112)

From *I*, *My*, and *You* to *Us*, *We*, and *Ours*

In *Learning and Leading With Habits of Mind*, authors Art Costa and Bena Kallick (2008) summarize the work of well-known educational psychologist and philosopher Jean Piaget. In his research and writing regarding cognitive development, Piaget identified conceptual frameworks that guide an individual's perceptual position including egocentric and allocentric. Though Piaget identified the frameworks to help educators better understand and work with young learners, we have discovered that those same frameworks help us better understand and explain the work of the effective leaders as they facilitate shared responsibility in their districts, schools, and teams.

When operating from an *egocentric* orientation, Piaget says people perceive situations and occurrences from their own points of view and then make determinations as to how they will respond, react, or allow their perceptual position to affect them on a personal level. In an *allocentric* orientation, people perceive situations, events, and occurrences from another person's point of view. When individuals function from an allocentric perceptual position, they "empathize with another's feelings, predict how others are thinking, and anticipate potential misunderstandings" (Costa & Kallick, 2008, p. 22). Effective leaders in PLCs lead from an allocentric place.

We are hard pressed to find any literature or research that suggests effective leaders are selfish or self-centered. In the interviews we conducted with effective leaders, we hardly ever heard *me* or *my*. These leaders speak and think in allocentric terms of *us*, *we*, and *ours*. In high-performing PLCs, we hear district, school, and teacher leaders speak about the important work "*we* are doing" and "*our* [collective] work with students." Moreover, we found that effective teacher leaders extend allocentric language to be inclusive with students, emphasizing, for example, "*our* students in fifth grade." Consider the allocentric language we heard from effective leaders regarding their work in becoming a PLC:

> We made a lot of mistakes over the past eight years, but we learn from them. We have created a culture where people are safe in making mistakes, and we actually celebrate when people try new things, and even though we might have screwed it up, we know how to make it better for next time. (District-level leader interview, summer 2010)

> Every single person in our school offers considerable value to the group at large, and we believe strongly that each person has a role in helping students to achieve, every single one. We work to make sure we are reaching our vision and purpose in the daily moments. To the extent that we can, we commit to help one another understand how our role is helping students learn; we are creating the right school culture for students. (Principal interview, summer 2010)

> In our school we are now focused on how all of our students are doing in the third grade, as opposed to how we used to operate, which was focused on my students, in my class. What's cool is we can even name all of the students in third grade, and we care about how Jamal is reading, even though he's not in our individual rooms. (Teacher interview, summer 2010)

The effective leaders in our research made word choices that reflected their vision of the collaborative culture they were hoping to create. We simply never heard a leader within a high-performing professional learning community use the phrases "*my* school," "*my* staff," or "*my* students." The leaders we met consistently spoke of "*our* students," the work "*we* are engaged in," and how changes will affect "*us*" as a school.

We do not pretend to believe that leaders can increase their success and effectiveness by simply replacing the inherently exclusive language of *I*, *you*, and *my* with the inclusive vernacular of *we*, *us*, and *ours*. Professional learning communities need more from their leaders than a loud proclamation that there is no *I* in *team*. We do know, however, that leaders can sometimes talk their way into new habits of mind. We also have found that the language leaders use tells us a lot about their leadership practice and priorities in leading change.

In *How the Way We Talk Can Change the Way We Work*, developmental psychologists and organizational theorists Kegan and Lahey (2001) found that the language leaders choose to use has a significant impact on the culture of an organization:

> All leaders are leading language communities. Though every person, in every setting, has some opportunity to influence the nature of the language, leaders have exponentially greater access and opportunity to share, alter, or ratify the existing language rules. . . . Leaders have no choice in this matter of being language leaders; it just goes with the territory. We have a choice to be thoughtful or intentional about this aspect of our leadership, or

whether to unmindfully ratify the existing drift in our community's favored
forms. We have the choice to be responsible or not for the meaning of our
leadership as it affects our language community. But we have no choice
about whether we are or are not language leaders. (p. 8)

Our research has shown us that the most effective leaders of PLCs work diligently
to ensure their language accurately reflects their efforts to facilitate a culture of shared
responsibility.

Enabling a Culture of Relational Trust

A leader's ability to facilitate a culture of shared responsibility is contingent on the
level of trust within a school. Leadership experts James Kouzes and Barry Posner assert
the importance of trust in facilitating shared responsibility: "Trust motivates people
to go beyond mere compliance with authority. It motivates them to reach for the best
within themselves" (2010, p. 77). Valerie von Frank (2010) writes further:

Where there's trust, people are more likely to innovate because they feel
less vulnerable and alone, they give leaders more latitude because they
believe in the leader's intentions, and people are able to coalesce around
action plans, leading to more progress in reform. They are more likely to
collaborate. (pp. 1–2)

Simply put, trust is the relational glue that enables and supports the hard work and
collective commitments required for a school to develop as a professional learning
community.

The effectiveness of leadership efforts to develop a collaborative school culture and
align systems to the vision, mission, values, and goals is directly proportional to the levels of trust that leaders have been able to facilitate within the school. In schools with
low levels of personal and organizational trust, the effort to build a collaborative culture
will be difficult at best and impossible at worst. In *Leading with Trust*, Susan Stephenson
states simply, "If there is distrust in a school, it almost certainly will prevent a true learning community from getting off the ground" (2009, p. 11).

Trust is a two-way street. Developing personal and organizational relationships built
on relational trust requires that individuals trust others and have demonstrated that
they themselves are trustworthy. Trust in individuals, within curriculum teams, and
within schools can be easily and quickly broken; it is best to develop relationships built
on authentic relational trust by consistent action over time. The effective leaders in our
study diligently aligned their words and actions to demonstrate that they are both trusting and trustworthy.

Vulnerability is the foundation of trust. In *Overcoming the Five Dysfunctions of a Team*,
Patrick Lencioni (2005) states, "For a team to establish real trust, team members, beginning with the leader, must be willing to take risks without a guarantee of success. They
will have to be vulnerable without knowing whether that vulnerability will be respected

and reciprocated" (p. 18). We found that the leaders of high-performing PLCs were very willing to be vulnerable. Due to their willingness to be vulnerable and their consistent actions over time, the leaders we met developed a culture of relational trust in their districts, schools, and collaborative teams.

In their groundbreaking research on trust in schools, Anthony Bryk and Barbara Schneider (2002) suggest that relational trust reflects a personal assessment by leaders and followers of four criteria:

1. **Respect**—Does he listen to me? Does she invite dialogue? Does he look for new ideas and consider all points of view?

2. **Competence**—Does she have the knowledge and skills to do the job? Do individual teachers and curriculum teams understand and have the skills to do the work?

3. **Personal Regard for Others**—Does he care about me as an individual? Does she care about my growth and development as an educator?

4. **Integrity**—Does he follow through with what he says? Does she keep her word? Has he lied to me before? (pp. 23–26)

Respect, competence, personal regard for others, and integrity are the essential elements of relational trust and must be constantly nurtured. A teacher leader in a middle school described the importance of trust in her relationship with her team in this way:

It is important that my actions match what I have to say. If my colleagues start seeing that my actions are different from what I preach, then I might be a person that they will not be able to trust. What I talk about and what I do should be the same.

In the absence of organizational trust, colleagues will be far less likely to have an action orientation and will be less willing to engage in the collective inquiry that is the backbone of a collaborative culture. In our research with effective leaders, we have found that although vulnerability precedes trust, trust is the essential ingredient in the empowerment that educators must feel to be willing to take risks (see fig. 4.1).

Vulnerability → Trust → Empowerment → Risk taking

Figure 4.1: Relational trust.

Kouzes and Posner (2010) put it this way:

There is a positive relationship between risk and trust. The more people trust, the more they'll risk. When people feel secure, because they trust that you and the organization will protect their welfare, they can focus their energies on meeting higher-order needs, such as forming strong and cohesive relationships, mastering tasks, achieving organizational objectives, gaining a greater sense of self-efficacy, learning new skills and knowledge necessary to prepare for future assignments, and pursuing activities that promote growth and develop potential. (p. 79)

In high-performing PLCs, leaders are tireless in their efforts to create a school culture based on relational trust. Members of the PLC need to know that their efforts—those that hit the mark and those that don't—will be recognized, supported, and celebrated as learning experiences by their leaders. When leaders build relationships on authentic relational trust, they nurture the commitment to collective inquiry and action orientation that often leads to new insights, high degrees of creativity, and professional learning for all members. Stephenson (2009) summarizes the research of Bryk and Schneider and their study of trust in the Chicago public schools in this way:

> Resoundingly, they found that schools with strong relational levels of trust—teacher to teacher, teacher to leader, teacher to parent—were much more likely to make academic gains than schools without strong levels of trust. In fact, if the low level of trust continued over time, they concluded, there was virtually no chance of the school improving student achievement. (p. 98)

While building a culture of trust is important for the relationships among members of collaborative teams within PLCs, it is also crucial to a school's achievement of helping all students learn.

Building Relational Trust

While there is no shortage of ideas, suggestions, and tips on how to develop trust, we have made an effort to identify the strategies we have seen and heard effective PLC leaders use. Although building a culture of relational trust is an inexact science, we have found that effective leaders are able to do so by intentionally developing and practicing strategies to (1) use clear and effective communication, (2) manage emotions, and (3) manage relationships.

Using Clear and Effective Communication

Although there may be any number of reasons that trust is absent in districts, schools, or teams, our work with educators has demonstrated that a lack of trust almost always involves the inability of a leader to clearly communicate priorities and expectations. The inaccurate information, confusing rhetoric, and mixed messages that some leaders convey to their colleagues is often the source of an integrity gap between leaders and followers. The effective leaders we met in our research shared that they considered effective communication essential to their daily work and the first ingredient in establishing trust with their colleagues. When leaders communicate their expectations clearly and effectively, they are in a much better position to develop a culture of relational trust.

We found that in their effort to use clear and effective communication, the effective leaders of high-performing PLCs succeed by:

- Facilitating clear, meaningful communication with their colleagues—
    - Practicing deep listening when in conversation with others

- ○ Paraphrasing back what they are hearing

- ○ Maintaining eye contact with those they are speaking with

- ○ Asking open-ended questions to seek understanding

- ○ Examining issues from multiple perspectives

- ○ Modeling positive, affirming nonverbal behaviors

- Demonstrating sensitivity to the stated and apparent needs of others

- Watching for group responses and tuning in to the emotional reaction of others

- Resolving manageable conflicts within meetings and moving large or complicated conflicts outside a meeting to small-group sessions

- Inviting, acknowledging, and responding appropriately to feedback

Managing Emotions

One of the more fascinating neuroscience discoveries in the past few years is that the makeup of the human brain is "sociable" and that humans are naturally drawn into "brain-to-brain linkup whenever we engage with another person" (Goleman, 2006, p. 4). The "neural bridge" that is established when we come into contact with others builds a neurological pathway that transfers emotions and emotional conditions from one person to another, which is to say, emotions are contagious (Goleman, 2006). We found that the most successful leaders within high-performing PLCs had an intuitive understanding and appreciation for the fact that their emotional state and condition affects their colleagues. Effective leaders pay particular attention to their emotional condition, and they practice skills and techniques throughout their day to ensure they do not intentionally or unintentionally fracture the culture of trust in their districts, schools, or teams. Nothing breaks the social and emotional bonds of relational trust faster than when a leader acts or reacts out of anger, fear, remorse, bitterness, or spite; the effect on others can be significant. We found that effective leaders manage emotions by:

- Embracing and exhibiting a calm demeanor and caring orientation toward others

- Setting aside personal interests in order to facilitate the best solution for the good of the group

- Following the RAIN Principle (Kornfield, 2009)—

- ○ Recognition of their emotions as they occur in the moment

- ○ Acceptance of their emotions as they are, not as they wish them to be

- ○ Investigation of why they are experiencing a heightened emotional state, understanding that the cause of nearly all emotions and subsequent reactions are rooted in past experiences and not the result of events in the present

○ Non-attachment to the emotion as a means to prevent resulting behaviors that might negatively impact themselves, their team, or the collective work

- Maintaining self-awareness of what emotions they are bringing (positive and negative) to their collaborative work by—

  ○ Examining the influences of cultural dynamics on beliefs, values, and boundaries in their collective work

  ○ Examining their own biases, assumptions, judgments, conventions, needs, and habits and the potential impact on others

  ○ Examining their personal pressure points or emotional hooks

- Facing and accepting emotional situations with a minimum of personal defensiveness

- Practicing letting go of judgments, attachments, and resentments that might interfere with their work with colleagues

Managing Relationships

In an effort to build a culture of relational trust, effective leaders spend considerable time managing their relationships with colleagues. Successful leaders understand that every interaction they have with their colleagues will serve as either a building block for improvement or a chip in the foundation of their collective work. In *Leading in a Culture of Change* (2001), Fullan discusses the importance of relationships and the necessity for leaders to carefully cultivate and tend these collegial relationships. At the same time, Fullan warns that relationships are not an end in and of themselves and that "relationships are indeed powerful, which means that they can also be powerfully wrong" (p. 65). The leaders we met in our research vividly described their collegial relationships and the never-ending work to manage the relationships effectively by:

- Resolving issues between colleagues with care, concern, and integrity

- Balancing their calming behavior with assertive expectations

- Making decisions based on what's best for students, not in service of adult autonomy or convenience

- Whenever possible, answering affirmatively with "Yes," recognizing that it may be a "Yes, if," "Yes, when," or "Yes, maybe"; always finding a way to respond to requests with by empowering others within agreed-upon parameters (Erkens, 2008a)

- Treating everyone equitably (not necessarily equally)

- Keeping their word and, in the rare circumstance that they cannot, bringing it to the group with an explanation for the change

- Avoiding blaming and shaming—not pointing fingers at others as the cause of unhealthy behavior or mind shifts

Enabling a culture of relational trust is an essential component of a leader's efforts to facilitate a culture of shared responsibility within PLCs. When Peter Drucker (2011) suggested that the only appropriate approach to change was "Ready, Fire, Aim," he did so assuming that high levels of relational trust existed in the organization. The risk-taking inherent within the action orientation of PLCs becomes safe and supported when leaders prioritize building relational trust in their daily work. The investment of time that leaders spend in developing a culture of relational trust pays dividends when individuals and teams experience the inevitable dissonance of creating and sustaining a collaborative learning culture.

Embracing Dissonance

In traditional schools, leaders spend considerable time attempting to maintain a relatively calm and disturbance-free culture. We find that many leaders are uncomfortable with the disorder and dissonance that meaningful change brings. Some leaders, in fact, simply find that they cannot handle the stress of leading significant change and improvement initiatives. In *Beyond School Improvement*, Robert Davidovich, Pauli Nikolay, Bonnie Laugerman, and Carol Commodore (2010) describe the phenomenon this way:

> Superintendents, principals, and teachers learn quickly that those above them and around them not do like disequilibrium, so they work for change without making too many waves. Unfortunately, that important state between stability and disorder—the one where innovation occurs—cannot be achieved without dissonance. Avoiding dissonance means that initiatives are sought that create minimal disruptions. These tend to be quick fixes and surface changes. Seeking such solutions eliminates the energy needed to break apart old ways so that new ones can form. (p. 106)

What makes matters worse is that leaders often develop feelings of insecurity and anxiety as conflict begins to manifest. This is especially true when they hear that their colleagues are questioning them and their decisions with comments such as:

- "There is very little trust between administration and teachers right now."
- "I'm not sure you appreciate how many people are upset with this initiative."
- "This seems like another top-down initiative."
- "I have never seen the morale in our schools so low."

As a result, leaders may question their leadership practice and interpret the disequilibrium as a negative reflection on not only their leadership, but also on them personally.

It's fair to say that most school leaders did not enter the education profession with high hopes of annoying people. To mitigate the anxiety they often feel when leading change initiatives, leaders tend to rely on "relationship building" as a basis for their leadership practice. In doing so, they risk creating a school culture in which administrators and teachers have to bargain for important work to be done and in which nurturing and healing strained relationships becomes more important than doing the actual work of becoming a learning community. We have seen leaders abandon improvement efforts completely in hopes that strained relationships with colleagues might quickly go back to normal. Effective leaders of high-performing PLCs are always mindful of their relationships with colleagues; however, they do not allow relationship building to trump the other prerequisites of successful leadership.

Leaders who are successfully guiding their schools along the continuum of becoming a PLC embrace individual and collective dissonance as an important component of the change process and an essential element in facilitating shared responsibility. Effective leaders are not only open to the questioning, testing, and challenging that accompanies individual and collective dissonance; the successful leaders we studied also went out of their way to actually engage their colleagues in the dynamic tension that spawns creativity and innovation.

Leon Festinger first articulated cognitive dissonance theory in 1956 by suggesting that a state of dissonance is produced when there is inconsistency between a person's beliefs and his or her experiences (Festinger, Riecken, & Schachter, 1956). In schools, individual and collective dissonance occur routinely as teachers and teams consider their beliefs in light of new experiences that demonstrate different and potentially more effective ways of doing things. Rather than running away from the disorder that often accompanies the change process, effective leaders understand and appreciate that dissonance is essential for organizational growth and improvement—and that it is absolutely required for meaningful adult learning. Dissonance occurs at the edges of people's comfort zones; professional improvement occurs when they move beyond it.

In their examination of effective leadership practices, Davidovich and colleagues (2010) come to a similar conclusion:

> Leaders who have learned to embrace dissonance . . . understand that change is about reordering and that transformative change is messy—it involves breaking down and letting go of old patterns so that new ones can emerge. They may not relish the messes, but they know that messes are an essential precursor to developing higher capacity. [Leaders] do not just merely value dissonance and its role in change, they consciously choose to be disturbed, which is the first attribute of innovation. (p. 104)

We found that effective leaders of high-performing PLCs were entirely comfortable with the disequilibrium created by introducing innovation and change; in fact, they went out of their way to facilitate professional development opportunities to experience individual and collective dissonance. Consider the following example of a collaborative conversation that a principal facilitated to enable dissonant thinking regarding his school's collective work:

In my role as the learning leader of the school I am constantly trying to pro-vide opportunities for thinking creatively and examining our individual and collective work to examine areas for improvement. At the start of this past year I facilitated a learning opportunity that is still paying dividends to this day. Having read Collins' book *Good to Great*, I was struck by his finding that leaders who built Good to Great organizations focused less on their To Do List than their Stop Doing Lists. That is to say, Good to Great organizations spend time focusing not just on creating and innovating new programs they have to consider what they need to stop doing as well. As a pretty good school it was hard for my teachers to think that we might be doing some things that we shouldn't be, so I facilitated a series of meetings in which we spent time critically examining our practices and programs in light of our guiding principle and asking ourselves if we were engaging in behaviors and actions that were inconsistent with student learning. Although it was initially hard for our teachers to admit that they might be doing things that were actually having a negative impact on students and student learning, once we really got into the conversations they realized that some things we do, like giving zeros, not accepting late work, sending students out into the hallway or to the dean for discipline issues, interrupting class time through the use of the intercom, were all actually inconsistent with our fundamental purpose. As hard as it was for our teachers to accept the idea that we were anything less than the outstanding school that we had received awards for, as we created our Stop Doing List we realized that we still have a long way to go. The conversations were hard on a few of our folks, however, in the end it was one of the best professional development experiences we had in a long, long time. (Personal communication, summer 2011)

While enabling and embracing dissonance can take a variety of forms, all of the lead-ers we met in our research clearly understood and appreciated the powerful learning opportunities that result when their colleagues think critically about their work and challenge assumptions about their practice. Rather than running away from the chal-lenging conversations, effective leaders go out of their way to encourage and facilitate experiences for their colleagues.

Resolving Conflict and Building Consensus

Most people view conflict as something to avoid. In fact, leaders in traditional schools spend time and energy worrying about how to prevent and respond to conflict. Leaders in high-performing PLCs, however, understand that most conflict is simply a manifes-tation of unresolved individual or collective dissonance, and this state of dynamic ten-sion provides opportunities to facilitate shared responsibility. Effective leaders do not shy away from conflict. They understand that *resolving* conflict and building consensus are important elements of their leadership practice.

While there is obviously more than one way to approach conflict resolution and con-sensus building, the following suggested strategies from Marcia Hughes and James

Terrell (2007) in *The Emotionally Intelligent Team* are worthwhile and are representative of what we heard from effective leaders:

- **Patience**—Effective leaders and "high performing teams listen to their members with open minds" (p. 125). If leaders choose to be impatient, the authors warn, they may pay significant consequences. Hughes and Terrell write, "Impatience is a choice" (p. 125). Effective leaders spend time listening to their colleagues and approach their comments, questions, and concerns with an open mind.

- **Perspective**—Effective leaders appreciate that perspectives differ. Understanding the unique and varied perspectives of their colleagues is an important function of effective leadership. The most effective leaders appreciate that, if treated as ideas or possibilities, differing perspectives can be a "team's greatest strength" (p. 125).

- **Intention and attention**—It is important for leaders to cultivate a culture of "personal intention" in which everyone commits to working together and to finding the best possible solutions to the issues the team is addressing (p. 125). Effective leaders help teams stay focused on those things that need attention.

- **Collaborative communication**—Effective leaders and truly collaborative teams must have a "shared commitment to spend the time required to work through issues" (p. 126). Leaders who are open to collaboration demonstrate a commitment to the team and their collective work. Effective leaders create a culture of interdependence, and they embrace the tensions and conflicts that will arise from close, proximate working relationships. The most effective leaders do not avoid difficult issues and conflicts; they know that to do so would be "the death knell for teams" (p. 126). Effective leaders embrace dissonance and conflict and use these times as an opportunity for innovation and improvement.

- **Empathy**—Leaders of collaborative teams demonstrate "care, concern, and respect" for each of their colleagues (p. 126). Hughes and Terrell (2007) write, "One way to work through a conflict on your team is by letting your teammates know that you are seriously considering what they are advocating, that you will attend to their perspectives, and that you respect their opinions and feelings" (p. 126). Effective leaders employ empathic leadership skills that demonstrate their sincere desire to help each member of the team improve and build his or her individual and the team's collective capacity.

- **Assertiveness**—Assertiveness, according to Hughes and Terrell (2007), "is found in the happy medium between being passive, which is the failure to speak up regarding an important issue, and being aggressive, which is expressing your point of view in a manner that takes it too far, leaving your teammates no room to disagree" (p. 126). It is important for leaders to be aware of their "volume and tone of voice, along with posture, gestures, facial features and other non-verbal signals . . . because empathy and assertiveness need to be blended for effective teamwork" (p. 126).

- **Humor**—Effective leaders appreciate and understand that humor, when used wisely, is the best "antidote" to conflict. Leaders know, however, that "humor can backfire if it is misconstrued as a put down or that the leader doesn't take the matter seriously" (p. 127). At the same time, the most effective leaders do not take themselves too seriously, and they are unafraid to practice self-deprecating humor to highlight areas for improvement and growth.

- **Gratitude**—Effective leaders make "gratitude a habit" (p. 127). Effective leaders understand that sometimes, the most effective leadership practices are simple acts of kindness that express gratitude and thanks for the hard work of others on the team. According to Hughes and Terrell (2007), teams build resilience when they "recognize and celebrate the many gifts they receive as a team" (p. 127).

- **Choice in conflict resolution style**—Collaborative teams have an identified and agreed-upon way to resolve conflict and build consensus. Effective leaders ensure that collaborative teams are consistently using their consensus-building and conflict resolution strategies (p. 130).

While the guidelines offered by Marcia Hughes and James Terrell (2007) serve as wonderful reminders of how teams should go about the work of conflict resolution and consensus building, their final point is an important reminder for leaders. Leaders in professional learning communities help teams identify a protocol that they agree to use to resolve the inevitable conflict that will arise. Healthy and productive teams have a clear understanding of how they will resolve conflict and build consensus, and they articulate specific strategies for doing so. In *Learning by Doing*, DuFour et al. (2010) offer the following regarding the importance of consensus building and the "standard that must be met in order to move forward":

> A group has arrived at consensus when:
>
> 1. All points of view have not merely been heard, but actively solicited.
>
> 2. The will of the group is evident even to those who most oppose it.
>   (p. 228)

The effective leaders we met understood that conflict and disagreement were not obstacles that had to be overcome or indicators of processes or relationships that were broken and in need of repair. In districts, schools, and teams that function at high levels of collaboration, disagreement and conflict are natural by-products of collective work. Successfully building consensus around areas of confusion or individual or collective dissonance often leads to greater levels of understanding and commitment. Effective leaders do not spend time hoping they will never have conflict or resistance; instead, they embrace the opportunity to resolve conflict by carefully responding to resisters in ways that help everyone learn and develop new strategies and practices that will drive improvement and facilitate deeper levels of commitment.

Caring to Confront: Responding to Resisters

When facilitating shared responsibility, it is just as important for leaders to respond to resistance and the resisters as it is to build clarity and consensus. Each of the leaders we interviewed for this research reported that responding to resisters, though typically not pleasant, was one of the most important functions in their leadership practice. Some of the leaders we met described the early struggles they had with responding to resisters; however, each of them was able to move from *fearing to confront* to *caring to confront*. Responding to resisters and confronting behaviors that are inconsistent with the vision, mission, values, and goals of the district, school, and curriculum teams are essential elements in facilitating shared responsibility.

The literature on PLCs clearly documents the importance of responding to resisters. In *Learning by Doing*, DuFour et al. (2010) describe the importance of responding to resisters in this way:

> Every organization will experience conflict, particularly when the organization is engaged in significant change. Every collective endeavor will include instances when people fail to honor agreed-upon priorities and collective commitments. . . . it typically will be the responsibility of the leader to communicate what is important and valued by demonstrating a willingness to confront when appropriate. Nothing will destroy the credibility of a leader faster than an unwillingness to address an obvious violation of what the organization contends is vital. A leader must not remain silent; he or she must be willing to act when people disregard the purposes and priorities of the organization. (p. 230)

The effective leaders we met were absolutely clear on the necessity of confronting individuals or teams that may be in violation of the school's purposes and priorities. While we fully expected to hear that responding to resisters was critical, we were interested in the virtual unanimity as to why. Consider these responses:

- "We care so much about this school . . . when we see something that is inconsistent with our goals, we have to respond."

- "When you care as much we do, you must also have the courage to confront."

The leaders in our research made it clear that they engage in the work of responding to resistors not for its own sake, but for the deep passion and care they have for their district, school, and teams.

In *The Art of Caring Confrontation* (2009), Sanford McDonnell provides a summary of guidelines and strategies for how to meaningfully and caringly confront behavior that may be inconsistent with agreed-upon vision, mission, values, and goals:

- **Confront caringly**—Confront only after showing real care for the other person, and confront only to express genuine concern.

- **Confront gently**—Speak tactfully, in a way you would like someone to speak to you about a sensitive matter.

- **Confront constructively**—Make your positive intentions clear at the start to minimize the possibility that others may interpret your comments as blaming, shaming, or punishing (the negative aspects of most confrontation).

- **Confront with acceptance and trust**—Assume that the other person's intentions are good even if his or her actions are problematic.

- **Confront clearly**—Report what you actually observe, what emotions you feel or sense that others feel, and what you conclude would be a good next step for the person you're confronting. (p. 1)

Responding to resisters may not be the most alluring component of leadership. Nevertheless, the effective leaders of high-performing PLCs have told us repeatedly that they considered this leadership practice the most critical to their success in facilitating shared responsibility.

Decoupling Position, Power, and Authority

One of the most significant challenges to facilitating a culture of shared responsibility is the belief that power and authority are dependent on formal positions and official titles. In our work with school districts, it is not uncommon for us to hear refrains such as:

- "How can I lead this initiative when I don't have any power? I'm not an assistant principal or department chair."

- "Before we move forward with common assessments with our teachers, as principals we need to wait until we get approval from the district office."

Leading effective and systemic change can be difficult; and in school systems that promulgate authority as a function of title and position, it may be nearly impossible.

In *Learning by Doing*, DuFour et al. (2010) instruct us that in schools that develop as PLCs, "every educator—every teacher, counselor, principal, central office member, and superintendent—will be called upon to redefine his or her role and responsibilities" (p. 248). We have found that in high-performing PLCs, roles and responsibilities have indeed changed significantly. The most effective leaders we interviewed helped every educator in their districts and schools understand that *everyone* has the power and authority to be leaders. In professional learning communities, leadership is less about position and title and more about the individual and collective commitments members make to one another in pursuit of their shared vision, mission, values, and goals.

Understanding the Sources of Authority

The effective leaders we have met over the years and those we included in our research understand completely that their effectiveness as a leader is not a reflection of their official title and formal position, but of a higher authority. In *Moral Leadership*, Thomas Sergiovanni (1992) identifies the five sources of authority that shape a leader's understanding of his or her role and relationship with those he or she leads: (1) bureaucratic authority, (2) psychological authority, (3) technical-rational authority, (4) professional authority, and (5) moral authority.

Leaders who rely on *bureaucratic authority* lead through "mandates, rules, regulations, job descriptions, and expectations" (Sergiovanni, 1992, p. 30). The use of bureaucratic authority reflects a value system that identifies teachers as subordinates in a hierarchical system and that requires supervisors to ensure accountability for results.

Leaders who rely on *psychological authority* find that teachers will follow them if they lead through their use of personal motivation and interpersonal skills. A leadership approach that focuses on psychological authority may enable a congenial work environment that focuses on "bartering" the interests of supervisors and teachers "so that each side gets what it wants" (Sergiovanni, 1992, p. 36).

Leaders who rely on *technical-rational authority* lead through the presentation of evidence "derived from logic and scientific research" (Sergiovanni, 1992, p. 31). These leaders use research to identify best practices, provide training and in-services, and monitor processes to "ensure compliance" (p. 36).

Leaders who rely on *professional authority* understand the importance of "seasoned craft knowledge and personal expertise" (Sergiovanni, 1992, p. 31). These leaders understand that teachers respond "in light of common socialization, professional values, accepted tenets of practice, and internalized expertise" (p. 36). As a result, teachers develop and respond to professional norms, their "practice becomes collective," and they require "little monitoring as their performance becomes expansive" (p. 36).

Leaders who rely on *moral authority* understand that their leadership is "derived from obligations and widely shared values, ideas, and ideals" (Sergiovanni, 1992, p. 31). These leaders work to "make explicit the values and beliefs that define the center of the school as a community," and teachers respond to the "community values for moral reasons as their practice becomes collective and their performance is expansive and sustained" (p. 37).

Although leaders must incorporate all five sources of authority into their practice, it is clear that in high-performing PLCs, leaders rely primarily on professional authority and moral authority as the basis for their leadership practice.

When leaders rely on professional and moral authority, they answer the *what* and *why* questions commonly asked in traditional school improvement initiatives differently. Effective leaders answer the *what* question of change and new initiatives by turning to the district and school mission and vision statements that articulate the "shared ideals that define" the community and the professional responsibilities of community members (Sergiovanni, 1992, p. 35). These leaders answer the *why* question by pointing to the collective commitments that community members made to one another in support of the vision, mission, values, and goals of the school. Effective PLC leaders rely primarily on moral authority to answer to the *why* and *what* questions "because [the work] is the right thing to do" (Sergiovanni, 1992, p. 37).

By relying on professional and moral authority, leaders move past the need to create significant accountability systems and formal leadership positions and titles, thus also eliminating power struggles. When an administrator, faculty, or staff member suggests, "I can't effect change on my team. I'm their colleague, not their boss," the effective leaders we met all had similar responses. They worked tirelessly to help everyone in their districts and schools understand that leadership in PLCs is not about title, position, power, or getting things done by making people do things. One leader might respond by saying:

> I would encourage you not to worry that you do not have positional power when you are working with your team. Instead you can help your teams understand how the individual and collective work of becoming a professional learning community is consistent with what we know is best practice in our profession and the research that demonstrates positive increases in student learning and achievement.

Still another leader might respond by suggesting,

> As we are engaging in collaborative conversations regarding our collective work, it is important to keep in mind that the decisions we make are not going to be based on "who's in charge" but rather, "what is best for our students."

While the leaders we researched had all heard, at some point, different variations on the theme that some members of their districts, schools, and teams felt powerless, they all responded by redirecting their colleagues' attention away from positions and titles toward the professional and moral authority that must guide our work in schools developing as professional learning communities. Having met hundreds of leaders, both ineffective and effective, we conclude that creating and sustaining structural and cultural change is only possible when leaders make the conscious choice to rely on moral and professional authority as a basis for their work with colleagues.

Facilitating shared responsibility is central to the thoughtful and intentional leadership required to build districts, schools, and teams as PLCs. One of the superintendents we interviewed reminded us of the importance of facilitating shared responsibility in the following story:

> Two years ago we were engaged in board of education and faculty negotiations. In one of the early sessions, things started to get a little bit heated, as negotiations sometimes do, and one of the teachers at the negotiations table said that people don't know how a particular leader in one of our schools makes decisions in general, and one decision in particular (that this teacher did not like). Before I could get a single word out of my mouth, another teacher on the faculty negotiating team said, "Hey, that's not true. All of the teachers know what happened and why it happened." And she added, "In fact, I was part of all that summer work and we all worked together to make sure that we shared everything with the faculty so that everyone knew what we were planning to do and why we were planning on

doing it. It would be unfair for us so sit here now and claim that we were not included in the process or kept in the loop."

I simply could not have said it better myself.

Given that much of how the United States does things in public schools was intentionally designed to mirror the work done in early 20th century factories and assembly lines, it makes complete sense to us that some school leaders would consider creation of a school structure and culture of accountability as their primary responsibility. In fact, we have seen many school leaders take immense pride in the assembly-line precision they have instilled in their schools. Our experience and research, however, have taught us that the most effective leaders in PLCs take on the more difficult and rewarding challenge of facilitating a culture of shared responsibility. By doing so, they enable high levels of personal and collective commitment that serve as the launching pad for new levels of student learning and achievement.

CHAPTER FIVE

Building Coherence and Clarity

Leadership is about going somewhere. If
you and your people don't know where you
are going, your leadership doesn't matter.

—Ken Blanchard

When we developed our initial assumptions for this project, we expected the leadership practice of building coherence and clarity to be the *first* order of business for leaders in professional learning communities. We eventually found that the three core practices we've described launched the work of becoming a learning community, and that building coherence and clarity is the foundational practice that underpins all other aspects of their leadership work. In other words, effective leaders engage teams in understanding the compelling *why* before, during, and after engaging in the work at hand. Moreover, the leaders we interviewed shared their own newfound understanding that they could not create coherence and clarity by simply defining and *sharing* the compelling why; instead, they had to engage staff in conversations so that staff explored and defined the compelling why *for themselves*. This strategy created meaning that took hold, and leaders no longer felt like they were constantly repeating the rationale. When leaders facilitate conversations so their colleagues can build coherence and clarity, they develop shared understanding for the organization's work, they articulate a clear rationale for improvement and change, they focus collective efforts, and they mobilize and energize shared passion for a common purpose.

We also discovered, however, that in some cases leaders engage in the core leadership practices without building coherence and clarity. While the "forced" and not "forged" approach might work to attain increased levels of student achievement, more often than not, the improvement efforts are unsustainable, and the successful initiatives eventually follow the leader out the door (Kouzes & Posner, 2007). When leaders do not make an intentional effort to build coherence and clarity, they virtually eliminate any chance for long-term sustainability of their improvement and change efforts.

Educational experts and organizational theorists alike acknowledge that changes in beliefs and attitudes are often the result of changes in practices that lead to better results. We have found this sequence of change—actions, results, then beliefs—to be true in our work with schools and educators across North America. However, in the absence of *organizational* coherence and clarity, the beliefs of a few, even when presented with strong conviction and authority, seldom have the staying power to carry the work forward if the leader leaves. The leadership practice of creating coherence and clarity must serve as a foundation for everything that an educational leader does throughout his or her work, and it is paramount to creating sustainable efforts and affecting school culture in the effort to build districts, schools, and teams as PLCs.

Focusing on the One Thing

It has become something of a fad in education to reference and utilize *Good to Great* (2001) by Jim Collins as a resource for our individual and collective work. Considering that Collins has proven to be one of the best-selling management and leadership authors of all time, that might not be such a bad idea. In fact, nearly all of the research findings on effective organizations can be highly instructive for us as educators. While *Good to Great* has served as a wonderful resource for many educators in their reflection on their practice, we believe that Collins's follow-up book is equally as, if not more, important for PLC leaders to consider.

In *How the Mighty Fall* (2009), Collins and his research team take on the daunting task of trying to determine why some of the original *Good to Great* companies suffered significant losses (and bankruptcies in some cases) following the dramatic downturn in the economy during the 2000s. In his early work, Collins (2001) stated that great organizations "simplify a complex world into a single organizing idea, a basic principle or concept that unifies and guides everything" (p. 91). In his 2009 work, Collins and his team found that the initial and first stage of decline in the once-great organizations was reflected in four significant mistakes made by managers and leaders. The lessons for education leaders in their efforts to create and sustain professional learning communities are significant:

1. **Success entitlement, arrogance**—Whatever success an organization had experienced was seen as "deserved" rather than a product of hard work and dedication. People within the organization began to believe that their success would continue into the future no matter what, and they took their current state of achievement for granted.

2. **Neglect of primary flywheel**—In all of the organizations that witnessed significant performance declines, the leaders became distracted by "extraneous threats and opportunities" (p. 43), and they neglected to focus on their guiding principle.

3. *What* **replaces** *why*—Leaders lost sight of the importance of the *why* question and the need to build coherence and clarity regarding their collective work. People no longer understood why they were doing important work.

4. **Decline in learning orientation**—Leaders lost the strong focus on learning and development across the organization that drove initial success. Organizational cultures were no longer focused on the important work of collaboration and collective inquiry.

While the specific decisions and actions that led to the "fall from grace" of the *Good to Great* organizations varied, Collins and his team found that the initial mistakes that leaders and managers made all contributed to a gradual movement and retreat from the fundamental purpose and guiding principle of the organization. Although schools and school leaders are clearly different from businesses and business leaders, the lessons of the fallen *Good to Great* companies are important reminders.

Every day, district-level leaders find themselves working through difficult decisions ranging from tax levies and financial issues to staffing levels and strategic plans. Being a school-level leader is similarly challenging; principals and assistant principals address problems with the buses, personnel issues, curriculum alignment, instructional supervision, and student discipline—all before the lunch period. Teacher leaders face challenges that may be even more vexing as they work with colleagues to make curriculum recommendations, develop shared lesson plans, map curriculum, and build balanced systems of assessments—all while implementing the goals, projects, and initiatives of the district. And is any challenge quite as daunting as those faced daily by teachers in their classrooms as they attempt to lead large groups of students through a learning trajectory that meets the needs of individual students, the goals and objectives of their courses, the pacing guides of the district, and the state and national standards in their disciplines? The effective leaders we met in our research understood this point clearly. They did not waiver in their belief that their primary responsibility as leaders was to build coherence and clarity throughout their districts, schools, and teams toward the most important thing, the fundamental purpose and guiding principle of their individual and collective work: facilitating high levels of learning for all.

First Things First: Simplify, Simplify, Simplify

In building coherence and clarity amid all the challenges educators at every level face, few aphorisms would serve school leaders better than the KISS (Keep it Simple, Silly) principle. Far too many schools suffer from "projectitis" (Fullan, 2001, p. 109). As Fullan suggests:

> In schools, for example, the problem is not the absence of innovations but the presence of too many disconnected, episodic, piecemeal superficially adorned projects. And it is not uncommon now to find school districts in which vastly different approaches to educational reform are being attempted at the same time. (2001, p. 109)

It is not uncommon for school leaders and schools to bite off more than they can chew. Educators know too well the damaging effects of reform efforts that place a priority on the quantity versus the quality of improvement initiatives. In *Finding Your Leadership Focus* (2011), Douglas Reeves warns against the dangers of "the serious and growing problem" of initiative fatigue:

> By initiative fatigue I mean the tendency of educational leaders and policymakers to mandate policies, procedures, and practices that must be implemented by teachers and school administrators, often with insufficient consideration of time, resources and emotional energy required to begin and sustain the initiatives. Even the sturdiest bridges have load limits for a reason, as they can bear tons of weight up to a limit, with trucks, trains, and cars all crossing the bridges without incident. Once the load limit is exceeded, however, even a small additional weight can lead to catastrophic consequences. (p. 1)

We have found that the most effective leaders make a concerted effort to keep things simple so that administrators, faculty, and staff understand the change and improvement initiatives they are proposing as credible, realistic, and *achievable* in the course of their daily work. New programs rarely have staying power if they are seen as simply a side effect of someone attending a conference or seminar. Such programs are often discarded shortly after they are proposed for a lack of collective efficacy, or alternatively they can sometimes continue without doing any meaningful work to move the initiative forward. Leaders are far more likely to facilitate collective efficacy and shared responsibility when they intentionally work to build coherence and clarity. Effective leaders in professional learning communities are able to *do* when they simplify the many and sometimes complex messages that teachers are hearing into a "single organizing idea" or guiding principle (Collins, 2001, p. 91).

Effective leaders make a focused effort to move away from the salad bar approach to district and school management in which schools and teachers are able to pick and choose from a variety of improvement initiatives in favor of a more simplified and targeted plan for improvement. For example, in response to the initiative fatigue that his district was experiencing, one of the superintendents we interviewed remarked:

> We made a conscious and deliberate effort to work with our district level leadership team to whittle down the number of initiatives from more than twenty to two. Following a collaborative process that involved district-level administrators, school principals, and teachers, we created a new strategic plan that was developed to focus work for the entire district on two very specific improvement initiatives: curricular alignment and the development of common formative assessments.

This simplified approach helped everyone in the school have a very clear picture of the work he or she needed to accomplish and, more importantly, a very clear understanding of *why* they needed to do the work in the first place.

In their effort to build a single, unified message, effective leaders are doing the following:

- Answering the *why* question before the *how* question
- Clearly communicating initiatives and priorities
- Framing collaborative conversations to ensure shared understanding
- Serving as a cultural barometer

Answering the *Why* Question Before the *How* Question

It was interesting to discover the significant learning and reflection that effective leaders shared regarding their own leadership struggles and failures in leading change and school improvement initiatives. Although we had expected a certain minimum level of self-reflection, the depth of personal analysis and the sheer determination effective leaders exhibited in learning from their mistakes and improving on their leadership practice impressed us.

One common mistake the leaders in our research made in their early leadership practice was failing to build shared knowledge among their faculty and staff regarding school improvement plans and initiatives. In our work with schools, we have had the opportunity to witness—and in many instances, we have been asked to help remedy—improvement initiatives that have gone awry as a result of failure to build shared knowledge and understanding. Consider the following example.

Returning to school in early August after a three-day Professional Learning Communities at Work™ summer institute, Principal Farkas and her school improvement team of four teacher leaders, the school counselor, and the dean of students set aside three days for planning the upcoming school year. Having had the opportunity to hear enlightening keynote presentations and informative, practical breakout sessions, the school improvement team was on a conference boost and was ready to get to work. After attending many sessions in which the presenters identified the benefits and importance of common formative assessments, the team decided it would develop a common formative assessment system for the coming school year in which all teachers would be responsible for working with their curriculum team to develop common assessments and implement them every three weeks.

Unfortunately, this story is not only true, but all too common. The very last words that teachers want to hear from their principal on the first day of school are, "Hello, welcome back everyone! I went to a conference this summer, and I have some great new ideas!"

Most educators notice instantly that change is coming, and change can be scary. The "conference boost" is a very real phenomenon and can cause significant damage to school culture. Many leaders spend time at conferences and institutes with leadership teams during the summer months, learning and getting excited for the upcoming school year with new ideas to improve their school, only to become frustrated by the lack of enthusiasm their colleagues demonstrate upon their return.

Principal Farkas and her team intended to focus on the right work, but they made a number of mistakes, the first and most significant of which was a failure to build shared knowledge and understanding regarding the importance of common formative assessments. In *Start With Why* (2009), Simon Sinek suggests that:

> When a WHY is clear, those who share that belief will be drawn to it and maybe want to take part in bringing it to life. If that belief is amplified, it can have the power to rally even more believers to raise their hand and declare, "I want to help." With a group of believers all rallying around a common purpose, cause or belief, amazing things can happen. But it takes more than inspiration to become great. Inspiration only starts the process; you need something more to drive a movement. (pp. 136–137)

Although Principal Farkas and her team were excited about and inspired by their summer learning and they felt they were asking teachers to do the right work, they clearly did not build coherence and clarity by developing a common purpose and shared commitment—they did not answer the *why* question before the *how* question.

Remarking on a failed effort to build coherence and clarity, one of the leaders in our research reported:

> I think that one of the biggest setbacks that we had when we first began the work is that we never took the time to set vision, values, and goals around our initiative. What that ended up causing for us was significant misalignment of priorities and level of false agreement to the core principles and ideas.

All too often, school leaders engage in change and improvement initiatives that very well may be the right thing to do, but prior to doing so, they fail to build a clear rationale for the change that everyone within the organization can understand and share. Having learned from early mistakes, the leaders in our research spent time with their staff developing a common understanding of why they were doing what they were doing and how the new initiative was critical to their continued improvement as a professional learning community.

The effective leaders in our research identified the following strategies for answering the *why* question before the *how* question: using data to identify a clear rationale for programs and initiatives, linking programs and initiatives to the district and school vision and values, and ensuring that programs and initiatives support a focus on learning approach.

Using Data to Identify a Clear Rationale for Programs and Initiatives

Few conversations in the educational profession generate as many opinions and heated discussions as the debate over the appropriate use of data in schools. On one end of the continuum, advocates for the use of data suggest that nothing less than full transparency and a wide-open approach to tracking, sorting, and sharing data is a prerequisite for driving school improvement programs forward. At the other end of the continuum, those opposed to the use of data typically suggest that, as educators, our fundamental purpose is to help develop the full human potential of each and every child, and the use of data serves to distract us from the more important work of developing the whole child. Regardless of one's personal opinion, there can be little debate that, in the era of accountability that was the 2000s, the use of data became a standard practice among those interested in tracking and sorting schools and districts. In fact, "data dialogues," "data days," and "data retreats," are so ubiquitous that our colleague Rick DuFour often jokes that it seems many educators have begun to "pray at the altar of comparison and longitudinal data." We have found that effective leaders in PLCs do not accept the use of data as the sole source of authority and instead use data in a careful, thoughtful, and meaningful way.

The challenge that educators face, given the tremendous amount of data that floods their districts, schools, and teams, is how to use data appropriately. Each and every one of the leaders in our research described bringing intentional focus to the discussions and dialogue concerning how to use data appropriately. The most common use of data among the leaders we studied was to help build a clear rationale for proposed changes and initiatives. Consider the following example from a district-level leader:

> We were one of the first districts in our state to fall into Improvement Status in 1998—that was a wakeup call for us. In some ways, it was the best thing that could have happened to us. We took it seriously. We did not say, "Oh, here is another label." What we asked was, How did we get the label? Where are we failing? Where are our shortcomings? We very quickly learned that we were doing a great job for some kids, but we needed to do a great job for all kids.

> As a result, we started a practice several years ago called our Principal Summit. Every year we publish our strategic plan so that everyone knows what is expected in terms of student growth, intervention strategies, etc. At the start of each school year, we bring our principals together three at a time and they do a forty-five minute presentation on their student achievement data over the last six-year period. In doing so, the principals share their data and describe their PLC practices and how they are building the capacity of their instructional leaders in the school in response to the areas of student need. We are deeply focused on building instructional leadership capacity at all levels. In their presentation, the principals are asked to identify trends and patterns in their data and to develop recommendations for improvement strategies. The principals will then go back and share with their staff all the elements of the Summit, and they begin working with their staff to make action plans for their collective work in response to the student achievement data.

> Everyone has come to understand that these are the things that we must do to improve. We have been able to change the culture here, and our teachers now understand that everything we do is based on meaningful data and student learning. As a result, everyone has a very clear understanding of what we are trying to do for students. (Superintendent interview, spring 2010)

The DRIP syndrome (Data Rich, Information Poor) is a real condition that often afflicts schools and school leaders. However, the cure is not a complete withdrawal from data or even a severe data diet. Instead, we found that effective leaders in PLCs make better choices in how they use the data they have. In high-performing PLCs, leaders use data to help create a compelling rationale for new programs and initiatives. In the absence of meaningful data, new programs and initiatives become a reflection of the leaders; with data focused on building coherence and clarity, the data helps provide a clear and compelling rationale for change.

Linking Programs and Initiatives to the District and School Vision and Values

We found that effective leaders in PLCs take time to facilitate a collaborative process that results in the creation of district and school vision and values statements. The danger that befalls many educators in traditional schools is that, once they do the heavy lifting of bringing people together to hammer out agreements and come to consensus on a vision and values statement, nothing much happens with the results of their collective work. After the cursory celebration of its completion and the first few months of paying homage through speeches and passing references in district and school communications, most vision and values statements spend more time on the shelf than in purposeful use as a guiding principle and a possible rationale for proposed changes and initiatives.

Effective leaders understand clearly that the vision and values statement serves an important role in their efforts to build coherence and clarity. When Bennis and Nanus (2007) defined a vision as "a target that beckons" (p. 82), they did so with the assumption that the target is not a moving one. In the midst of the ever-changing world of daily life in school systems, the vision and values statement can serve as an important target for leaders to shoot for when leading change. In high-functioning PLCs, effective leaders rely on the vision and values statement to provide the first and most important rationale for change programs and initiatives. As a result, when leaders link proposed changes and improvement initiatives to the collective vision and shared values, the answer to the *why* question becomes abundantly clear. A principal of a large middle school described his school's efforts to stay focused on the collective vision and values this way:

> We have shared vision and values that we collectively developed a few years ago. We operate on the premise that "Hope is not a strategy." We simply cannot hope that things will get better. We remind ourselves of Einstein's warning that "Insanity is doing the same thing over and over again, and expecting a different result." We know that our outcomes will not change, unless we have the courage to change the inputs. The second premise is that "We don't blame our kids." There is not a family in our district who doesn't send us the best kids they have every day, they did not keep the good ones at home today. So, if our kids do not have what we would like them to have when they come to us every day, it is our job to give it to them. Our third premise is, "What we do is not about teaching, it's

about learning." Good teaching is important to achieving student learning. Everything we do as a district and schools is based on our vision and values. As we make decisions, we need to be sure that any changes and improvements are consistent with the collective vision and values.

Building coherence and clarity is not a one-time event or a seasonal endeavor. Quite in contrast, it is a vital component of the daily practice of effective leaders in high-performing PLCs. Effective leaders demonstrate what we have believed to be true for a long time: utilizing the vision and values statement is the most important and essential strategy for leaders in creating and sustaining PLCs. Linking programs and initiatives to the vision and values statement provides leaders with the opportunity to exercise the "moral authority" that is essential to facilitating a culture of shared responsibility.

Ensuring That Programs and Initiatives Support a Focus on Learning

Of the three big ideas that drive a school as a PLC, a focus on learning is vital when building coherence and clarity regarding district and school goals, projects, and initiatives. In traditional schools, adult interests and priorities are significant, if not the most important, factors that drive programs and initiatives. In fact, the unfortunate reality of many schools is that they design the daily structure and culture with the needs and interests of the adults at the forefront.

While educators publicly claim that making decisions in relation to what is best for students is the sine qua non of schools, many leaders quietly reveal that in reality, most schools consider the autonomy and convenience of adults before they consider what is best for students. In high-performing PLCs, effective leaders are consistently willing to buck the status quo and put students at the heart of their decision making. Consider the following example from a high school leadership team:

> We knew for a few years that we had a problem with how we were scheduling students into their classes. Essentially, the process worked like this: sometime in the winter prior to the next school year, we would establish a course selection process in which students would identify the courses they would like to take. Once all of the students had finished their course selections, the department chairs would identify the number of sections for each division and specific courses to determine staffing levels for the following school year. Once staffing levels were determined, the department chairs would begin working on the master schedule by reviewing the faculty preferences and requests for their schedule. The master schedule would be built based on teacher requests, such as preferences for free periods, accommodations for coaching and cocurricular assignments at the beginning and/or end of the day, common prep periods with collaborative teams, lunch period requests, etc. Once the schedule was created with the adult requests prioritized, the students' course requests would be inputted by the student information system into the schedule that had been created.

We utilized this process for many, many years. In fact, we found that most comprehensive high schools in the United States created their schedule this way—with adult priorities inputted first. The problem is that nationally, and in our school, the data shows that once student course requests are inputted into the master schedule, fifty percent of the students requests were determined to be hard conflicts that could not be resolved, and students were called in by the counselor to make schedule changes. When we really started to think deeply about this process, we were stunned by how absolutely silly it is that half of our students could not take the courses they signed up for because of the constraints put on the schedule by the adults priorities for their schedule. We realized that the model was unsustainable and certainly not in the best interests of students.

The following year we allowed students to make their requests, and then we used the course selection data to develop the master schedule. Once the schedule was set, we then assigned teachers to the classes that needed to be taught and the periods during the day that they were scheduled in order to optimize the greatest number of students being able to take the greatest number of their requests. When we ran the master schedule after assigning teachers to the available courses and class periods, our hard conflict rate had dropped from fifty percent to eight percent. Of the eight percent, we were able to schedule five percent of those students by hand into the courses they requested. We only had three percent our students that needed to identify alternative courses. As much as this was a change in our practice of creating the master schedule, at the end of the day, it was clear that developing the master schedule based on the student course requests was clearly what was in the best interest of students.

The effective leaders in PLCs are consistently making efforts to prioritize programs and initiatives so that learning and consideration of what is best for students are the guiding principles of their daily work. In high-performing PLCs, they understand that answering the *why* is important before and during change efforts to create a shared purpose in ensuring high levels of learning for all students.

Clearly Communicating Priorities

One of the more significant findings in our research was also one of the most challenging for our leaders to identify about their own leadership practices. Some things become second nature for effective leaders, and the clear communication of shared purpose is no exception.

The daily lives of school leaders, whether they work in the district office, the principal's office, or in the classroom, are nothing short of frenetic. Obviously, school leaders have more than one role and responsibility, and building coherence and clarity is dependent on clearly communicating change and improvement priorities. It should come as no surprise to any school leader that clear communication and straightforward, honest articulation of district and school priorities is an important and essential component of effective leadership. As we learned more about the leaders in our research, it became clear that each considered clear communication to be an important element in their daily leadership practice. Effective leaders are intentional and thoughtful about when, where, and how they communicate district, school, and team priorities. Simply put, we cannot overstate the importance of clear communication.

Effective leaders understand that building coherence and clarity is not a one-time event or something they can accomplish through a mass email or beginning-of-the year speech to the district or school faculty. Schools that function as a PLC do so, in part, because their leaders spend time and energy building coherence and clarity and developing multiple strategies for clearly communicating their priorities, including developing a common vocabulary and a teachable viewpoint.

Developing a Common Vocabulary and Common Definitions

With so many acronyms flying around the hallways of schools—PRTI, PLC, SEL, SAT, ACT, NAEP—on a first hearing, you might think our districts, schools, and teams are run by the military. Given that our profession has a language of its own, many leaders make an effort to develop a common vocabulary to guide their work. The effective leaders we met knew that identifying terms wasn't enough, however; without common definitions, the common vocabulary would not help their efforts toward building coherence and clarity. We found that an essential strategy of district, school, and teacher leaders in their work to build shared knowledge and understanding is to spend quality time developing a common vocabulary *and* common definitions for the change initiatives they are leading.

In fact, many of the leaders considered doing so to be one of the most important and first steps in building their school as a PLC. One of the leaders we met described it in this way:

> We had so much difficulty at first trying to just get clarity around the ideas and concepts that we were hearing. Finally we just said, forget it, let's just define these terms ourselves, who cares what the experts say. So, we set out on a collaborative process with our faculty to define all of the terms that we have been struggling with. When it was all said and done, we had developed definitions that made sense to us for the terms that always seem to cause problems: objective, standard, target, summative assessment, formative assessment. We are in a much better place now to move forward. (Personal communication, summer 2011)

While there may be any number of reasons that a particular initiative might have difficulty taking root, the leaders in our research made sure that their efforts did not fail for a lack of clarity on basic terminology. We were delighted by their efforts to facilitate specific learning opportunities for their colleagues to develop a common vocabulary and shared understanding of key words.

The effective leaders we met were less concerned with whether they worked to define a common vocabulary that was consistent with the educational world at large, as much as they were concerned that everyone within their district, schools, and teams shared the same understanding and working knowledge.

Developing a Teachable Point of View

A leader's ability to clearly communicate district, school, and team priorities and build the necessary coherence and clarity to move change and improvement initiatives forward is entirely dependent on his or her willingness to "invest the time and emotional energy to engage those around him or her in dialogue that produces mutual understanding" (Sparks, 2005, p. 50).

Though developing "mutual understanding" is no easy task, the effective leaders we met experienced success when they worked to develop what Noel Tichy describes as a "teachable point of view." According to Tichy, a teachable point of view is a "cohesive set of ideas and concepts that a [leader] is able to articulate clearly to others" (as cited in Sparks, 2005, p. 51). In many ways, a teachable point of view is a conceptual framework of an organization or team's key ideas that clearly communicates a consistent message to all colleagues. Taking the time to sit down, think through, and then write out a teachable point of view is an important process that helps everyone develop clarity on shared practices and new understandings of the potential implications in individual and collective work. According to Tichy:

> Leaders come to understand their underlying assumptions about themselves, their organizations, and business in general. When implicit knowledge becomes explicit, it can then be questioned, refined, and honed, which benefits both the leader and the organization. (as cited in Sparks, 2005, p. 51)

In the day-to-day life of district, school, and team leadership, it is easy to lose focus on the guiding principle and the "one thing" that is supposed to lie at the heart of our work and drive our daily practice. Creating a teachable point of view helps district, school, and teacher leaders clarify their own thinking and understanding and develop ideas and strategies to clearly communicate with others in an effort to build coherence and clarity. One of the central office leaders we met described the importance of district and school leaders developing a teachable point of view in this way:

> One of the more successful practices that we utilize within our district with the leadership team is that we have all of the principals develop and practice their teachable point of view. For example, one of our district initiatives focuses on personalization of curriculum, instruction, and assessment, and we wanted everyone to develop a very clear understanding and picture of what personalization is. Last spring, we had all the principals spend time in some of our district leadership team meetings and develop a teachable point of view for personalization so that we could go around the district and have conversations with each staff member. So we had the principals develop their teachable point of view, practice sharing it with one another,

and then go out and have conversations with staff members. And then they documented the feedback that they heard back from everyone. We asked everyone what they thought after the principals shared their teachable point of view: What ideas do you like? What questions do you have? What suggestions for improvement would you make?

The principals then brought the feedback back to the district leadership team and we refined the vision based on the feedback. We documented more than five hundred different conversations that principals had with their staff members throughout the district. In these conversations, we talked about what personalization is and what it looks like—they were great! We then asked the principals to come back together and have collaborative conversations on what they learned from their colleagues.

Each of the principals are now working with their building leadership teams, and sharing the different things that they learned and what they might try to implement in the building. Working together on developing a teachable point of view helped the principals to develop a common language and the common message that is cascading throughout our schools. (Central office administrator interview, spring 2010)

The leaders in our research not only worked to create their own teachable points of view, they facilitated opportunities for their administrative and teacher colleagues to do the same. Developing a teachable point of view is not a simple task—it takes time, energy, and commitment. However, it is a critical task, and it "requires first doing the intellectual work of figuring out what our point of view is, and then the creative work of putting it into a form that makes it accessible and interesting to others" (Sparks, 2005, p. 52). Developing and utilizing a teachable point of view is an important strategy to help leaders build coherence and clarity. When leaders create a teachable point of view, they must explain their reasoning, challenge their assumptions, and clarify their thinking regarding important elements of creating and sustaining PLCs. Leaders with a teachable point of view are in a much better position to provide the support and guidance necessary and to develop learning opportunities for others within their districts, schools, and teams.

Framing Collaborative Conversations to Ensure Shared Understanding

One of the more interesting commonalities of the leaders in our research is that they all had experiences of participating in an unbelievable number of unproductive and seemingly needless meetings. In *Death by Meeting* (2004), Lencioni describes the problem with most meetings in this way:

Meetings are boring. They are tedious, unengaging, and dry. Even if people had nothing else to do with their time, the monotony of sitting through an uninspired staff meeting . . . would have to rank up there with the most painful activities of modern business culture. And when we consider that

> most of the people struggling through those meetings do indeed have other
> things to do, that pain is only amplified. (p. 223)

Although Lencioni is describing life in the business world, we have found this to be a common experience in many schools as well. Given that time is the one resource educators routinely identify as the most essential to their improvement efforts, it seems somewhat silly for administrators and teachers to spend such significant amounts of time in meetings that quickly devolve into topics often unrelated to our primary purpose as educators. In fact, one teacher leader described her experiences with meetings in a traditional school this way: "Our meetings were so completely unproductive and worthless that over time we began to realize that the School Improvement Team was the place that good ideas go to die" (Personal communication, 2009–2010 school year).

Though well intended, meetings can quickly become dysfunctional for any number of reasons. Here are the most common reasons we heard:

- Participants arrive late.
- Participants leave early.
- Facilitation is ineffective.
- There are no agendas.
- There are no minutes.
- Too many topics are identified for the meeting.
- No topics are identified for the meeting.
- There is no clearly articulated purpose for meeting.
- Focus is on topics that participants could deal with via email.
- Participants routinely talk over one another.
- Participants focus more on participating than listening.

Unfortunately, many of the meetings educators participate in during the daily life of schools look remarkably similar to the way children play in the sandbox, and they often consist of the same behaviors, figuratively speaking of course: throwing sand, stealing shovels, yelling, whining, and so on. In such meetings, educators do very little of the important work they need to accomplish, and more significantly, they often create strained and fractured relationships that upend and hinder their ability to move forward as leaders and schools working collaboratively.

We have noticed that in many schools, meetings often fall apart, and the sandbox behaviors kick in primarily when the meeting organizer did not provide clear communication regarding the meeting's purpose, the type of conversation to expect, and how the meeting was meant to build shared understanding and coherence and clarity. Lencioni describes the importance of having clearly articulated meeting purposes in this way: "To make our meetings more effective, we need to have multiple types of meetings, and clearly distinguish between the various purposes, formats, and timing of those meetings" (2004, p.

224). When one team member is looking to engage in a dialogic conversation to build new understanding and meaning, another team member is looking to defend an idea or push an agenda, and yet another is looking to simply get the answer to a pressing question, the meeting can quickly fall apart. Team members will leave the meeting frustrated and without the opportunity to further their own learning or have their immediate concerns addressed. Effective leaders in PLCs understand that meetings are not inherently bad; rather, poorly designed and ineffectively facilitated meetings are what turn them into frustrating experiences. In fact, bringing people together to work collaboratively will invariably involve some type of meetings. Effective leaders understand how to design meetings to be purposeful, productive, and focused on learning.

Understanding Collaborative Conversations

In PLCs, effective leaders resist having meetings for their own sake and avoid the pitfalls that come from doing so. Effective leaders learn that by creating *collaborative conversations* they enable participants to stay focused on the important work of creating powerful learning opportunities for everyone. Collaborative conversations are opportunities for

> focused group interaction guided by a skillful leader acting as a group coach who invites exploration of ideas, shared problem-solving, mutual goal setting, assessment of progress, group decision making, and professional insights to be exchanged among educators in order to expand collaboration, enhance quality teaching and increase student success. (Luidens & Tabor, 2008)

Contrary to the typical "death by meeting" that occurs in some school settings, *collaborative conversations* create the opportunity for purposeful and focused interaction in relation to important ideas and relevant work in various purposes and formats. We have witnessed many truly amazing meetings, which the leaders designed specifically to create collaborative conversations. It is not easy. Successful and productive meetings require thoughtful and careful planning. In fact, effective facilitators shared with us that they schedule the same amount of time for planning and preparation of collaborative conversations as they do for the meetings themselves.

Effective leaders bring their strong understanding of high-quality instruction to their leadership practice and their work with colleagues. They know it is absolutely essential that everyone in the district, schools, and teams has the opportunity to participate in meaningful conversation regarding their individual and collective work.

We have seen effective leaders build coherence and clarity by facilitating collaborative conversations for discussion, dialogue, and decision making. Although all three types of conversations have a place in and are important to a team's collaborative work, it is far more important that teams have the ability to recognize the distinctions among the three conversation types. It is also important that they develop protocols and habits of mind that allow for the collective understanding of what type of collaborative conversation is required for the issue at hand. Without a clear purpose for meetings as collaborative conversations designed for discussion, dialogue, and decision making, teams will revert to sandbox behaviors that prohibit collective learning and improvement.

Collaborative Conversations for Discussion

The primary purpose of collaborative conversations designed for discussion is to present information, identify alternative points of view, analyze perspectives, and take positions for the sake of argument and debate. Discussion is an important component of a team's learning trajectory as it allows participants to share information and analysis that enables deeper understanding of particular points of view. In collaborative conversations for discussion, leaders have the opportunity to help participants develop a deeper understanding of complex issues and often help teams "converge on a conclusion or course of action" (Senge, 2006, p. 230).

While there are many benefits to framing collaborative conversations for the purpose of discussion, there are also notable potential pitfalls. In *The Fifth Discipline* (2006), Senge summarizes David Bohm's characterization of discussion as

> something like a ping-pong game where we are hitting the ball back and forth between us. In conversations that are designed to be discussion oriented, the subject . . . may be analyzed and dissected from various points of view by those who take part. Clearly, this can be useful. Yet, the purpose of the game is normally to win and in this case winning means to have one's views accepted by the group. (p. 231)

District, school, and teacher leaders in PLCs know full well that meetings and conversations for the purposes of discussion are necessary for collaborative work. Meetings focused on discussion help participants gain clarity on process, develop timelines and protocols for implementation, and create organizational efficiencies. Nevertheless, effective leaders also understand that placing too much emphasis on discussion, with its inherent possibility of a "winning" mentality, is inconsistent with our fundamental purpose of creating a truly collaborative culture.

It is likewise essential to design meetings that focus on building shared knowledge, generating creativity and discovery, and facilitating learning through collaborative conversations for dialogue.

Collaborative Conversations for Dialogue

Dialogic conversations are generative and emphasize groups coming to an understanding rather than individuals making points and counterpoints (Senge, 2006). In collaborative conversations framed as dialogue, educators explore collective rather than individual meaning and develop new ideas on how to improve learning and achievement. They learn how to suspend assumptions and work diligently to understand how their own thinking may be enhanced by the thoughts and contributions of their colleagues (Senge, 2006). Collaborative conversations for dialogue often result in new meaning and collective understanding that would have been impossible to create without the intentional effort of colleagues to learn with and from one another.

These conversations require thoughtful facilitation and active participation among team members. Just as meetings developed for the purposes of decision making and discussion are more effective with the implementation of specific protocols, collaborative conversations for dialogue tend to be more open-ended and may require participants to exercise new skills so protocols are necessary. Coaching experts Peg Luidens and Marilyn Tabor (2008) have suggested that the effectiveness of dialogue meetings depends on the following skills for facilitators and participants:

- Shuttling perspectives
- Creating a collaborative culture among team members
- Clear planning and thoughtful facilitation
- Engaging team members in meaningful work
- Setting aside judgmental thinking
- Listening to multiple voices
- Using questions to prompt thinking
- Paraphrasing multiple voices
- Balancing human and situational needs

In their work helping schools and teams develop more meaningful relationships focused on student learning, Luidens and Tabor (2008) identify the following benefits of collaborative conversations:

- Group members develop a collective sense of responsibility for all students and a common sense of purpose that serves as a basis for action.
- A collective focus on the complexities of student learning emerges, and teaching becomes a collective endeavor rather than an assortment of isolated individual efforts.
- Group members begin talking to each other openly about student performance; the nature of learning; their subject matter; their teaching practices, situations, and challenges; and their own thoughts and ideas.
- Conversations become safe places in which to examine practices and acknowledge areas of need. There is openness to improvement and an encouragement to take risks and try new ideas.
- All group members contribute so that all feel honored for their experience.
- Conversations renew passion and hope, making group members feel professionally engaged, invigorated, challenged, and empowered.

If conversation is food for the soul, as an ancient Mexican proverb suggests, then collaborative conversations are food for a school's growth and development as a PLC.

Building coherence and clarity is an intentional act of leadership that requires leaders to continually improve on their ability to frame collaborative conversations that will ensure individual learning and build collective capacity.

Collaborative Conversations for Decision Making

Given all the practice educators have making decisions every day in their classrooms, one might think that decision making at the district, school, and team levels would be easy. Nothing could be further from the truth. In traditional schools, decision making is often a difficult and arduous task that leaves many participants feeling as if their colleagues did not adequately hear and consider their points of view.

Many meetings fail due to problems with the structure and facilitation of the meeting itself: lack of defined purpose (decision making, discussion, *or* dialogue, rather than all three); lack of appropriate and adequate planning for the meeting; and/or lack of a clear and articulated protocol for the designated purpose.

It is not uncommon in traditional schools to participate in meetings in which the decision-making process is reduced to simply posing questions for a team to consider: What goals should we adopt for the district this year? Where might we place the common formative assessments we will create for the first semester? Should we consider developing an intervention program for prealgebra students? All are good questions, but in and of themselves, they do not provide a clear decision-making protocol that leads to group consensus.

Effective leaders in PLCs do not leave decision making to chance. The leaders in our research all identified a decision-making process and protocol that constructed shared meaning and ensured every team member an opportunity to participate. Before a decision-making meeting occurs, effective leaders facilitate collaborative conversations for discussion and dialogue in earlier meetings. During those meetings, teams begin by exploring everyone's ideas and suggestions and investigating options. When the team gets to the decision-making meeting, there is no debating or discussing, no new ideas tossed into the mix, no opportunity for challenging assumptions and testing reasoning, as those conversations have already taken place. During the decision-making meeting, everyone is clear from the onset that the purpose of the meeting is decision making, and a specific protocol will drive the conversation and guide teams safely to an end result— the decision.

A Cultural Barometer

In his leadership classic *The Servant as Leader* (1991), Robert Greenleaf suggests, "Many attempts to communicate are nullified by saying too much" (p. 11). Effective leaders of PLCs remarked that they spend as much, if not more, time listening as they do talking. An elementary school principal described the importance of listening in this way:

I am constantly trying to get feedback from our leaders and teachers. If I am going to get a good idea of what is working and what is not working, then I need to be listening carefully to what our teachers and our teams are saying. I'm trying to live the mantra "Listen more, talk less." (Principal interview, spring 2010)

While effective leaders spend time in informal conversations, they also establish frequent opportunities to practice listening as they engage in collaborative conversations with various groups. Effective leaders engage in regular meetings with teachers, regular meetings with students, monthly meetings with parents, quarterly board of education meetings, and one-on-one meetings. Each of these meetings provide leaders with the opportunity to serve as a kind of cultural barometer to better understand the extent to which the district, school, and teams were moving closer to their collective vision, mission, values, and goals.

- **Regular meetings with teachers**—Each of the leaders we met held regular meetings with various groups and teams of teachers in order to listen to teachers and learn how their individual and collective work was progressing. Leaders expressed tremendous value in these regular opportunities to develop coherence and clarity regarding district initiatives.

- **Regular meetings with students**—Many of the leaders we met had regularly scheduled monthly meetings with students. We heard leaders suggest, for example, "If students are the reason we're here, then every once in a while, it makes sense to sit down with them and see how we are doing."

  The conversations with students focused on everything from the plans and details of homecoming week to how well teachers were providing regular descriptive feedback for the purpose of increased learning and achievement. Regular meetings with students serve as an important opportunity to check in and determine whether the school is meeting the needs of students and the extent to which the teachers are helping all students learn at high levels of achievement.

- **Monthly meetings with parents**—In addition to meeting regularly with students, effective leaders established regular meeting times with parents. Formal meetings with parents give leaders an opportunity to hear what they might not otherwise hear while talking with parents before and after school during drop-off and pick-up times. Regular and structured meetings also provide leaders an opportunity to hear parents discuss their impressions of and satisfaction with the school and the academic and cocurricular programs.

- **Quarterly board of education meetings**—Many districts have teaching team presentations as a regular component of their monthly board of education meetings. However, the effective leaders we met facilitated opportunities for the board of education to sit down for an extended meeting with teaching teams and engage in dialogue regarding the district's goals, projects, and initiatives, as well as the various practices and strategies that teams are employing to ensure student learning.

- **One-on-one meetings**—While more formal collaborative meetings are wonderful opportunities to check in and see how teams are progressing, effective leaders also make an intentional effort to establish one-on-one meetings with colleagues. Leaders use one-on-one conversations with colleagues to gain a deeper understanding of how well the school is progressing as a PLC and to practice the art of listening and asking thoughtful questions designed to determine the extent to which the culture of the school is focused on learning, collaboration, and results. Every one of the leaders we interviewed considered their one-on-one conversations with colleagues as one of the biggest leverage points to build coherence and clarity.

The journey toward becoming a PLC is first and foremost about orientation. Effective leaders at the district, school, and teacher levels fully understand that although clarity precedes competence, capacity building is key to helping everyone in the organization develop coherence and clarity regarding the shared vision, mission, values, and goals.

CHAPTER
SIX
Modeling Practices and Expectations

> I hear, I forget; I see, I remember; I do, I know.
>
> —Confucius

Leadership is neither a passive nor a periodic act. Effective school leaders in a professional learning community are relentless in their ongoing efforts to build the individual and collective capacity of their colleagues. As we spent time with leaders of high-performing PLCs, we found that successful leadership practice is less a result of soaring rhetoric and inspirational speeches than of intentional modeling. In fact, strong leaders used modeling as yet another way to create coherence and clarity regarding their collective work. We found that highly effective leaders spend time, attention, and effort modeling the practices and expectations they have for their colleagues and schools.

The importance of modeling has been well documented in the research and literature on leadership. In *The Leadership Challenge*, Kouzes and Posner (2007) describe the importance of modeling in this way:

> Constituents expect leaders to show up, to pay attention, and to participate directly in the process of getting extraordinary things done. Leaders take every opportunity to show others by their own example that they're deeply committed to the values and aspirations they espouse. Leading by example is how leaders make visions and values tangible. It's how they provide the evidence that they're personally committed. And that evidence is what people look for and admire in leaders—people whose direction they willingly follow. (p. 77)

While we fully expected to find that effective leaders in high-performing PLCs considered role modeling to be an important part of their leadership practice—who would ever suggest that being a role model is not a good idea?—we were inspired by *thoughtfulness* that the effective leaders brought to modeling. These leaders considered modeling to be a critical element in their leadership practice that required much more that spouting the typical axioms such as "I would never expect my colleagues to do something that I wouldn't do" or "I like to jump right in, roll up my shirt sleeves, and dig into the work." Effective leaders of high-performing PLCs intentionally model, in their speech and actions, the important work essential to creating a school culture and structure that supports high levels of learning for all students.

We found that modeling practices and expectations focused on the three core leadership practices of creating and sustaining a collaborative culture, aligning systems, and facilitating shared responsibility—and that modeling never happened by accident; it is always a thoughtful and deliberate act. Leaders at the district, school, and teacher team levels indicated they recognized the need for modeling and sought opportunities to model core practices whenever possible. The highlighted ring in figure 6.1 surrounds the core of the framework. Effective leaders model their expectations for each of the inner practices. In doing so, they extend opportunities for creating coherence and clarity as they *show* the way.

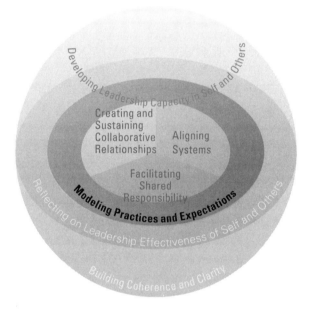

Figure 6.1: Modeling practices and expectations.

Effective leaders described with precision their ongoing efforts to plan how they would model practices and expectations. The most effective leaders spent nearly as much time planning how to serve as an effective model as they did actually modeling. We found that this modeling is so intentional, in fact, that it follows an algorithm of thirds for time allocation. Leaders spent approximately one third of their time planning for aligned and deliberate messages and efforts, one third of their time actually modeling those messages and efforts, and the final third of their time reflecting on the impact of the modeling. An outstanding fourth-grade teacher leader described the importance of modeling in this way:

> Modeling is very, very important in my daily work. However, it is just as
> important for me to consider how I am modeling the work that we are trying

to do as a district for my colleagues. Ultimately, I need to be sure that I am modeling the right work, so I spend time thinking through how I need to structure my work with colleagues so that they can see how we should be working collaboratively. (Personal communication, 2009–2010 school year)

Effective leaders give careful consideration to not only the time they spent modeling but also to *what* practices and expectations they were modeling to their colleagues. As with many of the practices and strategies of effective leaders, we found tremendous thoughtfulness and intentionality in the efforts of leaders to model specific teaching skills, craft knowledge, and personal characteristics.

Windows and Mirrors

Effective leaders are passionate about seeking both windows and mirrors regarding their efforts. They look outward to observe the impact of their speech, decisions, actions, and leadership on others just as much as they look inward to examine the effectiveness of their efforts. We found that leaders who serve as positive role models for the individual and collective work of becoming a high-performing PLC examine their impact in the following instructional target areas: teaching skills, craft knowledge, and personal qualities. Table 6.1 lists specific characteristics of leadership in each area as well as positive behaviors that support that characteristic in measurable ways.

Table 6.1: Modeling Instructional Target Areas

Positive Characteristics	Positive Behaviors
Teaching Skills	
Remains aware of role	Engages in self-talk relative to role
	Ties comments and actions to vision and values
Is explicit about what is modeled	Employs think-aloud strategies for identification of what is being done and why
Makes time for teaching	Engages in advanced planning
	Uses strategies for prioritizing decisions during instruction
Shows respect for learners' needs	Uses formative assessment strategies with timely feedback embedded in a caring orientation
Encourages reflection in learners	Asks timely, thought-provoking, open-ended questions regarding content and process
Craft Knowledge	
Develops depth and breadth of knowledge and skill regarding effective teaching and learning	Engages in best-practice research to study educational craft knowledge
	Uses action research strategies for focused practice specific to educational craft knowledge
	Shares insights regarding new learning with others

continued →

Positive Characteristics	Positive Behaviors
Develops depth and breadth of knowledge and skill regarding leading PLCs	Engages best-practice research to study PLC leadership craft knowledge
	Uses action research strategies for focused practice to learn by doing specific to PLC leadership craft knowledge
	Shares insights regarding new learning with others
Provides effective communication	Anchors comments to vision, mission, values, and goals
	Asks open, honest questions
	Responds to questions and concerns with clear and timely responses
	Employs best practices in offering feedback
Offers sound craft reasoning	Draws on research and experience to support decisions and dialogue opportunities
Personal Qualities	
Exhibits confidence and competence	Uses actions and words intended to demonstrate craft knowledge and skill
Displays sincerity	Remains sensitive to needs of self and others
	Remains true to the vision, mission, values, and goals in word and deed
Demonstrates reliability	Demonstrates consistent action over time
	Acts to follow through with commitments
Extends a caring orientation	Displays a willingness to solicit feedback, listen for understanding, anticipate needs, and respond in kind
Exudes honesty and integrity	Speaks the truth
	Confronts issues and unethical behavior to hold all accountable to organizational values and beliefs
Practices positive interpersonal skills	Chooses words carefully
	Attends to the will of the group
	Employs a spirit of playfulness and appropriate humor
	Responds with sensitivity to needs and concerns
Demonstrates a commitment to excellence	Creates a high standard for professionalism
	Uses organizationally identified or commonly accepted industrywide criteria and quality indicators to frame decisions for self and others
Exhibits collegial nature	Frames and facilitates collaborative conversations
	Invites participation from others

Adapted from Cruess, Cruess, & Steinert, 2008.

The list in table 6.1 is probably not a surprise, nor should it be. Educational leaders who want others to follow their lead must be able to impart their desired messages through quality teaching, they must be credible, and most importantly, they must be willing and able to lead by example.

Modeling Teaching Skills

To successfully model the practices and expectations of creating and sustaining a collaborative culture, aligning systems, and facilitating shared responsibility, leaders must develop an understanding of and an ability to employ effective teaching skills and strategies. Modeling is, first and foremost, a teaching strategy. Although craft knowledge and personal qualities are important characteristics for leaders as role models, effective teaching skills are an essential prerequisite. Teaching skills are the tools by which leaders transmit craft knowledge in any organization (Daloz Parks, 2005; Senge, 2006; Tichy, 2004), and they are similar to those that experienced teachers exhibit in the classroom daily. Effectively modeling teaching skills involves several facets, including role awareness, self-talk and think-aloud strategies, making time and planning for modeling, respecting learners' needs and formatively assessing progress, and encouraging reflection and asking questions.

Role Awareness

When modeling, effective leaders focus on their own behavior, such as attentiveness, appropriateness, and whether or not they are following agreed-upon norms. As a result, leaders are able to model the positive behaviors they hope to see in others. Being aware of one's role as a leader is an essential first step in successfully modeling practices and expectations. The leaders we met understand that as positional and referential leaders in their districts, schools, and teams, they are "always on"—others are continually watching and taking mental notes and cues on their speech, actions, and behavior.

Self-Talk and Think-Aloud Strategies

Many of the leaders we interviewed described in vivid detail their daily mental reflection and self-talk. For instance, one of the principals we met shared that throughout the day she asks herself, "Am I demonstrating the attitude and practicing the behaviors that I expect to see in my colleagues?" Another principal explains how his self-talk affects his modeling:

> I am deeply aware that my colleagues spend time watching how I behave and listening to what I say. I have found that I need to be on top of my game all of the time. If I'm not, I will get called out on it at best, or give tacit permission for others to misbehave at worst. (Personal communication, spring 2011)

Effective leaders also practice thinking aloud, a metacognitive strategy that enables leaders to engage in the active and explicit identification of the practices and expectations that are being discussed or modeled in that moment. Thinking aloud allows others to "see inside the leader's head" and make thoughts, feelings, beliefs, and reactions that are usually hidden explicit. It might reveal the feelings attached to a decision, the possible *what ifs* connected to different options under consideration, or the assumptions behind positive feedback given to teams or individuals. A teacher leader we met described her self-talk strategy:

> It is not uncommon for me to reflect aloud with my team. I often begin my comments at team meetings with "I wonder what it would look like if . . ."; or "If we make this decision, it is possible that . . ." For me, it helps me to share my thinking with my colleagues, and at the same time, I am able to help my colleagues think from a different perspective. (Personal communication, 2010–2011 school year)

We found that effective leaders also routinely engage in collaborative conversations and think-aloud strategies to clarify or identify the desired practices and expectations. Effective leaders shared the following prompts that help them initiate reflective dialogue and collaborative conversations:

- "I appreciate hearing the team say . . ."
- "As a result of our conversation, I am thinking differently about . . ."
- "The next time I am in a similar situation, I might consider . . ."
- "As we continue to work with our colleagues, I wonder if we might be able to . . ."
- "Having had the opportunity to hear everyone's thinking, I wonder if we should consider . . ."

By creating opportunities for collaborative conversations regarding their own speech, decisions, and actions, leaders demonstrate the ability to be self-reflective, solicit and accept feedback, and interact as learners themselves. As leaders engage others in collaborative conversations and use think-aloud strategies on their leadership practices, they reinforce the positive characteristics and behaviors they are attempting to model, and they demonstrate important teaching skills.

Making Time and Planning for Modeling

We often hear educators say there never seems to be enough time to fit in everything they need to do during the course of the normal school day. Given the time crunch experienced in most schools, and the maladies of "meeting-itis" and "initiative fatigue" that many educators suffer from, it would be easy for leaders to avoid scheduling opportunities for professional learning and development outside the normal school day. The most successful leaders we met, however, went to extraordinary lengths to create opportunities for professional growth and development on a minute-by-minute, day-by-day basis, and they took an active role in planning and strategizing to make the learning opportunities job-embedded and within the course of their colleagues' daily work.

Since no one seems to be providing school leaders with loads of *new* time, effective leaders are creative in using existing time in different ways. One of the principals we interviewed described how she began using staff meetings as learning opportunities. As she—and eventually her teacher leaders—led these collaborative conversations, they made sure to use facilitation strategies that would work as instructional strategies in the classroom. At the conclusion of each staff meeting, they routinely asked, "What strategies did you see us employ today, and how could you use those same strategies in your classroom?" If leaders are thoughtful and strategic about leveraging time to model practices and expectations, each moment can serve as a learning experience and an opportunity to reflect on quality teaching practices.

Respecting Learners' Needs and Formatively Assessing Progress

Effective leaders spend extensive time formatively assessing their colleagues' learning and providing appropriate and timely feedback to facilitate their professional learning and growth.

Modeling the work of formative assessment practices and skills is not only powerful, it is also necessary to maintain a clear perspective on the effectiveness of our individual and collective work. In our work with districts across North America, we have met many leaders who use formative assessment practices to guide their own decision making. A district-level staff development coordinator we met described the practice in this way:

> In the same way that teachers formatively assess student learning, I am constantly checking in to see if my colleagues are clear about our intended outcomes for staff development, where we are at in our learning, and whether we will need to spend more time working together to ensure that we are all on the same page. I think that it is important for teachers to see the leadership of the school assessing our own work in the way that we would expect teachers to assess student learning. (Central office administrator interview, spring 2010)

Effective leaders engage in the important practice of formatively assessing their progress because they understand that their most intentional efforts don't always go according to plan. According to Reeves (2006b), "'Messy' leadership—the practice of reviewing data, making midcourse corrections and focusing decision making on the greatest points of leverage—is superior to 'neat' leadership in which planning, processes, and procedures take precedence over achievement" (p. xi).

As he was monitoring for implementation in frequent, formative ways, one central office leader noted that the high school in his district was "feeling overwhelmed" by the district goals and initiatives and, like it or not, the "entire building was coming to a grinding halt" (Personal communication, 2009–2010 school year). In an effort to build coherence and clarity at the next staff meeting, he facilitated a series of carefully framed questions to elicit their concerns and frustrations without turning the session into a gripe opportunity that would only further serve to burden the staff with negative feelings. During that meeting, he found that the staff was overwhelmed with both the work of the PLCs and the work of the district initiatives. They felt disjointed with all of the meetings and confused regarding their focal points. Were they supposed to be functioning as PLCs, and if so, why not just work as PLCs during collaboration times? Why did they sometimes have to help with the district-level initiatives?

The leader quickly posted the four corollary questions of PLCs on the wall and created a series of posters with a single district initiative written on each. Then he asked the staff to get into small groups and discuss how each district initiative helped the entire system to answer the four questions and how—once answered—the systems put in place from each initiative would actually support the work of their individual teams in answering the four questions. At the end of that meeting, he reported a visible lifting of anxiety as staff began to understand that the work they were doing at the systems level (aligning grading systems, creating pyramids of intervention, and so on) was not different or extra, but in fact integral and supportive of the efforts they were engaged in as they worked in their collaborative teams. He was successful in respecting both the staff's concerns and the district's need to move the work forward. He helped smooth the pathway so the staff could see their way to success.

Encouraging Reflection and Asking Questions

We found the effective leaders we interviewed not only modeled personal and professional reflection, but they also made it a priority to create opportunities for their colleagues to spend time in meaningful reflection of their work in the core leadership practices. Just as skilled teachers create learning opportunities for students to consider important ideas and questions to push their thinking, effective leaders make it a priority to design thoughtful questions and dialogue opportunities that engage their colleagues in reflection on the content and process of modeling practices and expectations.

Consider the following situation in which one teacher leader used reflective dialogue to help her team. The teacher noted that her team was exasperated by the lack of parent involvement and support. Of course the team would like to help students learn, the complaint went, but teachers weren't getting the support they needed from home regarding homework, for example. It was frustrating and overwhelming. The teacher leader in this case recognized that the conversation could quickly turn into a shame game—either parents feeling shamed by teachers giving lectures on their responsibilities, or teachers feeling shamed by *her* giving a lecture on their duties. So she decided to lead the conversation with a series of reflective questions such as the following:

- How many of us at this table sometimes feel like we are so busy with this job that we end up taking our work home? And when we do that, how many of us are less available to our family than we would like to be?

- Is it fair to assume that the parents who aren't helping with homework are apathetic or nonsupportive, if we ourselves are sometimes unavailable to help our own families?

- The teacher leader made herself an example by stating, "Even though I understand the value of homework, I'm probably the least available to my kids in the evening, and it's not because I'm disengaged. I'm busy, but I also want my kids to do the work, to engage in problem solving, to recognize the value of practice, and to identify their own styles and strategies when it comes to addressing hurdles so they can build a sense of efficacy. I'm available in the tough moments, but I'm not sitting with them, timing them, monitoring their answers, or anything like some of the requirements we are placing on our parents with our home work."

- If we require others, such as parents or guardians, to engage in the homework with their students, how can we be certain about what our students actually know and can do based on the evidence they generate? Might overinvolvement be just as significant a problem for us as underinvolvement?

- What do we want for our learners, and what can we control within the course of our day to achieve that with our learners?

- Are there any strategies that we have already tried or could adopt for our upcoming unit assessments that will monitor student practice and learning while they are within our purview?

She concluded her reflective questions and the ensuing team dialogue by asserting her expectations for herself and the team:

> I know I am pretty tough on us as a team, but I'm pretty tough on me as an individual too. As a professional and as a team of professional colleagues, I really look to us to be the teacher that we would want our own children to have. Our learners are with us in the here and now and they want and deserve our best shot at teaching. It's hard work, but we've already proved we can do it! We can't stop now. (Teacher interview, spring 2010)

She summed up the experience by talking about how teams in her building stopped using *victim language*—excuses about circumstances they could not control—and began to use *efficacious language*—statements that demonstrate a commitment to focus on the right work. Because student learning was at stake, the team identified the issues requiring their resolve and highlighted the strengths on which they could draw to address their new commitments. Making time for reflective dialogue moved her team further toward their goals rather than simply telling them how things would be done or ignoring their concerns altogether.

Effective modeling of practices and expectations requires masterful teaching skills. As Senge (2006) notes:

> In a learning organization, leaders are designers, stewards *and teach-ers*. They are responsible for building organizations where people continu-ally expand their capabilities to understand complexity, clarify vision, and improve shared mental models—that is, they are responsible for learning. . . . Learning organizations will remain a "good idea" . . . until people take a stand for building such organizations. Taking this stand is the first leader-ship act, the start of inspiring (literally "to breathe life into") the vision of the learning organization. (p. 321, italics added)

The most effective leaders we met were master teachers. Leaders in high-performing PLCs understand that it is their responsibility to be continually involved in the process of teaching and learning with their colleagues. It is simply not enough that a leader was at one time an exemplary mathematics or social studies teacher; as a leader in a PLC, he or she must also become a teacher of the important content and skills of becoming a professional learning community. The effective leaders we met throughout our research considered their role as lead teacher within their district, schools, and teams as one of their most, if not *the* most, important responsibilities.

Modeling Craft Knowledge

On the continuum of power, expert power (for example, "I will demonstrate a strong understanding of our work") is far superior to coercive power (for example, "I will use rewards or punishments to make you do it") or even authority power (for example, "I have the appropriate job title or positional authority, so I can require you to do it con-tractually"). When leaders demonstrate expert power, others self-select to follow them (Denhardt, Denhardt, & Aristigueta, 2009). Expert power is based on expertise, or vis-ible and recognizable demonstrations of our craft in action. It is easily recognizable:

> The most direct way to find the [superhubs/trusted leaders] within any organization is simply to ask numerous people within the group, "When you have a work-related problem, from whom do you ask advice?" The names given most often are the superhubs. (Reeves, 2006a, p. 36)

Superhubs, as Reeves defines them, are people who are recognized and honored due to their craft knowledge. Highly successful educational leaders demonstrate a command of the core work (standards, curriculum, assessment, instruction, data analysis, classroom management, and so on) of our craft, making them superhubs.

Effective leaders are relentless learners. The effective leaders we have met are constantly refining and improving their skills and knowledge. If they are focused on an area of per-sonal growth, they are honest about it, and they find ways to address that gap. They work to develop or refine their personal depth and breadth of knowledge and skill regarding effective teaching and learning, sometimes inviting others to share their expertise in that area or facilitating conversations so collective expertise emerges. If a leader is notably engaging in beliefs or actions that do not demonstrate expertise in the core work, it is challenging at best to follow when he or she recommends significant changes or activates future-oriented next steps. Leaders cannot *model* if they do not understand and demonstrate quality teaching. Craft knowledge about curriculum, instruction, and assessment—core work in teaching—is critical to the success of modeling so others might learn.

Leading the growth of a school committed to ensuring high levels of learning for all students requires that leaders also demonstrate strong craft knowledge in all aspects of leading PLCs: the three big ideas, the six essential characteristics, and the four corollary questions (see table 6.2, page 130). Like any other school improvement effort or initiative, teams can implement the work of PLCs poorly just as often as they can implement it well. Professional learning communities require well-versed leaders who deeply understand the work in order to lead it. It is only through clarity that they can avoid "collaboration lite" or "coblaboration" about the wrong things (DuFour, 2003). As DuFour argues,

> We must do more than exhort people to work together. In order to estab-
> lish schools in which interdependence and collaboration are the new norm,
> we must create the structures and cultures that *embed* collaboration in the
> routine practices of our schools, ensure the collaborative efforts focus on
> the right work, and support educators as they build their capacity to work
> together rather than alone. (2011, p. 61)

This is not to suggest that leaders must master the work before actually beginning the work. Learning by doing is not only acceptable, it is desirable. At the same time, effective leaders have their own personal levels of coherence and clarity regarding their work, and they are careful to consider long-range implications before making decisions that would set their colleagues and their schools off in the wrong direction. DuFour (2011) notes:

> Schools can create artificial rather than meaningful and relevant teams.
> Educators can make excuses for low student achievement rather than
> developing strategies to improve student learning. Teams can concentrate
> on matters unrelated to student learning. Getting along can be a greater pri-
> ority than getting results. Administrators can micro-manage the process
> in ways that do not build collective capacity, or they can attempt to hold
> teams accountable for collaborating while failing to provide the time, sup-
> port, parameters, resources, and clarity that are crucial to the success of
> teams. (p. 61)

At a minimum, effective leaders make sure they understand and can demonstrate the craft knowledge regarding the work of PLCs.

The leaders we interviewed all demonstrated an understanding of the importance of shaping a school structure and culture built on a foundation of collaboration, with professionals who are passionate about ensuring learning for all students and a laser-like focus on evaluating their success based on results rather than intentions. The daily work of effective leaders in schools and in their collaborative teams was built on a strong conceptual understanding of the six characteristics of schools as PLCs and how to implement them in their schools.

Table 6.2: Craft Knowledge of Professional Learning Communities

The Big Ideas
1. Focus on Learning
2. Collaborative Culture
3. Focus on Results
The Six Characteristics
1. Shared Mission, Vision, Values, and Goals—All Focused on Student Learning
2. A Collaborative Culture With a Focus on Learning
3. Collective Inquiry Into Best Practice and Current Reality
4. Action Orientation: Learning by Doing
5. A Commitment to Continuous Improvement
6. Results Orientation
The Four Critical Questions
1. What is it that we expect our students to learn?
2. How will we know when they have learned it?
3. How will we respond when they don't learn?
4. How will we respond when they already know it?

Source: DuFour et al., 2008.

Wherever the work of PLCs was happening and significant gains in student achievement were made, we found effective leaders at all levels who were passionate students of PLC concepts. They took advantage of every opportunity to extend their learning and deepen their understanding of how to improve their schools. As students themselves, effective leaders are voracious readers, and they spend considerable time pursuing new ideas and strategies for how to improve their leadership practice and deepen their craft knowledge.

The most successful and effective leaders we met told us they saw every interaction with colleagues as an opportunity to shape conversations around their efforts to build a learning community culture. Although we heard from leaders that it was important to develop personal connections with their colleagues, we found they built those relationships more on a foundation of shared commitment to the three big ideas and six characteristics of a PLC and less on their plans for the weekend or movies they had seen at the local theatre.

Leaders with strong craft knowledge have the ability to engage in meaningful dialogue and clear communication regarding the individual and collective work of helping their school develop as a professional learning community. Creating concise messages, focused questions, and shared dialogue opportunities regarding learning were some of the more successful strategies that effective leaders used to model practices and expectations with their colleagues.

As they model practices and expectations, effective leaders also use sound reasoning. *Expertise* sits at the intersection of strong craft knowledge and solid reasoning in complex situations. *Sound craft reasoning* is the pinnacle at which expertise is recognized and celebrated. It may be one thing to wax philosophical regarding a concept and another thing entirely to integrate that concept. Integration requires sound decision making, persuasive arguments based in truth and proof, meaningful evidence gathered from personal experience or direct observation, and logical conclusions, judgments, and inferences grounded in a sincere desire to do what is best for the greater good.

In *Leadership Can Be Taught* (2005), Daloz Parks highlights the need for leaders who

> can deal with the intensification of systemic complexity emerging from the cybernetic, economic, political, and ecological realities that have created a more connected and interdependent world; and [who] can respond adaptively to the depth, scope, and pace of change that combined with complexity creates unprecedented conditions. (p. 2)

She continues by highlighting that the rapid and universally expanding landscape for leadership creates new moral complexities:

> Critical choices must be made within significantly changed conditions, a greater diversity of perspectives must be taken into account, assumed values are challenged, and there is a deepened hunger for leadership that can exercise a moral imagination and moral courage on behalf of the common good. (p. 2)

In such a context for leadership, there is no magic answer or lock-step program to solve emerging problems. Solid reasoning is required, and it is as much about mastery in an individual's personal work as it is about developing systemwide coherence and clarity regarding the paradigm shifts that education must undertake as a PLC.

Modeling Personal Qualities

In speaking of the important responsibility that doctors have in working with residents and interns and providing the necessary training and support for their future colleagues, Harvard Medical School professor Daniel Tosteson (1979) suggested the following regarding modeling practices and expectations: "We must acknowledge that the most important, indeed the only, thing we have to offer our students is ourselves. Everything else they can read in a book" (Cruess et al., 2008, p. 719). Tosteson reminds us that at the end of the day, the most effective leaders, regardless of their profession or the age of their students, must demonstrate a strong commitment to building the leadership capacity of others through continuous modeling of the practices and expectations they want to see reflected in those they lead.

A leader's personal qualities will influence his or her ability to successfully lead the work of becoming a PLC and to guide the leadership growth of colleagues. One of the most noticeable patterns we discovered in our research of effective leaders was that they all had the following strong personal qualities:

- Competence
- Sincerity

- Reliability

- A caring orientation

- Integrity

- Interpersonal skills

- A collegial nature

- A commitment to excellence

These personal qualities enabled them to go beyond the title of their position and naturally entice others to *want* to follow them. Their personal qualities were essential to building successful collaborative cultures within their districts, schools, and teams.

The leaders we met in our research are *competent*, talented, and skilled educators with a strong understanding of the knowledge, skills, and dispositions necessary for creating and sustaining their schools as PLCs. Their colleagues considered them to not only know what work they needed to do, but also to have the ability to actually *do* the work.

Effective leaders are also *sincere*. They make sure they use words and demonstrate actions that not only set a high bar of professionalism but that also are entirely consistent with the shared vision, mission, values, and goals. Teams consider leaders insincere when there is a misalignment among intentions, speech, and behaviors. There is no confusion in high-performing PLCs because the most effective leaders mean what they say and say what they mean. Ralph Waldo Emerson may have said it best: "What you do speaks so loudly that I cannot hear what you are saying" (Quotations Page, 2010).

One of the endearing characteristics of effective leaders is that their colleagues consider them *reliable*. Effective leaders are intentional in their efforts to choose words wisely, speak the truth, and then follow through with consistent action over time. Reliability is an important trait in leaders. While a team might view its leader as sincere and competent, if he or she has a history of not following through on commitments, the team will not view the leader as reliable. Successfully leading a school on its journey as a PLC requires leaders to follow through on their commitments and to keep their promises.

We also found that the effective leaders we met *cared deeply* about students, colleagues, and their school. A deep passion for their collective commitments was a common characteristic among the leaders in high-performing PLCs. We found that successful leaders care passionately about their work and the people with whom they work. It was not uncommon to hear leaders describe their colleagues as "family" and "friends" and to express a sincere desire to help each of their colleagues succeed both inside and outside the classroom. Effective leaders are responsive to the interests and needs of their colleagues, and they work diligently to help everyone achieve success in their individual and collective work. As a result, the members of the school community felt that their leaders were personally interested in them and made every attempt to reciprocate a strong passion for their collective work of becoming a PLC.

Effective leaders have *integrity*. Over the years, we have met many wonderful educators who have experienced high degrees of frustration when working with leaders who they believed lacked integrity. While it is difficult to point to a single cause for the challenges their schools face, a consistent theme emerges in conversations with these educators: their school leaders lack integrity. Kouzes and Posner (2007) highlight the importance of integrity in this way:

> Above all else, we as constituents must be able to believe in our leaders. We must believe that their word can be trusted, that they're personally passionate and enthusiastic about the work that they're doing, and they have the knowledge and skill to lead. (p. 37)

When school leaders have developed a high degree of integrity with their peers and colleagues, there is little question as to whether the leaders are doing what they believe are the right things for what they believe are the right reasons. Leadership is not easy work, and organizational and individual dissonance occurs regularly. In high-performing PLCs, such dissonance does not turn to dysfunction. Trust is a direct result of a leader's commitment to leading with integrity.

We did not find a single leader at the district, school, or team level who did not have *strong interpersonal skills*. The leaders we met were able to talk to and relate to everyone in their districts, schools, and teams. Effective leaders choose their words carefully, and they spend time paying attention to and attending to the needs of their collaborative teams. At the same time, we found all of the effective leaders to have a sense of humor and a strong resolve not to take themselves too seriously. We also found that effective leaders made it clear when working with others that they cared about the them and were sensitive to their needs and concerns.

Given their strong interpersonal skills, effective leaders also modeled a *collegial nature* that was contagious, not surprisingly. Working in collaboration with others is not something that is a burden or chore for effective leaders. Quite the contrary, effective leaders thrive in situations in which they have the opportunity to work with and learn from others. The most effective leaders consciously seek out and facilitate collaborative conversations to stretch their thinking, and they invite others to help them refine their ideas.

In their work to develop high-performing PLCs, effective leaders also demonstrate a strong *commitment to excellence*. Although it may be easier for leaders and managers to settle for something less than excellence, effective leaders are constantly pushing themselves and those they work with to reach for the very highest standards of professionalism and expertise. In their commitment to and pursuit of excellence, effective leaders have a low tolerance for behaviors and actions inconsistent with the collective vision and values statements, and they make a determined effort to facilitate and model a culture of shared responsibility for the agreed-upon standards for excellence. They do not shy away from crucial conversations in an effort to maintain high standards. Likewise, they take every opportunity available to recognize and celebrate the work of their colleagues that meets their high standards of excellence.

We know that we would be hard pressed to find a leader who would disagree with the suggestion that they serve as a role model for their colleagues each and every day. However, we found that highly effective leaders in PLCs spend extensive time, focus, and energy developing deep clarity regarding what exactly they should be modeling through their teaching skills, craft knowledge, and personal qualities. Suggesting that someone is a model is easy; actually serving as a role model is a much more challenging responsibility that effective leaders practice daily.

Case Studies: Modeling Practices and Expectations

Effective leaders in high-performing PLCs continuously examine and evaluate their leadership practice to more thoughtfully model the practices and expectations they have for themselves and for their colleagues within the district, across schools, and in the various grade levels and departments. The following examples show leaders at all levels engaged in the work of modeling practices and expectations.

A Teacher Models the Importance of Lesson Planning and Clarifying Learning Targets

Joan's district was engaged in a two-year process of examining, developing, and implementing formative assessment practices across the curriculum. Her district's emphasis on improving student achievement included a schoolwide initiative that would ensure that clearly articulated learning targets became an integral component of the curriculum. These learning targets were used as a focus for providing feedback to students and formative assessments. As a teacher leader in the Social Studies Department, Joan began to integrate learning targets and formative assessment into her curriculum and assessment practices during the first year of the initiative. For Joan, the practice of developing clearly defined learning targets within her curriculum and creating aligned formative assessments just seemed to make sense. She began to be intentional about using the language of "learning targets" and "formative assessment" with her colleagues in their weekly collaborative team meetings. In addition, she made a conscious effort to share examples of lessons and assessments that included clear targets, and she showed data demonstrating that having learning targets helped students learn important concepts and skills more effectively.

In both formal and informal collaboration opportunities, Joan made an effort to discuss the importance of learning targets and formative assessment and how she was beginning to see improved results with her students. In addition, when working with teachers individually, Joan asked her colleagues to consider how learning targets and formative assessment might serve as a basis for structuring and assessing instruction. Joan often referenced the Black and Wiliam study (1998), which demonstrates that low-achieving and learning disabled students experience greater learning gains than other students when provided with formative assessment.

While Joan was experiencing success in her own classroom, she knew that for the initiative to really have an impact on all students, it would be imperative for the Social

Studies Department as a whole to learn how to successfully develop clear learning targets and develop aligned formative assessment practices. To help her colleagues develop a deeper understanding, Joan helped plan and prepare for the Social Studies Department's first staff development session of the year. She worked with her fellow team leaders in the department to develop activities that would serve to model the importance of learning targets. The goal was that teachers could then emulate these activities in their curriculum teams as they developed learning targets for each course, aligned with content objectives, college readiness standards, and social and emotional learning standards.

Using a clearly defined lesson plan with articulated learning targets to guide their professional learning conversation, Joan and her colleagues facilitated activities in which teachers engaged in discussion that focused on defining key terms and identifying the components required for all course descriptions and syllabi. Once they came to an agreement on the essential components, they created a standardized template they would use for all courses in the division.

As she was facilitating the staff development session, Joan intentionally demonstrated the process of developing course descriptions that included learning targets and the supporting frequent formative assessments. Given their advanced planning and effort to develop clearly defined targets, Joan and her colleagues were able to provide a strong course description example for the department. To ensure that their work within the department was connected to the district and school's vision, mission, values, and goals, Joan and her colleagues included all the components the district had identified as essential:

- Course title
- Course description
- Content objectives
- College readiness standards
- Social-emotional learning objectives
- Learning targets associated with each category

Once they addressed all learning targets, Joan and her colleagues developed a series of formative assessment practices to evaluate the quality of the department's staff development. Each curricular team was required to develop a content objective, college readiness standard, social-emotional objective, and learning target. Joan and her colleagues then utilized a variety of collaborative protocols to model providing formative feedback to the teams regarding their work. After revising the course descriptions to incorporate the feedback, each curriculum team shared their work with the whole department (see fig 6.2, pages 136–137). In addition, each team shared their action plan for finalizing their course descriptions in the coming days and weeks.

Based on the extensive discussions, focused collaboration, and positive response to the staff development session, Joan and her colleagues felt that they were helping the Social Studies Department make positive forward movement toward the district initiatives. Most importantly, as Joan worked with her colleagues, she served as a model of the teaching skills and craft knowledge that would enable the district's initiative to be successful. As her colleagues observed Joan facilitate staff development using learning targets and formative assessment practices, they were able to see how doing so in their own classrooms would have a positive impact on students. In addition, by modeling the importance of planning, having targets, and providing feedback and assessment, Joan and her colleagues created a staff development session based on activities important for their individual and collective work, rather than a sit-and-get professional development session only loosely related to what they were doing in their classrooms and teams.

Division: Social Studies

Course: Social Studies Faculty Professional Development

Course Description: This professional development session is designed to offer social studies faculty members the opportunity to identify the essential elements of exemplary course descriptions for social studies courses that are aligned to the district's vision, mission, values, and goals and to curriculum, instruction, and assessment initiatives.

Professional Development Sessions Objectives and Learning Targets

Content Standards Objectives and Learning Targets

Content Objective 1:
By the end of the professional development sessions, social studies faculty members will develop a course description that reflects districtwide initiatives focusing on student-engaged learning, formative assessment, and social and emotional learning.

> **Content Learning Target A:**
> I will define coherent learning targets that address essential course content and skills and will reflect a focus on student-engaged learning and social and emotional learning standards.

> **Content Learning Target B:**
> I will write learning targets that enable meaningful formative assessment of student learning by teachers and students.

College Readiness Standards Objectives and Learning Targets

College Readiness Standards Objective 1:
By the end of the professional development sessions, social studies faculty members will be able to identify the essential college readiness standards that will be included in the social studies curriculum and course offerings.

> **College Readiness Standards Learning Target A:**
> I will be able to identify the essential college readiness standards appropriate for each course within the social studies curriculum and courses.

> **College Readiness Standards Learning Target B:**
> I will write college readiness standards learning targets that are aligned with each domain of the college readiness standards.

Social Emotional Learning Standards Objectives and Learning Targets

Social Emotional Learning Objective 1:
By the end of the professional development sessions, social studies faculty members will be able to demonstrate an understanding of relationship management skills.

> **Social Emotional Learning Target A:**
> I will be able to effectively cooperate and collaborate in my work with my colleagues during the professional development sessions.

> **Social Emotional Learning Target B:**
> I will actively seek and accept feedback on my behaviors and how I am working with my colleagues. I will incorporate the feedback into my ongoing collaborative work with colleagues.

Social Emotional Learning Objective 2:
By the end of the professional development sessions, social studies faculty members will be able to demonstrate an understanding of responsible decision-making skills.

> **Social Emotional Learning Target C:**
> I will demonstrate appropriate decision-making skills in my collaborative work with colleagues during the professional development sessions.

> **Social Emotional Learning Target D:**
> I will reflect on and evaluate my behavior during the professional development sessions in order to make improvements in my performance and in my ability to make sound decisions while working with colleagues.

Figure 6.2: Sample lesson design template for clarifying learning targets.

A Principal Models the Importance of Facilitating Shared Responsibility for Group Norms

Cynthia knew it was important for the teams in her building to develop norms, and she had asked each team to complete the task and share their norms in writing with her by the second week in September. As the year progressed, however, she noticed that teams had *set* norms, but they were not *executing* the norms! Old, unhealthy, and in some cases even unprofessional patterns of behavior (such as arriving late to meetings, engaging in sidebar conversations, completing other work while in the meetings, and so on) were still happening, and her staff seemed either unwilling or unable to confront those behaviors.

In the middle of the year, Cynthia decided she needed to address the issue by first calling attention to it. During a January staff meeting, every staff member received a small survey slip as he or she entered the room (see fig. 6.3, page 138).

She gave the staff a few minutes to fill in their responses. When she could see everyone was ready, she asked them to crumple their papers into a snowball and throw them across the room to someone on the other side. Then everyone bent down, picked up a snowball, and tossed it one more time. Cynthia then asked the staff to take a snowball near them, open it up, and move to the poster that had been hung in the room prior to the meeting that had the number that corresponded with item one, box one (I am comfortable confronting with a caring orientation) on their paper.

Directions: Do not put your name anywhere on this paper.

Please provide a rating for each of the following items.

Answer first for yourself, then for your team, then for the whole building. How well do we do in each of the following categories?

Use a scale of 1–4, with 1 being low and 4 being high.

	Self (I am)	**Team** (As a team we are)	**Building** (The entire staff is)
1. Comfortable confronting with a caring orientation			
2. Willing and able to be confronted with a caring orientation			

Figure 6.3: Confronting assessment.

Based on the responses, Cynthia created a bar graph at the front of the room showing the results for item one and then asked the staff to move to the part of the room that represented the answer on their page for item one, box two (as a team, we are comfortable confronting with a caring orientation). They repeated this process until she had a complete human bar graph showing the results of each prompt. Once everyone had a chance to survey the room and see the results, Cynthia randomly assigned teachers to different groups to discuss the results.

It was easy to see that although *individuals* felt they were comfortable confronting and even being confronted, their teams were slightly less so, and the building as a whole was barely able to do the work. The numbers got worse the further the confrontation was from the individual level. At this point, Cynthia posed two questions for their small-group discussion:

1. If our building is filled with individuals who are comfortable confronting and being confronted with a caring orientation, then why are we not doing it in our teams?

2. What are some strategies and actions we can use to begin doing the work on a team or building level?

Cynthia recorded their ideas and shared one of her own: she intended to model caring confrontation herself and to engage the staff in practicing the work of holding one another accountable to team norms in all future staff meetings. She facilitated the conversation, and the team agreed to the following:

*   We will always post the norms in a visible location during meetings.

*   We will use the language of the norms to confront.

*   We will call for a norm check the moment someone violates a norm.

- We will always self-evaluate and discuss our use of the norms at the end of each meeting.

She concluded the meeting by making sure everyone understood that the work of confronting broken norms would begin at the next meeting.

At the following staff meeting, six staff members followed their habitual practice of arriving late to the meeting, and one was even eight minutes late. Cynthia began the meeting on time, as that was a norm, but once the last person arrived and settled in for a few minutes, she stopped and said, "I want to point out that we have already broken one of our norms, and we agreed to hold each other accountable on the spot." They talked about whether the norm or the behavior would have to change if they were serious about their desired state of working together. Staff agreed the norm was important and that the behavior would have to change.

Nevertheless, following the meeting, a small group of concerned friends—which included the building's representative to the local teacher's union—approached Cynthia in her office. They began by stating that they were glad that she felt that caring confrontation was important in a learning community setting, and at her own urging, they were now practicing their efforts to care to confront. They told her the new efforts to enforce norms would only serve to embarrass people, as she had done that morning to their friends. One of Cynthia's oldest friends and colleagues told her that if she insisted on such a practice, she "was being insensitive to the needs of our staff, and that ultimately you would be hurting our culture by creating fear and breaking trust." She went on to say that, although she considered Cynthia a good friend, she was surprised that she "was not fulfilling her promise of treating everyone as professionals and creating a safe working environment for everyone." The building's union representative insisted that if she had any issues with staff regarding performance, she would need to handle it as a supervisor to an employee, behind closed doors, and within the parameters of the policies and practices the district and union had agreed on.

As uncomfortable as she was, Cynthia viewed the meeting as yet another opportunity to model the practices and expectations that the entire staff had committed to employ. She said:

> I believe that we all want to be in a school based in trust and professionalism, and trust will be built in our collective willingness to keep our promises to each other consistently over time. As a staff, we made promises both with our norms and with our agreements to challenge broken norms. It is all of our jobs—not just my job—to keep those promises. We have made a commitment to function as a learning community, and we must hold fast to the agreements of the group. As such, conversations like the one you and I are having right now need to happen in the group.
>
> If there are concerns about how things will play out or how they are being handled as far as the group is concerned, then we need to keep those conversations and concerns present before everyone. We break trust when we

step outside of the group and break the rules or change the decisions the group has publicly adopted. It would have been important to hear your concerns out loud this morning so everyone would have a chance to interact and come to workable resolutions by the group and for the group. If you would like to continue this conversation, then we will take it to the group where it belongs, for I will insist that each of us in this room keeps our collective promise to the staff. In the future, however, I invite you to begin from the place of group discussion with your concerns as well as with your great ideas on how we can maximize our ability to work together professionally in the interest of what's best for our learners.

Finally, I look to you as leaders who are willing to confront and take risks, such as you did today in coming here, to join me in taking public risks in creating shared responsibility and accountability to our promises so that there is a culture of norm keeping rather than a single norm-keeper working to reshape culture.

Cynthia closed the meeting by asking her visitors if they wanted to place their concerns on the staff agenda for the next meeting. They expressed the belief that to do so would only further embarrass their tardy friends from the recent issue.

While they did not necessarily look thrilled with the outcome as they left her office, Cynthia was certain they understood her intention to keep the group promises. Although they were initially distrusting of her willingness to call out broken norms, she was confident that, over time, they might gain trust in her efforts to be consistent with the promises they made to one another. It seemed like a short-term loss for a long-term gain, but Cynthia desperately wanted the long-term win for her staff.

A Central Office Team Models the Work of Creating Coherence and Clarity for Building Leaders

In a large, urban district, Carol, the assistant superintendent, recognized the need to support all of the buildings in developing a shared vision, mission, values, and goals. Experience had taught her that even when given a similar assignment, the collective group of buildings could return results that were as varied in completion and quality as any classroom of diverse learners might return assignments. Carol decided to help the central office team model the process of creating vision, mission, values, and goals every step of the way.

To begin, Carol asked the central office staff to map out a long-range plan for the work they needed to do. The team decided to begin by clarifying and aligning the organization's vision and mission statements. The team got busy designing a thirty-minute session on developing a collective vision statement. In their design, only ten minutes were set aside for definition and examples of vision work; the rest of the session involved facilitated dialogue among participants in order to flesh out everyone's ideas and thinking. When the vision module was ready, the central office team presented it to all administrators in a lesson study format. Administrators were told in advance that they should watch and engage in the session with a critical eye since they were going to be presenting it to their own buildings sometime in the next two weeks, and they would need to return from those sessions in their buildings with specific products for discussion and alignment.

After the principals and program directors experienced the session, Carol facilitated a process in which they offered their feedback, including suggestions for improvements, at which point the central office team agreed to refine the presentation based on their feedback and then distribute the exact handouts, slides, or any necessary materials to the buildings so they could all use the same teaching module.

Once the module was completed in each of the buildings, Carol and the central office team engaged the principals in a reflection and feedback session so they could refine the work for future efforts and could gather the evidence generated in each building and begin assimilating the results. The feedback proved invaluable for improved success with the next module design, which would focus on mission statements.

The process of designing, presenting to the principals, modifying based on feedback, distributing revised materials, empowering the principals to conduct the work in their buildings, and finally gathering the evidence for collective review and discussion remained the same for each specific module that the central office rolled out for the principals to do in their buildings. Over the course of the work, Carol and the central office team felt they had a firm handle on the collective voice of the organization, the principals felt supported in their efforts and clear about the purpose and products of their work, and their culture changed in tandem with new structures in dramatic and significant ways.

Leading to Learn

"Leader as teacher" is not about "teaching" people how to achieve their vision. It is about fostering learning for everyone (Senge, 2006, p. 356). Leaders cannot model anything in which they are not already engaged themselves or at least willing to try. Leaders model through who they are. Teaching skills, craft knowledge, and personal qualities are the keys of success for leaders employing expert power rather than relying on their positional authority.

John Maxwell (1998), leadership author and expert, asserts that true influence comes from strategic leadership that is consciously focused on intentional and consistent modeling. Strategic leaders think about what they do and say to walk their talk everywhere, every day. According to Mike Bossi, yet another leadership author and expert, "such leaders are trustworthy, competent and prepared; they consciously keep commitments, openly acknowledge errors and model how they learn from mistakes" (2008, p. 11). Effective leaders in high-performing PLCs know they are always on stage and that every opportunity is a learning opportunity, so they work to model their message with consistency and deep clarity.

CHAPTER SEVEN

Reflecting on Leadership Effectiveness of Self and Others

> Reflective practice is as much a state of
> mind as it is a set of activities.
>
> —Joseph Vaughan

The suggestion that reflection is a key practice for successful leadership is almost as old as the craft of leadership itself; unfortunately, what is valued and what is practiced are not always aligned. Leaders do not always practice reflection with a high degree of consistency or purposefulness. Leaders are busy—many view taking time to reflect as a luxury or wish-list item. For leaders trapped in hurried days and harried ways, it is easy to put off reflection for a better time without recognizing that reflection is the antidote to frenzy. The practice of reflecting on leadership effectiveness of self and others serves to maximize the effectiveness of all leadership practices and strategies. Effective leaders engage in reflection as a means of understanding and refining their leadership craft.

Both experience and observation have shown us that modeling *requires* reflection in order to maximize its own potency. The two practices must operate in tandem for the full range of benefits of modeling to occur. Even when modeling is explicit, it does not necessarily guarantee the recipients of the experience will translate the unspoken messages into new and desired learning that will lead to deep understanding or systems change. The leadership practice of engaging others in thoughtful and strategic reflection will move learning from modeling to a consistent, clear, and organizationally understood level. Most importantly, the leadership practice of reflection plays a significant role in developing coherence and clarity throughout the entire organization. All reflective moments—whether in group conversations or private thoughts—should help members further understand the work of collaboration so they can fully participate in the team or organization.

The remarkable leaders we interviewed refused to miss the opportunity to reflect—individually and collectively—regarding their work with PLCs. They offered many specific examples of times, places, and ways they could readily engage in reflective practice. They also offered many personal insights. One teacher leader stated:

> I am not naturally a relationship builder. . . . I'm your typical trailblazer. I'm the guy that is driven by ideas but not by relationships, . . . so in my learning team, one of the things that was happening was I that I thought my ideas were all legitimate, and I had credibility based on what I know . . . but I wasn't very influential in my own learning team. I mean the ideas that I was trying to get across were not being received particularly well by my colleagues, because I didn't have the kind of deep and meaningful relationships that a pioneer would have. So I recognized that I had to alter my own approach to how I wanted to be influential and I did that in a few ways: one way was that I tried pretty hard to develop some of those social interactions with people. I tried to show people that I value them. I tried to ask more questions than I'd give answers to, even though lots of times I felt like I knew what the answer was already. More importantly, I recognized a few individuals on my learning team, who did respect my knowledge and my credibility and who were influential with the rest of the learning team and so I tried to build them up as leaders. (Teacher leader interview, spring 2010)

For many of our interviewees, reflection was renewing and invigorating. It was how they cultivated the *learning* from their efforts of *doing*. Due to the time they devoted to reflection, they developed a strong self-awareness, clarity of focus, and an ego-strength—a healthy mental condition with a balanced perspective and an "I can" approach—that enabled them to acknowledge mistakes, even publicly as needed, and redirect their efforts appropriately.

Much has been written about the idea of "reflective practitioners" in education, and many models or theories regarding the frameworks for reflection already exist. In a professional context, *reflection* involves thinking about practices or experiences in a manner that continues the process of professional learning and generates new understandings for future applications. Reflection has been identified as an inquiry approach to teaching (York-Barr et al., 2001), an action tool for professional development in learning communities (Hord & Sommers, 2008), and an organizational pathway to explore and access tacit knowledge (Johansen, 2007). Whether done alone or in groups, reflection offers yet another way to create systemwide coherence and clarity on the organization's fundamental purpose. The process of reflection can be structured or unstructured, self-engaged or dialogic with others, or immersed in the past or forward thinking. In other words, there is no one right way to engage in the practice of reflection, and all personal styles can find comfort in some form of reflection activities.

Reflection is powerful, and we are hard pressed to find any examples of exemplary leaders who do *not* engage in reflective habits. Reflection looks and feels the same at all levels of the organization, and teachers, as well as building and central office administrators, can readily identify those peers they would deem reflective practitioners; in fact, they often use similar descriptors to describe the reflective peers they admire. Over the course of the last ten years, we have asked educators from all levels in school systems and from the far reaches of North America to share with us their definitions and descriptions of *reflective practitioners*. Variations of the following qualifiers appear on virtually every list:

- **Voracious readers**—Reflective practitioners read constantly; moreover, they make sure to read things that stretch their skills and their thinking. Such reading requires them to tap into diverse subject matter and point/counterpoint content regarding hot topics. They read less for the purpose of affirming their current thinking and more for the purpose of expanding their own learning.

- **Disciplined, open-minded inquirers**—More than simply considering the varied perspectives that appear before them, reflective practitioners seek them. They make sure to sample all of the ideas and concerns that are represented in a discussion so that they can carefully weigh and consider all options. They constantly survey the culture and the politics for the unspoken paradigms and inferences. They are active and careful listeners because they understand their personal perspective is myopic at worst and insufficient at best as a means to represent the organization's foremost interests or the will of the group.

- **Possibility thinkers**—Reflective practitioners lead with "yes." They seek ways to reach the possibility, sometimes challenging the current system and paradigms of thinking. They are more apt to invite all of the reasons and ways that inspired ideas can happen—solving complexities as they go—than they are to dwell on all of the reasons and ways that new ideas will not work. They are promoters and protectors of innovation within the organization.

- **Calculated risk takers**—Reflective practitioners are grounded in thoughtful consideration, and they challenge themselves to try new things. Although they take risks, they have carefully reviewed those risks with criteria specific to the practices at hand and then explored the risks through a decision-making schema to determine whether the benefits would outweigh the costs. Often, reflective practitioners generate back-up plans to guarantee some measure of success—or at least minimize opportunities for damage.

- **Public learners**—Reflective practitioners are always talking about what they are learning or what they are personally attempting or implementing based on their learning. They are constantly engaged in metacognition: they think about what they are learning, and they talk about how they are thinking about what they are learning. In addition, they seem ready to share their personal goals and discoveries on the journey. They acknowledge mistakes made along the way, and they commit to fixing errors and improving things as they move forward. For reflective practitioners, ego takes a backseat to learning, and learning is a social activity.

Reflective practitioners are, more often than not, humble. The more they know, the more humility they demonstrate, with the dawning recognition of just how much more they have yet to learn. While they can speak with authority on a given subject, they often reference how much more they are striving to learn and accomplish in that same arena. It is the age-old conundrum: "The more you know, the more you know you don't know." Humility is a critical aspect of being reflective; it enables others to approach reflective practioners with comfort so they too can learn with ease.

We could readily identify the strongest leaders we had the privilege to interview as reflective leaders. During our interactions with them, they were constantly exploring their own levels of effectiveness as leaders and their levels of effectiveness in creating other reflective practitioners within their teams and organizations. In fact, they seemed so seasoned in the work of reflection that the *practice* itself offered a zone of safety and comfort while they explored the sometimes troublesome terrain of *truth* about their own effectiveness.

When leaders practice reflection, they navigate their thoughts both privately and publicly. In other words, strong leaders consider their effectiveness privately, they seek feedback about their effectiveness publicly, and they invite a team or teams to consider their effectiveness privately and publicly as well. No matter the context for the work, some focal points remain constant during reflection:

- **Attend to the results**—What happened? What data or evidence can we explore regarding the results? Are we exploring *all sides* to the event, experience, decision, or issue at hand?

- **Attend to the antecedents of excellence**—What are the criteria or standards of quality for the past or future planned event, experience, decision, or issue? Did what happened meet with our expectations? Our criteria for quality? Beyond the results, why did it happen, how did it happen, and what caused or enabled it *to* happen?

- **Attend to the learning at the personal level**—What have I learned about my character? My philosophy? My patterns of behavior and beliefs? My presuppositions and assumptions? What do I now understand about my strengths and opportunities for growth as a leader?

- **Attend to the learning at the team and organizational levels**—What have we learned about our culture? Our organizational philosophy? Our patterns of behavior and beliefs? Our presuppositions and assumptions? What do we now understand about our strengths and opportunities for growth as leaders?

- **Adopt a forward posture**—What are the key insights worth replicating or sharing? How might we refine or systematize that which we are discussing? What must we avoid altogether in the future? What questions should we ask? What criteria must we consider? What haven't we considered?

Whether finding answers from reflection privately or publicly, the resulting reflective insights are best shared and explored in a manner that solidifies insights and broadens the learning for everyone involved. Strong leaders use reflection to explore the uncertain as a means to gain certainty.

Reflecting on the Individual's Leadership Effectiveness

Effective leaders are almost always reflecting on their own effectiveness, and in the absence of any formal framework for understanding leadership, they will self-select criteria, frameworks, and examples against which to measure their own performance. Ideally, PLC districts, schools, and teams will have shared understandings of quality and effectiveness regarding their expectations for leaders in the work of leading. Engaged learners, in this case reflective leaders, naturally ask themselves three questions (Chappuis, 2009, p. 11):

1. Where am I going?

2. Where am I now?

3. How can I close my gap?

In the absence of a common understanding of quality, leaders will not have a common, clear benchmark against which they can answer the three questions. To develop shared understanding, organizations must engage learning community leaders in spending time collectively studying leadership strategies and practices so they can build their own framework of leadership. They may, for example, spend time developing a clear understanding and shared definition of each key shared as follows. In their 2006 book *Sustainable Leadership*, Hargreaves and Fink offer a collection of leadership strategies and practices that references the research of others:

- Modeling and building strong and rewarding relationships by paying attention to the human side of school change (Evans, 1996)

- Establishing a high-trust environment (Bryk & Schneider, 2004)

- Developing and renewing a culture of learning and improvement at all levels through problem-solving, inquiry, and intelligent, evidence-informed decision making (Hargreaves & Stone-Johnson, 2004)

- Helping the school community develop and commit to a cohesive and compelling purpose that also prevents dissipation of initiative and effort

- Stimulating a culture of professional entrepreneurship in regard to innovations and ideas that benefit learning

- Establishing and enforcing grown up, professional norms of civil argument and productive debate (Westheimer, 1999)

- Ensuring that the voices of minority members of the culture always receive a proper hearing (Anderson & Toneri, 2002)

- Doing all this within an unswerving commitment to improving learning and achievement for all students, especially those who are furthest behind. (pp. 127–128)

Another popular model regarding leadership practices, based on the research of Kouzes and Posner (2007), spans all industries. They offer a framework for exemplary leadership:

- Model the way
- Inspire a shared vision
- Challenge the process
- Enable others to act
- Encourage the heart (p. 14)

Even when adopting a formal framework for leadership, it never works to simply hand leaders the framework and expect them to follow it in their work, in their own way, with their own personal interpretations. Leaders working within a PLC spend time getting clear about what each term or strategy might mean and what it looks like when employed with high levels of quality. The most effective leaders we have met go one step further by drawing on multiple bodies of research and cocreating their own framework for understanding and practicing leadership.

While developing a framework for leadership is important, it is more important for leaders to engage their teams in dialogue to develop a common understanding and shared vocabulary. Effective leaders who demonstrate high levels of commitment and standards of quality strive to exceed expectations, but first they make sure they're clear on what quality actually looks like.

The effective leaders we interviewed realized that before they could ask others on their teams or in their organizations to practice reflecting on quality and effectiveness, they first had to begin with the *self*, reflecting individually about their own effectiveness. Personal reflection requires the capacity to make the self vulnerable in order to acknowledge certain truths. It can feel risky and wildly uncomfortable, but strong leaders set aside ego and, in turn, end up building ego strength.

Checking the "Self"

In almost any setting, humans migrate toward charismatic leaders, whose captivating personality, ideas, and leadership qualities inspire, motivate, and ultimately unite an organization or team's efforts to move in a common direction quickly. Why not? The charismatic leader's mission is often worthy, and the speed with which he or she can lead change is preferable in any organization and may be highly desired in most educational settings, where slow and tedious process change is the well-documented norm. People naturally seek leaders who can innovate and accelerate change.

Charisma, in and of itself, is neither good nor bad; like any other natural talent or gift, it has both a light side (the aspect that inspires) and a dark side (the aspect that stifles). Too much of a good thing is seldom a good thing. If charismatic leaders do not pay attention to their own agendas and motivations with thoughtful reflection and vigilance, they can easily control rather than empower, they can usurp creativity rather than inspire the ingenuity of others, and they can compel followership rather than develop leadership.

Attending to personal agendas and motivation while balancing leadership efforts with organizational needs requires a balanced dollop of "humility and will" (Collins, 2001).

When strong will is present without the balance of humility, people will perceive the leader as a bulldozer, even if he or she is charming or charismatic along the way. There is an archetype, "the pattern of the hero," for charismatic leaders: such a leader enters a troubled setting with vision and purpose, inspires the troops, and challenges the status quo with radical decisions and actions that may or may not have been vetted. Such leaders sometimes make as many enemies as friends along the way, but they are frequently applauded for doing the difficult work that others secretly hoped someone else would soon do. Transforming the system seemingly overnight with hard evidence to prove their success, the charismatic leaders become famous—sometimes infamous—and the culture is disrupted to the point where something new—good or bad—must happen. Anyone who felt change was needed will view the charismatic leader as successful. Nonetheless, the dark side of charisma can emerge in the absence of a humility born out of commitment to the greater good and a willingness to reflect on the effectiveness of *self* as leader.

When change efforts are exclusive to a specific leader, the organization develops a stance of codependency rather than one of collective empowerment. Charismatic leaders, especially those whose perceived power advances them to the limelight, can focus too much on self, and success becomes wrapped up in their persona. Or charismatic leaders might focus too much on the agenda of change and not the capacity of the organization. Either error—by intent or by accident—can have dire consequences since the dark side of charisma can send an organization, once jettisoning to success, spiraling backward. Fullan, Cuttress, and Kilcher (2005) reference this phenomena when they state, "High-flying, charismatic leaders look like powerful change agents but are actually bad for business because too much revolves around the individuals themselves. Leadership, to be effective, must spread throughout the organization" (p. 57). The effective leaders we researched were motivated beyond self and were passionate about creating and sustaining their districts, schools, and teams as PLCs.

To avoid the pitfalls and the dark side of charisma, strong leaders use the process of reflection to balance their resilient will with healthy humility. Reeves (2006b) offers insight into the concepts of resilience and will combined in the practices of educational leaders: "Reflective leaders take time to think about the lessons learned, record their small wins and setbacks, document conflicts between values and practice, identify the difference between idiosyncratic behavior and long-term pathologies, and notice trends that emerge over time" (p. 49).

Finding and Sharing Tacit Knowledge

Like master teachers who seem to flow with the *art* of teaching and frequently struggle to define the *science* of their craft, masterful leaders often struggle to isolate the daily leadership practices they readily access to influence positive change within their systems. It is a common phenomenon across all industries: "Perhaps the only thing that matters in leadership is the part that we struggle to capture and bottle" (Daloz Parks, 2005, p. ix). This is most likely due to the fact that strong leaders often approach their leadership efforts from a place of tacit knowledge—knowledge based on beliefs, values, and profound understanding from past experiences and actions. Such intricate ways of knowing are often expressed as insights, intuitions, and inspirations. Tacit knowledge is "not easily visible and expressible. Tacit knowledge is highly personal and hard to formalize, making it difficult to communicate and share with others" (Fullan, 2001, p. 80).

Observers often think that leaders who operate from a place of tacit knowledge are just naturally talented. Adding to the mystique, such leaders also seem to struggle with naming and claiming their own leadership practices. In fact, many of the effective leaders we interviewed were able to reflect on their own capabilities and areas for growth, but often found it difficult to articulate the variables of their individual success. They often struggle to articulate their own strengths; likewise, they seldom realize that the tacit knowledge they employ daily and intuitively for success is unique—not naturally owned or understood by all.

One of the many benefits of PLCs is that they work to make explicit that which is understood to master educators. PLCs engage educators in sharing their tacit knowledge with one another. The work of turning the unspoken wisdom of a few into the explicit knowledge of many is what Fullan (2001) suggests all successful organizations do: "Successful organizations access tacit knowledge. Their success is found in the intricate interaction inside and outside the organization—interaction that converts tacit knowledge to explicit knowledge on an on-going basis" (p. 80). It makes sense, then, that we would want successful leaders to begin sharing their tacit knowledge with one another on what works when leading the work of PLCs. Reflection, then, is a critical tool to explore tacit knowledge.

Strong leaders spend time considering their personal strengths as well as their weaknesses, and they seek opportunities to grow and develop their personal leadership capacity. They make reflection an integral part of their leadership algorithm for implementing something new—reflection before, during, and after is simply a necessity if they are to do their work well. Educators cannot leave reflection to chance: if it's on the back burner, they will never have time to get to it. So leaders find time daily—quiet car rides from work, silent moments with a book or a pen, a doodling process while sitting still—to explore their thoughts, actions, and overall effectiveness of their personal leadership in a given situation.

Although the act of reflection is non-negotiable for strong leaders, everyone has their own reflection style. Reflective leaders seek mediums that allow them to clarify and document their thinking. At best, chronicling thoughts enables reflective leaders to remember and ultimately activate key insights, and at worst, it provides them with a healthy chuckle as they look back on their personal growth over time. Journaling, blogging, or writing in almost any fashion is a great way to settle in with one's thoughts. Doodling, graphic organizers, to-do notes in calendars, think-alouds, verbalizing thoughts into handheld recording devices, or engaging in dialogue opportunities are nonwritten alternatives for the work of reflection. In the end, any of these choices can be useful as long as they smooth the way for personal reflection to occur.

Reflecting on the Team or the Organization's Leadership Effectiveness

Strong leaders engage members of the organization in personal and public reflection opportunities. Such work extends learning and creates *social knowing*—understandings that exist through conversations rather than in any one individual's head. Leaders create coherence and clarity when they conduct the work of social knowing: "knowledge exists between the contributors. It is knowledge that has no knower. Social knowing changes who does the knowing and how, more than it changes the what of the knowledge" (Weinberger, 2007, pp. 143–144). When leaders design such opportunities with care, the resulting social knowledge promotes a clear rationale and compelling purpose to activate collective ownership of the organization's work.

Having already reflected on their own leadership effectiveness individually, strong leaders can begin collective reflection by modeling their personal reflection efforts. The work is truly a journey for everyone, leaders included, and effective leaders make that concept clear by sharing their own evolving understandings along the way. At the organizational level, the questions of reflection move from an individual to a collective focus. As leaders begin engaging others in the work of reflection, it is critical that they provide the necessary content and materials for a full and healthy reflective dialogue. They must enter such conversations with the necessary documents and materials to address the critical questions:

- Where are we going?
  - Goals, quality indicators, and criteria for success
  - Research and promising practices
- Where are we now?
  - Key evidence or data
  - Internal and external interpretation and validation of relevant evidence and data
  - Organizational biases, assumptions, or inferences
  - Personal biases, assumptions, or inferences
  - Feedback
- What can we begin to do to close our gap?
  - Decision-making matrices
  - Protocols for exploratory thinking or brainstorming options
  - Planning tools

To be responsive, effective leaders begin the conversation with empathy, remaining sensitive to both the organization's need for the work and the capacity of those positioned to do the work.

There is an art to asking the right questions. Some questions, such as, "Have you stopped tricking your learners with irrelevant test questions?" can disempower, or worse, threaten the recipients. Answering that loaded question with either a *yes* or a *no* is often self-incriminating. A loaded question does more harm than simply shame the recipient, which is usually the inquirer's intent. It reveals a coercive or untrustworthy nature in the one asking the question, and it generates a negative tone that affects culture, often negating previous efforts to build community.

To lead the reflective process, effective leaders frame *provocative questions*—questions designed to compel participants to engage in meaningful and insightful ways. Quality questions can produce a variety of desirable outcomes: they can generate clarity, challenge assumptions and paradigms, invite collaborative problem solving, promote divergent thinking, engage critical reflections, synthesize learning, encourage innovative solutions, and create a culture of dialogue and learning. Quality questions are much more than spontaneous, free-formed thoughts. Done well, they must be worthy of answering and they are provocative enough to compel participation. Arriving at the answer to the right question is as worthy and exciting as the finding the answer itself. In fact, since using the right question can have such a positive impact, many of the leaders we interviewed lead their work with colleagues by asking questions rather than offering suggestions or asserting edicts. Instead, they asked open-ended, challenging, and non-judgmental questions:

- **Teacher leaders**—If we look at our SMART goal and the results of our most recent common assessment, does it seem feasible that we will make our goal by the end of this year? If not, what are some things we can do to close the gap between the two?

- **Building administrators**—We have agreed that if students are to practice in advance of summative assessments, homework completion is so important that we are willing to hold them accountable for completing it in our pyramid of interventions. Are we certain, before we send students to the homework lab, that we are tying the homework to specific learning targets found in our summative assessments and that the students can see the targets in the homework? How can we make those learning targets transparent to both the students and the homework helpers in the lab?

- **Central office**—It is a district goal to have all power standards posted as part of our guaranteed, viable, and visible curriculum on our school websites, in our reporting processes, and in our communications to parents. What will happen to trust and rapport, both internally and externally, if one school does not complete the task?

The questions that leaders pose for reflection move through various levels of complexity on behalf of those engaged in the work (see table 7.1). No tier is more important than another, and each will help build coherence and clarity, but the tiers do build on one another and increase in rigor as participants engage in different levels of thinking.

In Table 7.1, we provide examples regarding the depth of questioning that can happen with profound reflection. Effective leaders clarify their purpose in asking individuals in the system to reflect, and they craft questions that will align with the purposes.

Table 7.1: Descriptors and Examples of Levels of Complexity in the Reflection Process

Reflection Efforts	Purpose	Examples
Tier 1	The first level is specific to the here and now. This is by far the most popular kind of reflection, as it follows an event or effort and asks us to reflect on effectiveness. While Tier 1 questions can focus on the future, they do so within the confines of the specific event or effort. The answers inform but seldom transform our next steps.	How did it go? What did we learn? What must we do now?
Tier 2	The second level moves reflection beyond the event and works to create a shared understanding across the organization. It generates thoughts and ideas about possible implications for any proposed change. It likewise creates culminating, teachable points of view that are intentionally shared because discussions of clarity are continued by everyone across the organization.	Given all that we have tried in the past, what is our working theory of change for future initiatives? How does this initiative support our long-term work to become a PLC? How might it help us? Hinder us?
Tier 3	The third and highest tier moves reflection beyond the confines and paradigms that hold us in traditional patterns. We engage imaginations in disciplined inquiry and possibility thinking to construct new conceptual frameworks for the future of education.	How does our expertise perpetuate traditional paradigms? How might we move beyond our expertise to capture the essence of education in future designs? With our existing resources, how can we move into abundance thinking and redesign our schools? What might be the pitfalls and delights of a classroom with no walls? How can we design interventions and enrichments that are so engaging that they exceed the confines of the school day and capture the commitment of our learners?

One of the superintendents we interviewed shared the following reflective practice as a means to model the work of developing coherence and clarity:

> One of the important modeling practices that we began a few years ago in our district leadership team meetings involves having one of the administrators (central office and principals alike took turns) practice developing their teachable point of view with the larger group. Last spring, we used our district vision statement as the framework and said, "Okay instead of just

having it here on a piece of paper, let's go around the room and have a conversation about how we can bring this vision to life."

In the last two months, we asked our district office personnel to have conversation with each staff member. So we developed and then practiced
our teachable point of view around the vision statement; then we went out
and had conversations with folks and we documented what they heard
back from our colleagues. As we practiced, we realized that just sharing
the teachable point of view wasn't enough, so we engaged our colleagues
in conversation and then pursued an inquiry dialogue regarding their first
impressions of the vision statement; we wanted to know what they thought
of it in general. Was there anything they specifically liked? What's different than they expected? What can they accept? What can't they accept?
Any ideas for improvement? And we brought all that feedback back to the
district leadership team and refined the vision based on everyone's input.
We documented 500 conversations that we had with administrators, faculty, and staff members from throughout the district.

The only way we were able to pull it off is that we practiced, practiced,
practiced. As a result, we started to see many of our principals modeling
the development of a teachable point of view with their faculty and staff.
In one of our schools, the principal brought everyone together in a faculty
meeting, and they engaged in a dialogue about personalization and teaching. After the conversation, the principal asked everyone to write their own
teachable point of view about personalization. The principal gave them a
week to work on it and when they came back together the next week everyone rotated through small groups and they shared with three other staff
members and then they came back and refined it again and then he had
them do that again this fall.

Although each of the principals are working with their leadership teams on
different themes, they are implementing the use of a teachable points of
view in their buildings, which is allowing for the development of a common
language and a common key message that kind of carries and cascades
throughout the schools. This has been a very purposeful project that has
helped to push out our message regarding the district vision statement, and
it has helped everyone get clear on what it is we're trying to do as a district
leadership team. By asking people to take the time to develop a teachable
point of view and practice it with their colleagues, they develop an understanding about themselves and about why we're doing it, and they take the
time to push back a little bit when they need to do. Modeling and practicing the development of a teachable point of view has helped us examine
our systems and structures and pause to reflect and determine why we are
doing the work and if we can be doing it better. (Central office interview,
spring 2010)

When leaders engage others in reflective dialogue, they strive to capture the essence of
their collective work and the energy of their group and translate that into organizational

stories. If reflective practices are going to inform and transform systems, then sharing the insights, learning, and direction of reflective conversations is critical to continuing the work as part of the fabric of the organization. Strong leaders use the reflective work of various groups to shape and share the desired messages that will help co-create the desired cultural tapestry. Stories make the experiences of a few accessible to all. Retelling the reflective and imaginative work of a group shares an existing story while simultaneously creating a new one in other corners of the organization. Stories invite and connect us. They move the ordinary to inspirational.

In their book *The Leadership Engine* (2002), authors Tichy and Cohen state:

> Stories are a powerful tool for engaging people emotionally and intellectually and for leading them into the future. And the best leaders use them to do exactly that. . . . Successful leaders must have teachable points of view about ideas, values, energy and edge. It is through stories, however, that they tie them together and teach and energize others to move from the present into a winning future. (p. 236)

Of course, the stories that effective educators choose to promote are the ones they value and celebrate as a means of helping move the organization forward.

Using Celebrations and Honoring Processes

Effective leaders activate celebrations as a means to both cultivate intrinsic rewards and engage the organization in collective reflection and learning. In doing so, they acknowledge the values and practices that align with the organization's overall mission and vision. Kouzes and Posner (2007) suggest that the practice of engaging an organization in celebration is vital to the work of supporting change and creating clarity on what is worth valuing: "It's part of a leader's job to show appreciation for people's contributions and to create a culture of celebration. . . . Encouragement is curiously serious business" (pp. 22–23). Effective leaders base celebrations on organizational values. Done well, celebrations publicly acknowledge the behaviors and results worth replicating across the system, and they expand a leader's opportunity to create coherence and clarity in the purpose and direction of the organization. Quality celebrations extend the learning to a broader audience and context and remind us of the importance of our ultimate goal (Kramer, 2008).

In education, few have the financial resources to throw parties for the purposes of celebration. The good news is that a learning celebration doesn't require cookies, punch, rock bands, shaved heads, pig kissing, parades, or sparkles and noisemakers. Kovalik and Olsen (2002) suggest it isn't the rewards that matter: "Celebrating accomplishments is far different from receiving a reward" (p. 17.3). More importantly, the extrinsic rewards of trophies or parties, though admittedly exciting at times, seldom, if ever, create the drive necessary to motivate individuals intrinsically to replicate an action or carry the momentum forward.

In *Drive*, Pink (2009) debunks the theory that rewards increase productivity and organizational success:

> Researchers such as Harvard Business School's Teresa Amabile have found that external rewards and punishments—both carrots and sticks—can work nicely for algorithmic tasks [following an established set of guidelines to reach a specific, and guaranteed conclusion]. But they can be devastating for heuristic ones [a task that has no algorithm and requires experimentation with possibilities to devise novel solutions]. (p. 40)

He goes on to highlight the importance of creating intrinsic motivation to organizational success in right-brained, creative, and complex tasks that today's work world must navigate daily. Rewards and punishments actually work against creativity (Pink, 2009).

So, if educators opt out of parties and rewards for work well done, how do they celebrate? They can still accomplish quality celebration and recognition through quality feedback. This is not to suggest that everyone wants a public display of praise at all. In fact, even praise, when tied to intelligence or other isolated personal traits, has an adverse effect on most individuals—not just the shy ones. In her continued research on motivation and learning, Stanford University researcher and author Carol Dweck (2007) states:

> Many believe that (1) praising students' intelligence builds their confidence and motivation to learn, and (2) students' inherent intelligence is the major cause of their achievement in school. Our research has shown that the first belief is false and the second can be harmful—even for the most competent students. (p. 34)

Dweck is referring to her paradigm-shifting research about students in classrooms, but we believe it also ties to leadership work with adults. Praise, when tied to intelligence, the self, or even isolated tasks, has negative ramifications: it creates a fixed mindset, or worse, a dependency on others for continued feedback to move forward (Chappuis, 2009; Dweck, 2006; Hattie & Timperley, 2007). It does not promote the desired state of a self-directed, self-regulated learning literacy with which learners continue to learn and strive to improve.

Providing quality feedback is a reflection strategy that enables staff to continue to learn and grow as they address their knowing-doing gap. But not all feedback is helpful; in fact, many times, even if it is simply positive, feedback might be detrimental (Chappuis, 2009; Hattie & Timperley, 2007. In addition to being accurate, timely, and supportive of learning, feedback must tie to replicable processes and efforts worth improving over time. In essence, quality feedback should lead to reflection regarding what went well and how one might repeat or improve on it in the future.

How might quality feedback sound? It takes a little more time, but it is well worth the effort in the end. It requires a tone of appreciation for the specifics of success or for the parts that will ultimately lead to success (see table 7.2). It can be hard to offer quality descriptive feedback, especially intervention feedback, since so few are comfortable with conflict. Table 7.2 offers examples of how quality feedback might sound at each leadership level of the organization.

Table 7.2: Quality Success and Intervention Feedback Examples for Every PLC Leadership Level

	Not This (specific to tasks or individuals)	**But This** (specific to processes or self-regulatory efforts)
Teacher Leaders (success feedback)	We did a great job on our most recent common assessment.	When we all participated in the development process and wrote our common assessments in advance of our instruction, we were able to generate amazing results for our learners. Our data are impressive! What do you think of our data and our process? What should we continue doing so we keep getting great results?
Teacher Leaders (intervention feedback)	Our most recent intervention for our struggling students did not work. Apparently, we are missing the mark.	We have agreed that we did not close the gap for our learners with our recent intervention strategies. I know everyone on this team to be passionate, creative, and committed. We've all had previous success with helping challenging learners. I'd like to ask each of us to think about our most challenging learner—someone we won over in favor of learning. Let's identify what we individually did to help that learner, and then let's share our strategies to see if we can't find some common denominators to weave into our collective intervention efforts. I remain confident that we have what it takes to meet the needs of our learners.
Building Administrators (success feedback)	Wow. You are such an amazing team. You fight fair and address the "unspeakables." I wish other teams could be like you. Kudos to you!	I appreciated the team's skill and commitment to work through difficult conversations. I noticed you made sure you heard from all of the team members, and you stayed with the issue until you arrived at consensus. I think your success was in the way you individually demonstrated a willingness to trust the professional judgment of your colleague even though his or her opinion did not initially align with your own. And I am grateful that you have addressed sensitive issues, such as differing educational philosophies and grading practices, with a tone of respect but a firm commitment to come to a shared understanding and practice for the benefit of the team, and ultimately the learners in our classrooms.

continued →

	Not This (specific to tasks or individuals)	**But This** (specific to processes or self-regulatory efforts)
Building Administrators (intervention feedback)	This team is all over the map. Every time you head toward a decision, you sidetrack yourselves or sabotage others. It's just not healthy.	I have noticed that this team is committed to making careful decisions, so you spend a lot of time on them, and you have many divergent ideas that can help you form strong and original solutions to complex problems. It will be helpful if you identify and follow a set of team norms and decision-making protocols that help you channel all of your creative energy in productive and time-saving ways. I can help you access and practice those tools, and I am confident that you will feel less stressed and more focused in short order.
Central Office (success feedback)	Highview School won an achievement award for its outstanding student achievement results. Let's all give them a round of applause!	On Tuesday, the local newspaper will run a story on Highview's recent student achievement results, but there is more to this story than just the numbers. We celebrate the Highview staff's commitment to functioning collaboratively, to using the processes of a common core curriculum measured by common assessments, to designing targeted responses for their learners, and to staying the course and working through the challenges when things didn't go perfectly. We know there were times when it wasn't easy. And we want all the schools in this district to know that although Highview led the way, their accomplishments are accessible for all of us. They have offered us a model to follow, and we in the central office are committed to supporting all of us in achieving those results for all of our students. We are ONE district working toward the success of all of our learners.
Central Office (intervention feedback)	We do not believe that the principals in this district are focused on the right work. Our agenda items are not being addressed, so it would seem that you are not helping. You are spending too much time navigating the little things.	We understand that the day-to-day life of a principal can be chaotic, and we trust that you are spending your time navigating complex situations. At the same time, we have agreed to focus our core work on student learning, and we've worked together as an administrative team to specify the details of our collaborative work. We are a dedicated, talented group of educators committed to doing what's best for our learners—teachers and students alike. Let's spend some time talking about what might be getting in the way of us moving forward at our recommended pace. What's happening? What can we do differently? How can the central office team help support your efforts in managing your buildings while working on our core agreements?

Even growth or intervention feedback must build on partial knowledge in order to move teams and individuals forward. It must start with a tone of success or the possibility of attaining success.

The Power of Celebration

If a celebration is to serve as a reflective opportunity, then great care must go into its design and implementation. There are criteria for success regarding what or who gets celebrated, how and when the celebration happens, and even who will facilitate the celebration, and what will be highlighted or minimized in the process (see table 7.3). Whitten and Anderson (2010) sum up best what many experts acknowledge: "When we celebrate our hard-earned successes we also fortify our effective strategies by deepening our insight and developing more effective strategies for continuing the work" (p. 19). There is true power in the role that celebration plays in framing a culture.

Table 7.3 outlines considerations regarding *what* to celebrate and *how* to celebrate, with thoughtful planning and appropriate tone on behalf of the one *facilitating* the celebration so that the event itself becomes yet another learning opportunity and a chance to build coherence and clarity across the organization with shared values and commitments.

Table 7.3: Considerations for Celebration as a Reflective Opportunity

The Celebrated (people, events, or accomplishments)	The Celebration (ideas that honor)	The Celebrator (presenter of gratitude)
Generates data or evidence that can be trusted as reliable and accurate Offers a genuine cause for celebration Aligns with what the team or organization is striving to foster, support, develop, and so on (For example, if you desire collaboration, do not call out and celebrate the work of individuals. Highlight the work of teams instead.) Serves as a model that can and should be replicated	Celebrations gallery—a showcase evidencing recent team successes Honoring circles—a process in which a circle is formed and individuals are recognized for the specific contributions they have made to the team or organization's success (can be used for individuals or teams) Handwritten notes of gratitude Public expressions of gratitude—internal to building or beyond (for example, letters to the editor) A passport card or certificate—an offer to complete a task for the recipients	Is authentic and sincere Is informed of key details, such as hurdles, problems, successes, characteristics, and so on Highlights specifics worth replicating and keeps the focus appropriately on point Maintains a tone of honoring but avoids over-the-top gushing Avoids accidently sending wrong messages: • The event or person is too heroic; others can't do it • The celebrator is misinformed; others don't see the same value or traits being recognized and may even have evidence to the contrary Avoids praise by sticking to the impressive facts if at all possible Avoids making the presentation about the speaker (celebrator)

Celebration is a powerful tool to leverage the lessons of current growth and encourage continued change throughout the organization. What a team or organization values is what gets celebrated, and what gets celebrated is what gets done. Kouzes and Posner (2007) believe that celebration, done well, can support the desired culture and positively influence individual acts: "When you set the example that communicates the message 'Around here we say thanks, show appreciation, and have fun,' others will follow your lead. The organization will develop a culture of celebration and recognition" (p. 322).

In summary, effective leaders use reflection to teach, to inspire, and to cocreate. Reflection requires listening deeply and developing carefully crafted questions and responses all aimed at *learning*. Reflection is the tool used to guide the learning of PLCs. Merlyn, the magician, summed it up best in *The Once and Future King*:

> "The best thing for being sad," replied Merlyn . . . "is to learn something. That is the only thing that never fails. . . . That is the only thing which the mind can never exhaust, never alienate, never be tortured by, never fear or distrust, and never dream of regretting. Learning is the thing for you." (White, 1958, p. 183)

CHAPTER
EIGHT

Developing Leadership Capacity in Self and Others

> I start with the premise that the function of leadership is to produce more leaders, not more followers.
>
> —Ralph Nader

After we began writing this book, one of us had the opportunity to work with a wonderful educational leader, Jeff, who had done phenomenal work in transforming two different schools to function as PLCs. In each of those two schools, Jeff and his staff achieved incredible student achievement results while operating as PLCs. Though he had since retired from his role as principal, it was quickly evident that he was loved and respected by his peers, as virtually everyone in the room—teacher and administrator alike—flocked to greet him when he entered the training space in which we would be working. During a break, I shared my observations with Jeff that everyone there clearly respected and admired him. "Well," he said, "that's easy to explain. Each school here has a leader at their table *right now* who I worked to develop into a leader when we worked together in my first school—and they are each remarkable leaders in their own right." At that point, he was able to highlight the strengths of each of the leaders with whom he had worked, and it was immediately evident that the respect and admiration were mutual.

Since he was talking about developing leadership capacity, I excitedly shared the practice as we were exploring it and explained how we were beginning to understand it from our research for this book. He looked a little troubled and said quietly, "But it doesn't work."

I was stunned. "Excuse me?" I stammered. "You have leaders all around the room because you built their leadership capacity. What do you mean *it doesn't work*?"

"Well," Jeff responded, "not long after I left that first school, the district discovered them to be strong leaders too and moved them to new buildings just as the district had moved me. Then that school—the one they all left—had no remaining PLC leaders, and it fell back into old patterns and less desirable results. It didn't work," he insisted. "I built the capacity, but then they were taken away."

"Oh," I said. "You built their capacity to be strong leaders themselves, but did you build their capacity to build other strong leaders?"

It was Jeff's turn to be puzzled. "No," he confessed thoughtfully, "I didn't do that. I mentored them to be leaders to guide the PLC work. I did not mentor them to mentor other leaders of the work."

It turns out that Jeff's story is not unusual. Frequently, educational systems will move leaders who successfully transform a school to another school in need of improvement. The success of the original school after a strong leader's departure hinges on the capacity of those remaining to sustain the work. The final practice, building leadership capacity, is as much about developing leaders who can facilitate the first six leadership practices to guide PLC work as it is about developing leaders who build capacity in other leaders. A school's and a school leader's success with this last practice marks the difference between becoming a great PLC school and sustaining great PLC work—even after, *especially after*, a strong leader's departure.

One might wonder if we haven't been talking about this all along. Aren't monitoring, modeling, and reflecting all contributing factors to the work of developing leadership capacity? Absolutely. However, leaders can employ the individual practices themselves but stop short of developing *other leaders* who can accomplish that same work. Educators can lead by example, but that will not guarantee that their teams will fully embrace and integrate leadership practices. Without this last intentional leadership practice, a leader's effort to develop the leadership capacity in others is equivalent to the scattering of wild oats with the hopes that the seed will land on at least some fertile ground. This leadership practice is far more specific and deliberate. It is leadership by design.

Can leadership be taught? We, along with a myriad of published experts and the experienced, successful PLC leaders we interviewed, believe it can (Daloz Parks, 2005; DuFour et al., 2008; Reeves, 2006b; Tichy, 2004; Tichy & Cohen, 2002). We have found many wonderful examples of leadership development in action. We confess, not all of the leaders we interviewed for this book leveraged this final leadership practice, which only served to verify for us that schools really can achieve greatness in short order by doing most of the work well, but they will not be able to expect longevity from their efforts unless they engage this last crucial practice. Those who do, the few who stood out, were truly remarkable. They were the leaders that we both agreed we would be willing to follow ourselves—as did the members of their organizations. They were fierce in their efforts and unwavering in their conviction that they must devote attention to the practice of developing leadership capacity in others daily. Simultaneously, they remained humble servants and vulnerable learners, unthreatened by those who they helped become even stronger leaders than they themselves would ever attest to being.

We have learned that the leadership practice of developing leadership capacity in self and others must be systemic: it cannot be left to the "leader as hero" myth or to the finger-crossing anticipation and hope that selected leaders will just know how to do the right work in the right way. Effective leaders must develop the leadership capacity of others with an eye to the future in the anticipated absence of existing leaders, and finally, it must be done with a tremendous blend of strength and humility. Developing future leaders is both an organizational responsibility and a personal commitment on behalf of all existing leaders within the organization.

The work of school leadership and educational reform is complex, and we have observed just how much of a difference PLCs can make in the lives of teachers and students. It is not enough to have only a few leaders make it happen. In exploring what effective leaders do, we found that the most effective leaders draw forth the collective wisdom and the tacit knowledge of many successful individual leaders for the community's growth and well-being. There is always a need to help leaders understand what highly successful leaders intuitively know and seem to be able to do. The call for leadership development at the systems level is not new, but schools continue to struggle with how it might look.

Developing Leadership Capacity in Self

Jack Welch, the former CEO of General Electric, is often quoted as having said, "Before you are a leader, success is all about growing yourself. When you become a leader, success is all about growing others." While we agree that leadership is about growing the capacity of others, we assert that success is still about growing yourself. Like teaching, leadership is one of those complex tasks in which no one ever feels he or she has arrived. Each day brings new challenges and new opportunities to explore and expand our own knowledge and skills in dynamic new ways.

Effective leaders continually study and reflect on their own practice as leaders by reading, writing, attending conferences, practicing new strategies, self-recruiting strong leaders to operate as mentors, and employing their own conscious acts and personal reviews to determine the effectiveness of their efforts. One of the principals we interviewed highlighted a variety of strategies he used to continue his personal growth: he reads to remain current in the field at large and leadership specifically; he identifies and observes other strong leaders, trying to isolate their skills and strategies as they work with others; and he seeks honest feedback—the good and the bad from his staff (Principal interview, spring 2010).

Feedback is critical to a leader's success: "We're all aware that the higher you rise in an organization, the less feedback you get about your performance. You have to be prepared to regularly assess yourself" (Hill & Lineback, 2011, p. 129). Leaders who solicit feedback, especially feedback offered day-to-day from key stakeholder groups, don't need to wait for performance reviews to find their personal growth areas and strengths.

Renowned author and leadership expert Peter Drucker suggested that leaders begin their work by first knowing themselves. However, in "Managing Oneself," originally printed in his book in 1999 (and due to its staying power then reprinted as an article by the *Harvard Business Review* in 2005 and 2010), Drucker states that knowing and managing oneself is not always easy: "Most people think they know what they are good at. They are usually wrong. More often, people know what they are not good at—and even then more people are wrong than right" (2011, p. 5). Drucker recommends that leaders engage in a practice of "feedback analysis" so they might see the truth about their effectiveness and not be lost in an overinflated or misguided sense of self.

In feedback analysis, leaders take the time to record their decisions, actions, and anticipated outcomes. Once the true results are available—and this could take hours, weeks, or months—leaders should compare the actual results with the anticipated results to determine their own effectiveness. Drucker suggests from personal experience that the practice will be revealing and the results possibly surprising. He encourages leaders to explore their personal answers to questions regarding their strengths, work processes, learning processes, personal values as aligned to organizational values, and opportunities for contribution within the organization.

Drucker (2011) extends the challenge of personal management and development to all leaders with the exertion:

> The challenges of managing oneself may seem obvious, if not elementary. And the answers may seem self-evident to the point of appearing naive. But managing oneself requires new and unprecedented things from the individual, and especially from the knowledge worker. (p. 62)

Successful leaders already demonstrate a sense of efficacy, speaking and acting on an implicit belief that they have the capacity to make a difference in their work. It is precisely that sense of leadership efficacy that enables successful leaders to demonstrate wisdom in leadership decisions, accept responsibility for their day-to-day work, and express confidence and courage in demanding situations. Equally important, that sense of leadership efficacy emboldens leaders to stretch beyond their current capacity to take the necessary risks and accept new challenges that will continue their personal development as leaders (see fig. 8.1).

Figure 8.1 provides the traditional image of increasing personal leadership capacity and making the "climb" up the organizational chart of responsibilities. Individuals accomplish this work by adding to their knowledge and skills through formal training and experiential learning.

In addition to understanding their strengths and opportunities for growth as leaders, effective leaders continue

Knowledge and Skill by Way of Experiences and Exposure

Leadership Capacity

Figure 8.1: Learning for individual leadership capacity.

to develop their own capacity to lead by stretching themselves. They strive to develop their knowledge and skills by taking on greater leadership challenges within an existing role and even accepting new roles, as they are able. Like all quality learning experiences, learning about leadership is a spiraled process: each new experience offers an iterative opportunity for learning. The leadership learning spiral extends the learning to another level, deepening the necessary knowledge and skills by building on the previous learning with each successive encounter over time. As the levels of difficulty and sophistication increase in a leader's practice, he or she will relate new learning to previous learning, and the leader's competency will likely increase. It is a powerful way to learn. Leadership is rife with on-the-job learning opportunities. Hill and Lineback (2011) sum up what many experts believe and express: "Progress will only come from your work experience: from trying and learning, observing and interacting with others, experimenting, and sometimes pushing yourself beyond the bounds of comfort—and then assessing yourself . . . again and again" (p. 131).

Developing Leadership Capacity in Others

Figure 8.2 portrays expanding collective leadership capacity such that learning experiences become shared opportunities to expand understanding and skill regarding what works with effective leadership.

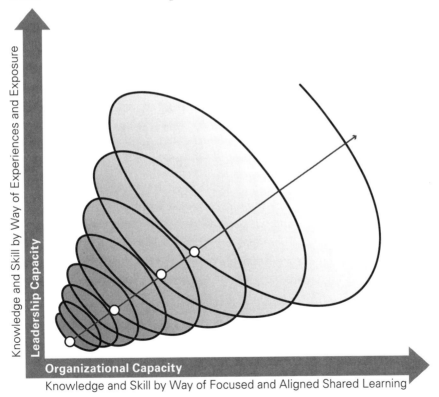

Figure 8.2: Learning for organizational leadership capacity.

Individual leaders can choose to grow their capacity over time by accepting new roles and responsibilities. Organizations benefit when they select the right leaders for the right work. An organization can best expand its leadership capacity by developing the knowledge and skills of all its leaders through focused and aligned shared learning opportunities. It is the work of PLCs at the leadership level. Collaboratively, our shared understandings benefit the collective well-being of the individual leaders within the organization and the organization at large in its capacity to develop leaders. Reeves (2006b) notes:

> Leverage for improved organizational performance happens through networks, not individuals. If the only source of inspiration for improvement is the imprecations of the individual leader, then islands of excellence may result and be recognized, but long-term system-wide improvement will continue to be an illusion. (p. 52)

Any organization that begins the work of developing leadership capacity in others must first acknowledge and respond to the existing paradigms that may undermine the desired direction in leadership development: (1) there will always be a hierarchy, so there will always be a *we* and a *they*; (2) good teaching is good leading, so good teachers will already know how to lead; and (3) efforts to help require doing all of the work. Left unaddressed, these three paradigms will block the organization's progress toward building internal leadership capacity.

Overcoming the "We/They" Myth

In organizations of any size, there will be politics. It's natural:

> It unavoidably arises from three features inherent in all organizations: *division of labor*, which creates disparate groups and even conflicting goals and priorities; *interdependence*, which means that none of those groups can do their work without the others; and *scarce resources*, for which groups necessarily compete. (Hill & Lineback, 2011, p. 128)

To operate effectively in their organizations' political environments, effective leaders acknowledge that politics exist but work to build relationships in and around those politics, connecting key players, ideas, and resources wherever they can (Hill & Lineback, 2011). While politics can create the potential for dysfunctional behaviors and patterns to emerge, a leader's exhibition of such behaviors or patterns *is a choice*. Leaders always have the option to take the high road.

One such dysfunctional pattern in the face of a division of labor is using we/they language, which we have already acknowledged effective PLC leaders avoid. It usually sounds something like "we'd like to do that, but *they* haven't allowed us," or "*they* are making our work harder," and so on. When individuals fall into we/they language, they often do so thinking that sharing their perspective clearly puts the villainy (if there is any) on the side of "they" and not "we." But it doesn't always work that way: it's the old adage that if someone engages in finger pointing, there are always three curled fingers pointing back to the original source. As Morriss, Ely, and Frei (2011) write:

> One particularly toxic behavior is the act of turning those you don't get along with into two-dimensional enemies. Distorting other people is a common response to conflict, but it carries significant leadership costs. It severs your links to reality, making you reliably incapable of exerting influence. As you turn others into caricatures, you risk becoming a caricature yourself. (p. 162)

There is no room for we/they language in organizations striving to cocreate healthy responses to student learning. And there is no room for we/they language in organizations committed to developing the leadership capacity of *all*. There is no *we*. There is no *they*. There is just *us*. Highly effective PLC leaders redirect such language every time they hear it from others.

Overcoming the "Good Teachers Already Know How to Lead" Myth

Inherent in this misunderstanding are two assumptions: (1) good leaders will self-identify, self-motivate, and self-improve, and (2) if teaching and leading are so closely related, then leaders don't need to do a lot of work for leadership development in the field of education. In the past, the work of leadership development has always been left up to individuals: "Many managers underestimate the transformational challenges of their roles—or they become complacent and stop growing and improving. At best they learn to get by; at worst they become terrible [leaders]" (Hill & Lineback, 2011, p. 127). Good teachers might make good leaders, but it doesn't mean educators opt out of the responsibility to make transparent the work of leadership. Good teaching and good leading *are* closely related; still, educators are better served by highlighting the close linkages. Effective leaders help people make the necessary connections in the commonalities between teaching and leading, rather than simply assuming that good teachers will naturally become good leaders.

Overcoming the "There Is No Such Thing as Too Much Help" Myth

Some well-intentioned leaders accidently overhelp. Since the staff is clearly busy, they step in and do the hard work for the staff. Frankly, it feels good to be needed and appreciated, so leaders like to offer support. In such a case, leaders become invaluable, and others learn to count on them. Likewise, it is easy to overhelp in the efforts to support new leaders by removing the challenging tasks from their plates. In truth, however, leaders' efforts to support often disempower the teams they are asking to step up and lead. If current leaders take the work from new leaders, then the new leaders never have to learn the work and develop their capacity to lead. Sometimes support arrives at the expense of empowerment. When leaders truly empower teams and individuals, they still require them to engage in the right work (see table 8.1, page 168). Table 8.1 outlines the differences between supporting others and empowering others. Effective leaders work to anticipate the impact of their efforts by focusing on comments and strategies that empower others.

Table 8.1: The Differences Supporting and Empowering Others

	Support	Empower
Definition	To *support* a team is to assist the members in their performance, advocate for their needs, or provide them with necessary resources. When we support, we serve as a foundation for their efforts.	To *empower* a team is to give it the power or authority to control the outcome of its work. When we empower, we set guidelines and then work to create stronger, more confident, self-sufficient groups.
Purpose	To offer services to thwart crisis or complications	To build team capacity to cocreate systems that will prevent the need for ongoing services
Potential Problems	Accepting a long-term role or task that disengages the team from its core work Sometimes building dependency	Turning over all power outside the tight parameters for creative decision making Sometimes creating a free-for-all and having trouble marshaling everyone in the same direction
Appropriate Times	Stressful moments—a single pass to help a team through a tough spot	At all times—even challenging ones—when the work is core to the desired outcome and the individual or team must develop ownership in the process and products
Potential Leaders and Team Members	Viewed as customers or recipients	Viewed as creative and powerful coproducers

Just as leaders must empower teams to do the right work, they must also empower future leaders to do the right leadership work. When leaders do the desired work themselves, they lose the opportunity to build their own leadership capacity as well as that of others, since they opt out of developing and refining their own skills around empowering others. Likewise, the recipients lose both the opportunity to learn and refine their own skills around the necessary work and the experience of watching leaders model the work of empowering others.

Developing Leadership Capacity Systems

It seems somewhat odd to us that educational institutions, which exist to develop those that they serve, have stopped seriously short of fully developing those that they employ. Effective leaders strive to create an educational system that fully embraces developing all of its people. When leaders find ways to develop other leaders, they stand a better chance of keeping quality people, stretching the skills of individuals, building the capacity of the organization, and most importantly, maintaining the momentum and culture we spend so much time trying to establish. When new leaders enter a system, they most often begin their leadership efforts under *their* personal vision for the organization—they likely believe they were hired for their vision—rather than continuing the existing work. Culture and focus shift in an endless stream of head-spinning change. Reeves (2002) writes:

> Most school systems are far better served by identifying and developing leaders from among their own colleagues than by hiring from other systems or relying exclusively upon the leadership preparation program of a local university. Moreover, schools must create a low-risk way for a prospective leader to pursue an internship, gain leadership experience, and confront the possibility that the path of leadership does not suit the person. (p. 160)

The work of developing leadership capacity in others is critical to the well-being of any organization.

The effective leaders we interviewed considered many ways to develop leadership capacity. One superintendent offered his perspective:

> My principals all understand that my objective for them is for them to be the best that we can be, but we will never get there. It is all about constant improvement. So they know my focus for them and with them is about getting better. It is about leading, about developing sound, solid, instructional learning leadership. They have to be good managers, but that is not good enough anymore. (Superintendent interview, spring 2010)

He went on to highlight how he manages leadership development collaboratively with his administrators. It is a constant conversation in his school district.

The idea of developing leadership opportunities and pathways can be challenging for two significant reasons that often become barriers to our ability to respond with creative options:

1. With limited resources, educational leaders often fall into scarcity thinking.

2. Education is a relatively flat organization; there are not many leveled opportunities for educators.

However, sometimes the challenges—the space between the proverbial rock and hard place—provide refreshing opportunities for necessity and creativity to mix. It is in that space that effective leaders generate new possibilities and powerfully fresh insights. Effective leaders view challenges as an opportunity to learn new strategies and refine their own leadership skills. Effective leaders leverage those challenges to illuminate the possibilities in unlikely circumstances.

Moving From Scarcity Thinking to Abundance Thinking

When people are engaged in scarcity thinking, they say things like: "there isn't enough," "more is better," and "that's just the way it is." The underlying premise of scarcity thinking is that of limited resources (such as time, money, opportunities, support) in the face of massive need or compelling desires. In education, the theory of scarcity permeates budget conversations, so much so that it seeps into day-to-day conversations and becomes engrained in the fabric of our reality. Sadly, it is often hard to recognize when we are living in that mode.

Quite in contrast to scarcity thinking is abundance thinking, which begins with the belief that we are enough; we have all we need to do the right things for learning, and whatever happens will lead to new opportunities for learning and improvement. There are some fundamental truths to support abundance thinking: resources are never constant—we grow what we value, and together we're better. These are detailed here:

- **There are no guarantees with resources**—If any pattern has emerged with consistency in educational finance, it is the pattern of economic peaks and valleys. No matter the direction of the resource swing, it is never about how much we have, but what we do with what we have. Even with scarce resources, remarkable things can still happen, just as with abundant resources, stagnating or debilitating things can still happen. Success is never based on the availability of resources; rather, it is based on the attitudes and the strategies of leaders who leverage their resources in powerful ways. In other words, resources can neither be the excuse as to why change cannot happen, nor can they be the cause as to why something did happen. How educational leaders *think* about what they have at their disposal at a given moment allows for successful change. Effective leaders leverage challenges to become resources. It is akin to the fable in which an animal is trapped in a well. As he tries to climb out, the dirt from the crumbling walls nearly buries him. Instead of collapsing in dismay, he shakes the dirt from his back and steps up, eventually elevating his position to the point that he has filled the hole into which he fell, and he can walk away. Effective leaders think outside the box and find new ways to explore and benefit from what they have.

- **We can grow what we value**—To truly practice abundance thinking, effective leaders always need to use their resources, even the limited ones, to reflect the organization's vision, mission, values, and goals. Effective leaders spend their existing resources (such as time, energy, commitment, money, and so on) in ways that invest in the things the organization will cherish and promote. By investing in things that really matter, effective leaders generate *organizational appreciation*, which means the limited resources grow in value and perceived availability because they are so visible. The existing resources become *more* in ways that really matter.

- **Together, we're better**—Much has already been written about the power of collaboration, but this concept applies even when experiencing healthy competition. When similar but competing stores, such as fast food restaurants, grocery stores, gas stations, and shops, all congregate in the same area, they generate a stronger consumer base. It might seem counterintuitive to put a new store next to a competitor. Nevertheless, due to that shared slice of real estate, the new store will have better visibility and a stronger consumer base when it is directly connected to a neighborhood of like resources. In the end, more people will go there since there are more options from which to choose and everyone benefits. Effective leaders highlight success in a manner that inspires others to engage in that same work. Moreover, they pool the organization's resources and engage teams in possibility thinking and collaborative problem solving to spread the wealth of availability and possibility.

A scarcity thinker will personally hoard, preferentially distribute, or even prioritize and then eliminate resources in an effort to preserve some degree of the status quo. An abundance thinker will open up resources and examine new possibilities from a place of opportunity, values, and collaboration. Scarcity thinking is sure to cause pain at the loss of the status quo, whereas abundance thinking will divert attention from loss to focus on intrigue, creation, and empowered choice.

It would be easy when developing leadership pathways to begin from a place of scarcity thinking with such comments as "we don't have enough financial resources to build pathway options and promote from within" or "we don't have the time or the resources to develop leadership capacity learning opportunities." Effective leaders, though, avoid scarcity talk and always lead from the abundance perspective with comments such as "our organization is filled with amazingly talented, dedicated, and creative educators who want to do what's best for our learners," "we have all of the necessary skills and talents to develop leaders and create a culture rich with learning opportunities," and "we all have the capacity to be positive and successful leaders."

What are the opportunities for *all* educators? How can leaders create a shared commitment and expectation so that everyone chooses to lead in some way? Effective leaders generate the collective will and wisdom to think with abundance, even in financially distressing times. The same concept of abundance thinking applies to the work of developing motivation. If educational leaders begin from the perspective that there is a deficit of motivation among colleagues and staff, their decisions and actions will overcompensate to inspire. They will use rewards and threats of punishments to force individuals to be motivated. However, when they begin from the perspective that there is an abundance of motivation and potential for motivation, they spend more time helping staff connect to a shared moral purpose that brings educators together, and the inspiration and motivation take hold on their own.

As we highlighted earlier, Pink's book, *Drive: The Surprising Truth About What Motivates Us* (2009), helps educators understand motivation differently. According to Pink, motivation 2.0—the carrot or stick strategy of the industrial era—relies on the promise of rewards or the threat of punishments to engage specific desired behaviors or results. But motivation 2.0 is an outdated, inaccurate model for getting things to happen today. In fact, Pink highlights the research conducted with a group of MIT students in which they determined that "when the task called for 'even rudimentary cognitive skill,' a larger reward led to poorer performance" (2009, p. 76). The work of leadership requires far more than the mechanical skills required to benefit from the use of rewards. It requires motivation 3.0 strategies (Pink, 2009).

Leadership is complex and dynamic; it often demands conceptual, breakthrough thinking. This provides an opportunity for educators to rethink our current systems— such as motivational systems—so we can align our efforts to build leadership capacity in new and creative ways. Leaders who understand that individuals are better motivated through "autonomy, mastery, and purpose"—the ingredients of motivation 3.0—will find better ways to invite and engage their staff (Pink, 2009, p. 79).

Because of limited resources, educational organizations often struggle with the concepts of developing leadership capacity and creating leadership pathways internally. Funds are limited. We suggest that educators begin to think outside the box on the resource front. We are not suggesting that individuals should not be paid for their work. Quite the contrary. Pink states, "The starting point, of course, is to ensure that the baseline rewards—wages, salaries, benefits, and so on—are adequate and fair. Without a healthy baseline, motivation of any sort is difficult and often impossible" (2009, p. 74). What we are suggesting is that if educators make the work a cultural norm—that is, if they expect everyone to engage in the work of leadership development in the various forms that appeal to their strengths and interests—then the systems in place can provide natural extensions to supporting our core work. The work of PLCs requires true leadership from everyone.

Creating a Career Lattice

The idea of a career ladder is less desirable than it once was. Not everyone wants to move up the ladder. For many, lateral moves can offer different responsibilities and more potential and excitement for job creativity and skill alignment than hierarchical moves in which the mere idea of adding more responsibilities causes concern. Education is a relatively flat organization, with only three hierarchical levels for educators to climb— from teacher to principal to superintendent. Education needs great leaders at *each* level. A career lattice provides such opportunities and builds leadership pathways for everyone.

In reality, educators must acknowledge that there must be leaders in all roles across the organization, especially in a PLC culture. So, all educators are already somewhere on the career lattice:

> Today, teacher leaders must adopt a new frame of mind and a collaborative way of working to lead from *within* the classroom—the heart of change in education. To lead from the classroom in a manner that impacts student learning in significant ways, teacher leaders across North America are assuming four critical roles in their classrooms and with their learning communities: collaborator, action researcher, reflective practitioner, and learner advocate. (Erkens, 2008b, pp. 11–12)

We have been suggesting throughout this book that leaders on each level of the organization must serve as collaborators, action researchers, reflective practitioners, and
learner advocates. The work of effective leadership requires all of these roles.

A challenge in developing a formally identifiable career lattice will be to create a norm
in which everyone extends their individual leadership skills by participating in additional roles. New and different roles might be short term (such as serving on a task force),
longer term (such as filling a two-year seat on a district curriculum committee), or even
more permanent (such as serving as a trainer for one of the district's in-house initiatives). The expectations of the roles will determine whether a district or school offers or
requires stipends or release time. Regardless, leadership development discussions and
opportunities should be available to everyone. Although a close connection between
teaching and leading exists, a skill in one area does not automatically inform the other.

The career lattice (see fig. 8.3, page 175) identifies a host of common roles we have found
in our travels. It helps educators see lateral and hierarchical career options and pathways.
In a hierarchical organization, the leadership capacity axis points upward to illustrate the
preferred pathway. The organizational capacity axis also shows lateral growth options by
pointing forward. Note that in lateral career moves, there is no hierarchy, and so there
is no proper sequence to the options a leader would select on a given rung of the career
ladder. The undivided rows show the organization's existing hierarchical structure
moving up the table—from the classroom to the boardroom. The rows with multiple
columns reveal lateral movement options for leaders who choose to remain at their
current hierarchical level but desire to continue stretching their knowledge and skills as
leaders. Effective leadership is required at all levels, and leaders require options for new
responsibilities and opportunities without necessarily leaving their positions.

Tier A is the foundation of a PLC; it involves leadership from teachers who work most
closely with the learners. When teachers leave Tier A, they do so to move "up" the career
ladder to Tier B (building administration) or Tier C (central office administration). Tier
A involves all classroom teachers leading from within the classroom by engaging in the
PLC leadership activities of collaborating, conducting action research, advocating for
all learners, and reflecting on the effectiveness of current practices for the purposes of
improving them. When teachers move up through Tier A, they make a lateral rather than
hierarchical move because additional responsibilities are added beyond the classroom—
such as mentoring, coaching (peer or instructional), or serving on a building leadership
team. Pay and title may not change.

With the appropriate license in hand, an educator can make a hierarchical move
to Tier B and become a building administrator—an assistant principal, vice principal,
or principal. Leaders in Tier B are also engaging in the work of collaboration, action
research, learner advocacy, and reflection. As building leaders move up through Tier
B, they keep their full-time roles and extend their responsibilities beyond the school
in which they work. Often, these are assistant or vice principals accepting additional
roles as they work toward the title of principal, or they are principals extending their

leadership to the system at large. The roles may involve task-specific or longer-term positions. For example, an assistant principal might fill a two-year role on the district curriculum council, and a principal might serve on a six-month task force regarding the district's strategic goal to build an internal leadership academy.

Because few educational systems build internal pathways for learning central office (Tier C) work, we suggest creating options for building leaders to safely explore central office level leadership. It is as much about the individual leader discovering if he or she would be interested in such work as it is about the system exploring the skills and virtuosities of the interested leader. Such roles might involve fulfilling an internship, leading a district initiative team, or serving as the district's technology coordinator while continuing work as a building assistant principal.

In Tier C, all district administrators work to support the work of collaborative teams and schools. They lead by example, also serving as collaborator, action researcher, learner advocate—for staff and students—and reflective practitioner. The Tier C hierarchy often nurtures future leaders; for instance, the director of teaching and learning moves into the assistant superintendent role, while the current assistant superintendent naturally progresses to the superintendent role. Organizations can maintain consistency in culture and expectations when they develop capacity and work to hire from within. This does not imply that organizations only hire from within. School systems that engage in the work of career and leadership development still post their positions outside the system and interview their candidates with a keen eye to those who will best align with and lead their existing efforts.

Formalizing Training

Some of the moves on a career lattice might involve moving up. In such a case, the organization would be wise to create its own institutes and internship opportunities:

> A leadership university would need to focus its work on four pillars: people, strategies, organization, and systems. If . . . you remain focused on the four key areas . . . , you produce leaders who think deeply about their present and future positions and about your organization. If they are uncomfortable with such a challenge, you are far better off to know it during a leadership institute than after a few months on the job. (Reeves, 2002, p. 164)

Internal leadership institutes create opportunities for long-term conversations and ongoing observations regarding the participants' competencies and skills.

More importantly, such institutes or academies create a structured system and a cohesive culture in which to explore the work of leadership and create shared knowledge. Organizations can customize internal, formal training opportunities to align with the criteria and performance standards that they have selected as a leadership framework. The tools leaders create to monitor progress are best introduced in learning environments in which individuals can self-assess, set goals, and work to meet the organization's needs and requirements.

Leadership Capacity (vertical axis)

Tier C

Leading From the Central Office on Collaborative Teams
Who: All district administrators
What: Leadership roles to support collaborative teams in a PLC district
When: All of the time

Collaborator, Action Researcher, Learner Advocate (for staff and students), and Reflective Practitioner			
District Leadership Academy Trainer (internal training cadre)	Internship	Chairing / Leading a District Initiative Team	Accepting a half-time role to serve as a district coordinator

Leading as a Central Office Administrator in District Efforts / Career Pathways
Who: Building administrators desiring to step into central office administrative roles
What: Leadership roles to support collaborative teams in a PLC building or district
When: Designated times as needed; remain in office role

District Training Team (internal training cadre)	District Initiative Team	Special Events / Projects Team Leader	District Curriculum Council

Tier B

Leading as a Building Administrator in District Efforts / Career Pathways
Who: Building administrators desiring to step into central office administrative roles
What: Leadership roles to support collaborative teams in a PLC building or district
When: Designated times as needed; remain in office role

Leading as Building Administrator With Collaborative Teams
Who: All building administrators
What: Leadership roles to support collaborative teams in a PLC building
When: All of the time

Collaborator, Action Researcher, Learner Advocate, and Reflective Practitioner			
Internship	Curriculum Coordinator	Dean of Students	Grant / Project Manager (inter/intra district)

Tier A

Leading as Teacher on a Career Pathway
Who: Classroom teachers desiring to step into administrative roles
What: Leadership roles to support collaborative teams in a PLC building
When: Most often full positions, all of the time

District Training Team (internal training cadre)	Math / Literacy or Instructional Coach	District Initiative Team	Special Events / Projects Team Leader	District Curriculum or PD Council

Leading as Teacher in District Efforts
Who: Classroom teachers as volunteers or invitees into leadership options
What: Leadership roles to support collaborative teams in PLC buildings/district
When: Designated times/release dates as needed; remain in classroom if possible

Mentor	Peer Coach	Instructional Coach	Team Leader	Building Leadership Team Member

Leading as Teacher in Building Efforts
Who: Classroom teachers as volunteers or invitees into leadership options
What: Leadership roles to support collaborative teams in a PLC building
When: Designated times as needed; remain in classroom if possible

Leading From the Classroom on Collaborative Teams
Who: All classroom teachers
What: Leadership roles in collaborative teams
When: All of the time

Collaborator, Action Researcher, Learner Advocate, and Reflective Practitioner

Organizational Capacity (horizontal axis)

Figure 8.3: **Sample career lattice.**

More and more school districts have begun this work. One of the superintendents we interviewed shared the highlights of his leadership development program, which was grant funded:

> We have our PLC Leadership program [in which] we are building capacity for instructional leaders through formal training. We have training going on today . . . and the expectation would be that the principal would be in attendance at every training session along with teacher leaders at the site. We invest a lot of release time, because we have a whole team coming in for conversations and we have them in cohorts. We have three cohorts running right now and they are in various levels in training. . . . The focus [of] our work is building capacity, building leadership across all lines. It is very formal and very structured.

He went on to share that his model is being studied through formal evaluation efforts in partnership with the local university. Internal learning opportunities are better, he says, since "you cannot depend on a training program to simply take; it is the informal piece that really drives the implementation of the formal piece" (Superintendent interview, spring 2010). With formal internal leadership capacity building efforts, the conversation continues beyond the classroom walls. The return on investment is significant.

Spreading Shared Learning Beyond the Classroom

The conversation about leadership development does not stop with the end of the leadership institute or academy session. Effective leaders weave the conversation into the fabric of daily work. Daloz Parks (2005) writes, "When leadership is understood as an activity . . . there is less attention to be paid to the transactions of power and influence and more attention given to the question of whether or not progress is being made on [complex] issues" (p. 10).

There are learning processes that enable the conversation to continue in the moment of leadership activities. Such conversations both create shared understanding and generate organizational results against which to measure success:

- Case studies

- Action research

- Lesson study

All these approaches enable participants to distill the learning from real time, in-the-moment work.

Case studies allow participants to explore ideas and options for complex problems. When a case study—an actual event that has already happened or a unique upcoming situation or problem that will require leadership—is discussed, it provides participants the opportunity to explore results or options collectively and to make meaning regarding leadership practices that work and those that do not. Sometimes educators come upon a case study in which they can readily explore best practices—how, for example, did another district successfully change their grading practices and policies? What worked for them and how might it work (or not) for another district? In our own research, we noticed that the best case studies came directly from opportune moments that emerged unexpectedly. We learned to find generalizable lessons in the moment, explore the quality indicators that made them worthy of discussing or replicating, and then consider alternatives that might help other educators understand and address their own complex issues. If systems use the case study approach, they can take the time to develop a shared framework for leadership, construct an accommodating rubric for quality leadership practices, and then invite participants to explore their own plausible responses and tools to address leadership issues. Such work creates coherence and clarity around the leadership framework and simultaneously helps leaders solve complex problems.

Another powerful learning practice for developing leadership capacity involves employing action research. *Action research*, a type of applied research, is a form of disciplined inquiry that practitioners conduct to improve practices in educational settings. It uses an array of methodologies and approaches, both quantitative and qualitative. Conversations that inform leadership practice can happen throughout the duration of the action research. Participants can discuss the frame of their individual questions, their criteria for quality, their tools for gathering data, their templates and protocols for their leadership work, and most importantly, their findings from the action research effort. Each phase is a powerful tool for unpacking our understanding of quality leadership. Just examining the leadership artifacts we create, for example, can inform the entire system of what has been created and is available internally as well as provide an opportunity for exploring quality relative to our work. The action research process is most powerful when used as a strategy to support key learning. It provides the option to implement a practice and gather data on its effectiveness. Used in this manner, the results offer leaders the reality of the attained leadership curriculum to serve as a mirror to the intended curriculum and the implemented curriculum.

Another powerful on-the-job learning opportunity is *lesson study*. Though teams do not often use it to support developing leadership capacity, it is a perfect tool when the strategies involved require presenting change initiatives or new information to a staff. The purpose of lesson study has always been to help teachers design better lessons to improve teaching. If leaders apply it to designing and delivering internal workshops, then the process engages those who design and deliver the workshops and provides them an opportunity to discuss what works when leading change with and among their peers. Lesson studies allow current and future leaders to discuss a selected issue from the perspective of leaders. Is the topic of discussion a worthy leadership issue? Have leaders in the system accurately identified the nuances and complications? Have the leaders designed a lesson to address the issue? Will others in the organization appreciate the lesson? What would it take for them to embrace the practices the lesson study team is teaching or encouraging? Certainly the critique of the workshop content—in advance of the final delivery of the content—helps inform all leaders about the best way to approach the learning opportunities they are providing as they lead staff into new ventures. The lesson study process provides an opportunity for those involved to examine their work relative to the leadership criteria and frameworks held by the organization.

Whether formal or informal discussions occur, effective leaders are constantly learning how to improve their leadership practice. The most effective leaders we met engage colleagues in healthy discussions on their leadership journey so that learning happens both in formal settings and informal conversations. Effective leaders are compelled to continue their learning and are eager to share their newest conundrums or insights with anyone willing to listen.

Rife with dualities, leadership is about enabling dissonance while sustaining stability (Fullan, 2001); it is about providing support and pressure (DuFour et al., 2006); it is about making tough calls while engaging the system in making crucial decisions (Judgment, 2007); and it is about establishing parameters while engaging people in challenging the status quo (DuFour et al., 2008). In short, leadership is about designing and navigating change:

> Effective leadership addresses problems that require people to move from a familiar but inadequate equilibrium—through disequilibrium—to a more adequate equilibrium. That is, today's complex conditions require acts of leadership that assist people in moving beyond the edge of familiar patterns into the unknown terrain of greater complexity, new learning, and new behaviors, usually requiring loss, grief, conflict, risk, stress, and creativity. (Daloz Parks, 2005, p. 9)

Leadership requires strong skill sets, clarity of purpose and direction, and cultural awareness. When we work to build leadership capacity across the organization, we build a sense of collective efficacy: a shared understanding that we have the capacity—the strength, wisdom, skill, and responsibility—to make a difference through our work, and we are willing and compelled to do so.

Case Studies: Developing Leadership Capacity From Every Level

We gathered the following case studies from real experiences in professional learning community settings. These case studies show how the various leadership roles build capacity for leaders and those they lead.

A Teacher Develops Leadership Capacity in Her Team

Clemé had been the go-to team leader for years. She was not only the most skilled at facilitating and organizing meetings, she was also beloved and trusted—a natural fit for a leader. There was no formal process for deciding Clemé was the leader. It just happened by default. Repeatedly.

Clemé noticed that her teammates were demonstrating eagerness and a readiness to engage in leadership activities, so she facilitated a conversation during which she highlighted the characteristics of healthy teams and thereby convinced them that they would benefit from sharing the role rather than always deferring the role to her. She formalized a process and engaged the team in identifying a new team leader: Shanna. But the transition did not happen simply because the team leader title was now bestowed on Shanna. Not only did Shanna need support in learning how to organize and facilitate the team meetings, but the team also needed to learn new patterns of behavior as they continued to defer to Clemé.

Clemé could clearly see a new role for her own leadership. First, she dedicated time to helping Shanna in her new role. She met with Shanna in advance of their team meetings to help her develop agendas, identify facilitation strategies for team engagement, anticipate possible complications, and prepare supporting resources. After every meeting, she met with Shanna for a brief reflection regarding the meeting, highlighting the strengths she saw in Shanna's leadership style whenever she could. Shanna soon began coming to their planning meetings with her own plan already mapped out.

Second, Clemé needed to help the team reshape old patterns during the meetings. By sheer habit, all heads would swing to Clemé for first responses to any discussion item. If the team asked a question, often looking in Clemé's direction, she would turn her gaze to Shanna and ask, "Shanna, what are your thoughts on that?" If Shanna posed a question and the team turned to Clemé for an answer, Clemé would respond, "So what do we think, team?" Clemé did participate in all discussions because she did not want it to seem as if she was either the team leader or a nonparticipant, but she always began by encouraging the other members to begin first. Eventually, the team learned to trust its own wisdom and rhythm, and Clemé could be more of an equal contributor on the team during their meetings.

Even though they had developed their own internal balance, Clemé noticed that when outside stakeholders were involved and began deferring to her, her team would fall back into its old patterns and publicly defer to her as well. Clemé wanted to break this habit too, but with outside stakeholders deferring to her and few opportunities to change the pattern over time, she knew her strategy would have to be much different. She decided to arrange a literacy meeting for the upcoming parent night, scheduled to occur at the same time that her team would overview the curriculum expectations with parents for the new semester. Clemé could have changed the time of her event, but she trusted that Shanna would run a fantastic meeting, that the parents would develop a new sense of equilibrium with the team in her absence, and that the team members would shine more brightly in her absence for this one event. Again, she helped Shanna prepare and assured her things would run smoothly. As it turned out, Clemé was right. The evening went off without a hitch, the team developed a new sense of public leadership, and Clemé was able to participate as an equal contributing member in all future events.

A Building Administration Team Develops Leadership Capacity Among Teachers

Marcus, a principal, created a guiding coalition in his building to support the building goal of understanding and implementing more formative assessments to support student learning. He knew that he would need to support the team's learning about formative assessment, that he would need to engage them in using the concepts in their classrooms, and that he would need to develop their leadership skills and knowledge so they could lead the rest of the school in implementing the work.

The team began with reading and understanding about formative classroom assessment. They met several times in an organized study effort. After the initial meeting, Marcus was sure to have his teacher leaders take turns facilitating upcoming sessions so they were already beginning the work of leadership development as a guiding coalition. After a session of discussing the reading assignment and exploring the implications of formative assessment on their school system, Marcus would invite closing reflections about how the meeting had gone and what they had learned about quality facilitation of meetings through the process.

Once the team had a shared definition and understanding of formative assessment, they each formed a specific application or strategy question with which they would explore the work of formative assessments in their individual classrooms. Marcus wanted them to be resident experts in the building so that their peers could easily follow them. He wanted them to be able to share from experience what worked, how it worked, and what tools they had created that helped it work.

With data and tools in hand, the guiding coalition began sharing their learning and results with the staff. For this phase, Marcus asked the team members to prepare to serve as trainers for the rest of the building. To do that, they identified key topics and people on the team who would best present each key topic to the entire staff in mini workshops. Marcus made sure everyone would be presenting at some point throughout the year. Then they began the process of lesson study. Each presentation team prepared their workshop for the staff and presented it in advance to the guiding coalition. The guiding coalition offered feedback for improvements, but the majority of the discussion was always aimed at how best to lead the work with their peers. How might they structure the activities so learning happened? How might they highlight their own research findings as well as the key ideas in ways that made the learning palatable?

At the conclusion of each mini workshop, the trainers for that session would pose a question and activity with which they would engage all of the staff—those in their grade levels and not part of the guiding coalition—in the work itself. The guiding coalition continued to meet, and team members returned with updates on their progress at the team level with formative assessments. Again, Marcus would close the meetings with conversations about leading this work with their peers. What were the best ways to lead their colleagues toward engaging in the right work and learning from it along the way?

Marcus always shared his own learning and understanding about leadership with the team as they progressed on the journey—highlighting related resources as appropriate.

Marcus developed a strong core of teacher leaders who now not only understand how to lead the work themselves, they also understand from his modeling and their shared planning how to *develop* other teacher leaders within their grade-level teams. Today, he asserts that his team leaders are stronger teacher leaders than he ever was, and they can probably run his building better than he can, too!

A Central Office Team Builds Leadership Capacity in the Assistant Principals

A large, urban district made the commitment to promote from within when and if an appropriate candidate was available. This did not preclude the district from finding suitable candidates outside the district, but it did focus their efforts and commitment to develop leaders by first identifying strong candidates and then developing learning opportunities and career opportunities for their success.

Elise moved up through the ranks herself, beginning as teacher and eventually switching from the role of principal to her current role as an assistant superintendent. Together with Tim, the director of professional development, she engaged the assistant principals from their schools in a yearlong action research project. In Elise's cluster schools, the assistant principals are consistently groomed for future principal positions, and they take their participation in their leadership development efforts very seriously. Last year, each assistant principal in Elise's cluster of schools was asked to identify an action research question relative to his or her leadership efforts in developing and strengthening the work of classroom interventions—a district initiative—at the classroom level in their individual buildings.

The assistant principals got together multiple times during the year to support their efforts. First, they spent time crafting, sharing, and ultimately refining their individual action research questions. Each principal had a specific but individualized question relative to leading the work of classroom interventions. Their questions looked something like the following:

- How can I facilitate the development of common formative assessments to increase a team's capacity to intervene with struggling learners accurately and effectively?

- How might I use my expertise in reading and formative assessment to help teachers analyze data and respond with targeted interventions that ultimately lead to increased student achievement?

- How can I best support the English department teams in designing and delivering strategic and effective targeted interventions that close the state reading-assessment achievement gap and raise the bar for all?

- How can I support the special education department's development of targeted intervention strategies and resources to support the work of grade-level teams planning interventions in the mainstreamed classroom?

Once the questions were framed, the assistant principals identified the leadership practices and strategies they were going to employ to answer their questions, and they met again to discuss valid and reliable ways to assess the results of their leadership. They spent considerable time identifying existing tools or cocreating specific tools with which to evaluate their efforts. Their tools were as much about student achievement results as they were about highlighting the specific tasks or products generated under their leadership and surveying staff about how they felt regarding their work as leaders along the way.

Finally, the assistant principals gathered in spring to share their results in a minimum of two forums: once as a share fair with their colleagues and once within their own buildings. The share fair was a powerful learning experience among the administration. They learned as much from hearing about their peers' efforts as they did from exploring their own. The building presentations were equally important. When the assistant principals shared their action research efforts and findings with staff, they taught the value of targeted interventions as they shared their results, they demonstrated the power of conducting action research as a learning tool, and they modeled their personal commitment to developing leadership capacity in self and others. Under Elise's watch, the assistant principals are constantly exploring and modeling their leadership craft so they will be ready for principal positions someday.

EPILOGUE

We are fascinated by leaders and successful leadership practices. What an educational leader does or doesn't do and the effect the practices have on districts, schools, teachers, and students is a matter of intense curiosity on our part.

Over the years, we have had the opportunity to work with and learn from many outstanding and highly effective leaders. We have also had the blessing of being able to work with and coach leaders who have struggled in their leadership role and needed guidance and support. We have come to the conclusion, as many others have before us, that the "great man theory" of leadership does not hold true in districts, schools, and teams. Leadership—*effective* leadership—can in fact be taught, and more importantly *learned*, by everyone with intention and will.

We certainly do not want to suggest that the seven leadership strategies and the supporting practices we identified here are the all-inclusive one-stop shop for leadership effectiveness. However, we do know that when leaders engage in the essential work of the seven leadership practices, they are in a better position to develop their organizations as high-performing PLCs and sustain the results for the long run.

Leadership does not need to be wrapped in a mysterious black box only to be unlocked and understood by a select few. We believe that all who endeavor to take on leadership roles in schools can learn the strategies and practices of effective leadership. We have seen it happen. And we have witnessed amazing results.

The focus for our work has been on understanding what effective leaders actually *do* to bring about meaningful change and improvement when developing as PLCs. We spent time isolating the specific leadership practices and strategies of the remarkable leaders in high-performing professional learning communities. There is an amazing synergy—a passion—for leadership that was evident in the talented leaders who informed the findings of our research.

In his classic leadership essay *The Servant as Leader* (1991), Robert Greenleaf describes the leaders we had the privilege to interview:

> The servant-leader is servant first . . . It begins with the natural feeling that one wants to serve, to serve first. Then conscious choice brings one to aspire to lead. That person is sharply different from one who is leader first, perhaps because of the need to assuage an unusual power drive or to acquire material possessions . . . The difference manifests itself in the care taken by the servant-first to make sure that other people's highest priority needs are being served. The best test, and difficult to administer, is: Do those served grow as persons? Do they, while being served, become healthier, wiser, freer, more autonomous, more likely themselves to become servants? (p. 7)

The first priority for the highly effective leaders in PLCs was to serve. We heard this over and over again from the leaders we interviewed. Although they are entirely focused on ensuring high levels of learning for all students by creating and sustaining PLCs, they know that to do so they must be fully committed to building the individual and collective capacity of those they serve. Many consider doing so the most important function of their leadership practice. We could not agree more.

Emotionally and Socially Intelligent Leaders

The effective leaders we interviewed demonstrated the intrapersonal and interpersonal characteristics that differentiate them from those who may otherwise struggle in their leadership role. These characteristics provided the something else—the something different that made the leaders we interviewed remarkable in the eyes of many, including their own followers. These very characteristics make many question whether leadership can be taught or if leaders are born. We believe that when isolated and practiced with humility and will, these characteristics are teachable and can be learned.

In *Primal Leadership*, Daniel Goleman and colleagues (2002) provide a framework that identifies the personal and social competencies that we found to be extremely apparent in the effective leaders we met who are successfully leading high-performing PLCs. These competencies include self-awareness, self-management, social awareness, and relationship management.

Self-Awareness

Leaders who are self-aware have a solid "understanding of their own emotions, strengths, and weaknesses," and they have an appreciation for how their actions and words affect others (Goleman et al., p. 40). The effective leaders of PLCs that we met all had a very solid understanding and appreciation for how their emotions and actions affect their colleagues and students. Effective leaders spend considerable time in reflection. They engage in a seemingly constant inner dialogue regarding their behaviors and practices and how they affect the lives of others.

For years, the intuitive approach that many leaders bring to their practice has fascinated us. In fact, we heard from quite a few of the leaders in this research that sometimes they seem to "just know" what the right thing to do is. We wanted to know more about what makes "trusting your gut" different from "random acts of practice." What we have learned from effective leaders is that the ability to trust one's gut and make good decisions as a result is directly tied to, and even proportional to, the amount of time spent in reflection. The more self-aware leaders are, the more confident they become in making decisions aligned to their own personal ideals and the shared vision, mission, values, and goals of the district and school. With such personal focus, remarkable leaders make decisions that might feel intuitive, but that are actually founded on sound judgment, tacit knowledge based on past experience, professional expertise, and skill. A strong understanding of oneself and a deep commitment to reflection enable leaders to make decisions entirely consistent with the agreed-upon values and ideals. Trusting your gut is not clairvoyant leadership; it is self-awareness in action among effective leaders.

Self-Management

When leaders have a firm understanding of their emotions, and they have a clear idea of how their behaviors and actions might impact others, they are able to engage in self-management. Given how little training and development are provided to educational leaders, and the little time that many leaders give to self-reflection, it is not uncommon to find leaders who have a difficult time managing their thoughts, feelings, and actions. Leaders who are unable to do so run the risk of creating organizational disharmony and incoherence in their districts, schools, and teams, and they may cause personal irritation and unhappiness in those with whom they work closely. In schools working to develop as PLCs, the close proximity of working in collaboration makes it obvious when a leader is unable to control and effectively manage his or her emotions. In his investigation of the impact of emotions on leadership, Goleman writes, "How a leader feels thus becomes more than just a private matter; given the reality of emotional leakage, a leader's emotions have public consequences" (Goleman et al., 2002, p. 46).

The effective leaders we researched for this project all gave thoughtful attention and consideration to controlling their feelings and impulses, and they worked to create a relatively disturbance-free and emotionally calm organizational culture. While effective leaders do not ignore their thoughts, feelings, and actions, they do actively work to be sure that their own emotional highs and lows do not negatively affect their colleagues. Goleman et al. (2002) suggest that when leaders "stay in control of their feelings and impulses, they craft an environment of trust, comfort, and fairness" (p. 47). This was certainly true for the district, school, and teacher leaders we included in this research.

Social Awareness

While it is very important that effective leaders have the personal competencies of self-awareness and self-management, in order to have a positive and sustainable impact, leaders must also have social awareness—the primary attribute of which is empathy. Having empathy—being in tune with others and how they feel—is vital to a district's, school's, or team leader's ability to effectively engage the seven practices of *Leading by Design*. When describing how leaders employ empathy in their daily work, Goleman et al. write, "By being attuned to how others feel in the moment, a leader can say and do what's appropriate—whether it be to calm fears, assuage anger, or join in good spirits" (2002, p. 49). Empathy helps leaders develop a more accurate understanding of the shared values and current reality of their districts, schools, and teams. Goleman et al. (2002) further state:

> By the same token, a leader who lacks empathy will unwittingly be off-key, and so speak and act in ways that set off negative reactions. Empathy, which includes listening and taking other people's perspectives—allows

leaders to tune into the emotional channels between people . . . and staying
attuned lets them fine-tune their message to keep it in synch. (p. 49)

We have come to believe that *empathy* is the single most important interpersonal
factor in a leader's ability to develop his or her districts, schools, and teams as PLCs.
Empathy allows leaders to effectively help their colleagues overcome fears and anxieties,
meet challenges head on, and bring people together. The hard work of developing PLCs
needs leadership that recognizes the difficulty in challenging assumptions and altering
the status quo. Empathy prevents effective leaders from taking themselves too seriously
or taking their colleagues for granted as they engage in their collective work. We have
seen the chaos and damage that nonempathetic leadership can have on districts, schools,
and teams. The results are not pretty. The leaders we researched for this project were all
empathic leaders who understood that their commitment to serve must be rooted in an
understanding and awareness of others.

Relationship Management

One of the most distinguishing characteristics of the effective leaders we have met is
their ability to use their own emotional intelligence to successfully influence and serve
others. In many ways, the *Leadership by Design* framework rests on a leader's ability to
effectively handle the complex relationships that exist in districts, schools, and teams.
The leaders we met all had a knack for finding common ground and building rapport,
which is essential in creating and sustaining the collaborative relationships that are the
glue of a PLC. Goleman et al. (2002) describe it in this way: "The triad of self-awareness,
self-management, and empathy all come together in . . . relationship management" (p. 51).

While relationship management is important, it is important to note that effective leaders don't manage relationships for their own sake. In fact, we have met far too many leaders who suggest that relationship building is their most important role as a leader. In the
reality of educational leadership, relationship building and relationship management
are two very, very different things. For many leaders in traditional schools, building and
maintaining relationships is a priority that trumps all others—they make, or avoid, decisions based on the potential impact on their relationships. Generally, the more likely a
decision will cause discord in a relationship, the less likely a leader is willing to make it.
Relationship management, on the other hand, rests on the assumption that nothing will
be done effectively, nor as well, if it is not done collaboratively. Effective leaders use their
skills of self-awareness, self-management, and empathy to create opportunities for people
to collaborate with one another in pursuit of shared commitments and common work.

We learned from the effective leaders in this research that, while it is vital that we work
to close the knowing-doing gap in our efforts to develop as PLCs, leadership is as much
about who we are as it is what we do. The personal competencies of self-awareness and self-
management and the social competencies of social awareness and relationship management are the fuel that drives the seven leadership practices and the supporting strategies
of the *Leading by Design* framework. Moreover, we know that researchers and practitioners

have identified and defined leadership competencies. If the competencies can be isolated, you can teach them. If you can practice them, you can learn them. Although it is not easy, we believe that anyone willing to try can become highly effective leaders.

Leading to Learn, Learning to Lead

The leaders we met during the course of this project did not begin their teaching careers with aspirations for district, school, or even teacher leadership positions. In fact, many of the highly effective leaders we met shared with us that they did not move into leadership by making a formal decision to do so; most were informally nominated by colleagues who saw strong leadership potential and capabilities in them. When they did make the decision to leave the classroom and their students, each leader we met described that decision as the single most difficult of their professional career. Accepting a formal leadership role is a highly personal decision and one that is only done with contemplation and care. These leaders understood that by accepting a leadership position, they had an opportunity as well as a responsibility to serve. In order to do so, they felt compelled to understand themselves as a leader, and they spent time investing in learning and growing their capacity to lead.

In a speech prepared for delivery on November 22, 1963, President John F. Kennedy wrote, "Leadership and learning are indispensable to each other" (John F. Kennedy Presidential Library and Museum, n.d.). Though never spoken, President Kennedy's words echo though decades and ring out loudly to us today. We will be forever grateful to the leaders who took the time to meet with us, answer our seemingly never-ending questions, and share their strategies and practices for creating and sustaining PLCs in their districts, schools, and teaching teams. We are thankful for all they have taught us, and everything we have learned about *leading by design*.

REFERENCES AND RESOURCES

Augsburger, D. (2009). *Caring enough to confront: How to understand and express your deepest feelings toward others.* Ventura, CA: Regal Books.

Bennis, W. (2005). Foreword. In S. Daloz Parks, *Leadership can be taught: A bold approach for a complex world* (pp. ix–xii). Boston: Harvard Business School Press.

Bennis, W., & Nanus, B. (2007). *Leaders: Strategies for taking charge.* New York: Harper & Row.

Black, P., & Wiliam, D. (1998). Inside the black box: Raising standards through classroom assessments. *Phi Delta Kappan, 80*(2), 139–148.

Bossi, M. (2008). Six dimensions of leadership. *Leadership, 37*(3), 8–12.

Bryk, A., & Schneider, B. (2002). *Trust in schools: A core resource for improvement.* New York: Russell Sage Foundation.

Chappuis, J. (2009). *Seven strategies of assessment for learning.* Portland, OR: Educational Testing Service.

Collins, J. (2001). *Good to great. Why some companies make the leap . . . and others don't.* New York: HarperCollins.

Collins, J. (2005). *Good to great in the social sectors: A monograph to accompany good to great.* New York: HarperCollins.

Collins, J. (2009). *How the mighty fall.* New York: HarperCollins.

Costa, A. (2007). *The school as a home for the mind: Creating mindful curriculum, instruction, and dialogue.* Thousand Oaks, CA: Corwin Press.

Costa, A. (2008). The thought-filled curriculum. *Educational Leadership, 65*(5), 20–24.

Costa, A., & Kallick, B. (Eds.). (2008). *Learning and leading with habits of mind: 16 essential characteristics of success.* Alexandria, VA: Association of Supervision and Curriculum Development.

Crow, T. (2008). Interview with Richard Elmore: Practicing professionals. *Journal of Staff Development, 29*(2), 42–47.

Cruess, S. R., Cruess, R. L., & Steinert, Y. (2008). Role modelling: Making the most of a powerful teaching strategy. *British Medical Journal, 336,* 718–720.

Daloz Parks, S. (2005). *Leadership can be taught: A bold approach for a complex world.* Boston: Harvard Business School Press.

Danielson, C. (2007). *Enhancing professional practice: A framework for teaching* (2nd ed.). Alexandria, VA: Association of Supervision and Curriculum Development.

Davidovich, R., Nikolay, P., Laugerman, B., & Commodore, C. (2010). *Beyond school improvement: The journey to innovative leadership.* Thousand Oaks, CA: Corwin Press.

Denhardt, R. B., Denhardt, J. V., & Aristigueta, M. P. (2009). *Managing human behavior in public and nonprofit organizations* (2nd ed.). Thousand Oaks, CA: SAGE.

Drucker, P. F. (2011). Managing oneself. In Harvard Business Review Press, *HBR's 10 must reads: The essentials* (pp. 43–62). Boston: Author.

Druskat, V. U., Sala, F., & Mount, G. (Eds.). (2006). *Linking emotional intelligence and perfor-mance at work: Current research evidence with individuals and groups.* Mahwah, NJ: Erlbaum.

DuFour, R. (2003). Leading edge: "Collaboration lite" puts student achievement on a starvation diet. *Journal of Staff Development, 24*(3), 63–64.

DuFour, R. (2007). In praise of top-down leadership: What drives your school improve-ment efforts—Evidence of best practice or the pursuit of universal buy-in? *School Administrator, 10*(64), 38–42.

DuFour, R. (2011). Work together: But only if you want to. *Phi Delta Kappan, 92*(5), 57–61.

DuFour, R., & DuFour, R. (2010). The role of professional learning communities in advancing 21st century skills. In J. Bellanca & R. Brandt (Eds.), *21st century skills: Rethinking how students learn* (pp. 77–95). Bloomington, IN: Solution Tree Press.

DuFour, R., DuFour, R., & Eaker, R. (2008). *Revisiting professional learning communities at work: New insights for improving schools.* Bloomington, IN: Solution Tree Press.

DuFour, R., DuFour, R., Eaker, R., & Many, T. (2006). *Learning by doing: A handbook for profes-sional learning communities at work.* Bloomington, IN: Solution Tree Press.

DuFour, R., DuFour, R., Eaker, R., & Many, T. (2010). *Learning by doing: A handbook for profes-sional learning communities at work* (2nd ed.). Bloomington, IN: Solution Tree Press.

Dweck, C. (2006). *Mindset: The new psychology of success.* New York: Ballantine Books.

Dweck, C. (2007). The perils and promises of praise. *Educational Leadership, 65*(2), 34–39.

Eaker, R., & Keating, J. (2009). A districtwide approach to professional learning: Learning by doing in a professional learning community. *Journal of Staff Development, 30*(5), 50–55.

Eisenstat, R., Beer, M., Foote, N., Fredberg, T., & Norrgren, F. (2008). The uncompromising leader. *Harvard Business Review, 86*(7–8), 50–57.

Elmore R. (2002). *Bridging the gap between standards and achievement: Report on the imperative for professional development in education.* Washington, DC: Shanker Institute.

Elmore, R. (2004). *School reform from the inside out: Policy, practice, and performance.* Cambridge, MA: Harvard Education Press.

Elmore, R. (2008). Practicing professionals. *Journal of Staff Development, 29*(2), 42–47.

Erkens, C. (2008a). Growing teacher leadership. In A. Buffum, C. Erkens, C. Hinman, S. Huff, L. G. Jessie, T. L. Martin, et al., *The collaborative administrator: Working together as a professional learning community* (pp. 39–53). Bloomington, IN: Solution Tree Press.

Erkens, C. (2008b). The new teacher leader: Transforming education from inside the classroom. In C. Erkens, C. Jakicic, L. G. Jessie, D. King, S. V. Kramer, T. W. Many, et al., *The col-laborative teacher: Working together as a professional learning community* (pp. 11–28). Bloomington, IN: Solution Tree Press.

Farren, C. (1999). A smart team makes the difference. *Human Resource Professional, 12*(1), 12–16.

Festinger, L., Riecken, H. W., & Schachter, S. (1956). *When prophecy fails.* Minneapolis: University of Minnesota Press.

Fullan, M. (2001). *Leading in a culture of change.* San Francisco: Jossey-Bass.

Fullan, M. (2006). Leading professional learning: Think "system" and not "individual school" if the goal is to fundamentally change the culture of schools. *School Administrator, 63*(10), 10–14. Accessed at EBSCO*host* database on December 2, 2011.

Fullan, M. (2008). *The six secrets of change: What the best leaders do to help their organizations survive and thrive.* San Francisco: Jossey-Bass.

Fullan, M. (2011). *The moral imperative realized.* Thousand Oaks, CA: Corwin Press.

Fullan, M., Cuttress, C., & Kilcher, A. (2005). Eight forces for leaders of change. *Journal of Staff Development, 26*(4), 54–64.

Garmston, R., & Wellman, B. (2009). *The adaptive school: A sourcebook for developing collaborative groups.* Norwood, MA: Christopher-Gordon.

Goleman, D. (2006). *Social intelligence.* New York: Bantam Books.

Goleman, D., Boyatzis, R. E., & McKee, A. (2002). *Primal leadership: Realizing the power of emotional intelligence.* Boston: Harvard Business School Press.

Greenleaf, R. (1991). *The servant as leader.* Indianapolis, IN: Greenleaf Center.

Guskey, T. R. (2009). *Practical solutions for serious problems in standards-based grading.* Thousand Oaks, CA: Corwin Press.

Hargreaves, A., & Fink, D. (2006). *Sustainable leadership.* San Francisco: Jossey-Bass.

Hattie, J., & Timperley, H. (2007). The power of feedback. *Review of Educational Research, 77*(1), 81–112.

Hill, L. A., & Lineback, K. (2011). Are you a good boss—Or a great one? *Harvard Business Review, 89*(1/2), 124–131.

Hord, S. M., & Sommers, W. A. (2008). *Leading professional learning communities: Voices from research and practice.* Thousand Oaks, CA: Corwin Press.

Hughes, M., & Terrell, J. (2007). *The emotionally intelligent team: Understanding and developing the behaviors of success.* San Francisco: Jossey-Bass.

Intrator, S. M., & Scribner, M. (Eds.). (2003). *Teaching with fire: Poetry that sustains the courage to teach.* San Francisco: Jossey-Bass.

Jacobs, H. H., & Johnson, A. (2009). *The curriculum mapping planner: Templates, tools, and resources for effective professional development.* Alexandria, VA: Association of Supervision and Curriculum Development.

Johansen, B. (2007). *Get there early: Sensing the future to compete in the present.* San Francisco: Berrett-Koehler.

John F. Kennedy Presidential Library and Museum. (n.d.). *Remarks prepared for delivery at the trade mart in Dallas, November 22, 1963.* Accessed at www.jfklibrary.org/Research/Ready-Reference/JFK-Speeches/Remarks-Prepared-for-Delivery-at-the-Trade-Mart-in-Dallas-November-22-1963.aspx on November 4, 2011.

Judgment: How winning leaders make great calls. (2007, November 19). *Businessweek,* 68–72. (Reprinted from *Judgment: How winning leaders make great calls,* by N. M. Tichy & W. G. Bennis, 2007, New York: Portfolio)

Kegan, R., & Lahey, L. (2001). *How the way we talk can change the way we work: Seven languages for transformation.* San Francisco: Jossey-Bass.

Kornfield, J. (2009). *The wiseheart: A guide to the universal teachings of Buddhist psychology.* New York: Random House.

Kouzes, J., & Posner, B. (2002). *The leadership challenge* (3rd ed.). San Francisco: Jossey-Bass.

Kouzes, J., & Posner, B. (2003). Challenge is the opportunity for greatness. *Leader to Leader, 28,* 16–23.

Kouzes, J., & Posner, B. (2007). *The leadership challenge* (4th ed.). San Francisco: Jossey-Bass.

Kouzes, J., & Posner, B. (2010). *The truth about leadership: The no-fads, heart-of-the-matter facts you need to know.* San Francisco: Jossey-Bass.

Kovalik, S., & Olsen, K. (2002). *Exceeding expectations: A user's guide to implementing brain research in the classroom.* Covington, WA: Books for Educators.

Kramer, K. (2008). Learning celebrations. *School Library Media Activities Monthly, 24*(9), 39–41.

Lencioni, P. (2004). *Death by meeting: A leadership fable—About solving the most painful problem in business.* San Francisco: Jossey-Bass.

Lencioni, P. (2005). *Overcoming the five dysfunctions of a team: A field guide for leaders, managers, and facilitators.* San Francisco: Jossey-Bass.

Lieberman, A., & Miller, L. (2004). *Teacher leadership.* San Francisco: Jossey-Bass.

Luidens, P., & Tabor, M. (2008). Leadership through collaborative conversation: Leaders coaching groups for sustained change [Workshop handouts].

Marzano, R. (2007). *The art and science of teaching.* Alexandria, VA: Association of Supervision and Curriculum Development.

Marzano, R. (2010). *Formative assessment and standards-based grading.* Bloomington, IN: Marzano Research Laboratory.

Marzano, R., Schooling, P., & Toth, M. (2010). *Creating an aligned system to develop great teachers within the federal race to the top initiative* [White paper]. Accessed at www.iobservation .com/whitepapers on August 2, 2011.

Marzano, R., Waters, T., & McNulty, B. (2005). *School leadership that works: From research to results.* Alexandria, VA: Association of Supervision and Curriculum Development.

Maxwell, J. C. (1998). *The 21 irrefutable laws of leadership.* Nashville, TN: Thomas Nelson.

McDonnell, S. N. (2009). The art of caring confrontation. *Educational Leadership: Revisiting Social Responsibility, 66.* Accessed at www.ascd.org/publications/educational-leadership /summer09/vol66/num10/The-Art-of-Caring-Confrontation.aspx on August 2, 2011.

Morriss, A., Ely, R. J., & Frei, F. X. (2011). Managing yourself: Stop holding yourself back. *Harvard Business Review, 89*(1/2), 160–163.

National Commission on Teaching and America's Future. (2003). *No dream denied: A pledge to America's children.* Washington, DC: Author.

O'Connor, K. (2010). *A repair kit for grading: Fifteen fixes for broken grades* (2nd ed.). Old Tappan, NJ: Pearson Assessment Training Institute.

Patterson, K., Grenny, J., Maxfield, D., McMillan, R., & Switzler, A. (2008). *Influencer: The power to change anything.* New York: McGraw-Hill.

Pfeffer, J., & Sutton, R. I. (2000). *The knowing-doing gap: How smart companies turn knowledge into action.* Boston: Harvard Business School Press.

Pfeffer, J., & Sutton, R. I. (2006). *Hard facts, dangerous half-truths and total nonsense: Profiting from evidence-based management.* Boston: Harvard Business Press.

Pink, D. (2009). *Drive: The surprising truth about what motivates us.* New York: Riverhead Books.

Quotations Page. (2010). Quotation #2323 from Laura Moncur's motivational quotations. Accessed at www.quotationspage.com/quote/2323.html on November 5, 2011.

Reeves, D. (2002). *The daily disciplines of leadership: How to improve student achievement, staff motivation, and personal organization.* San Francisco: Jossey-Bass.

Reeves, D. (2006a). Of hubs, bridges, and networks. *Educational Leadership, 63*(8), 32–37.

Reeves, D. (2006b). *The learning leader: How to focus school improvement for better results.* Alexandria, VA: Association of Supervision and Curriculum Development.

Reeves, D. (2007). From the bell curve to the mountain: A new vision for achievement, assessment, and equity. In D. Reeves (Ed.), *Ahead of the curve: The power of assessment to transform teaching and learning* (pp. 1–12). Bloomington, IN: Solution Tree Press.

Reeves, D. (2010). *Elements of grading: A guide to effective practice.* Bloomington, IN: Solution Tree Press.

Reeves, D. (2011). *Finding your leadership focus: What matters most for student results.* New York: Teachers College Press.

Sawchuk, S. (2010). Professional development at a crossroads. *Education Week, 30*(11), s2–s4.

Schmoker, M. (2004). Learning communities at the crossroads: A response to Joyce and Cook. *Phi Delta Kappan, 86*(1), 84–89.

Schofeld, J. W. (1990). Increasing the generalizability of qualitative research. In E. Eisner & A. Peshkin (Eds.), *Qualitative inquiry in education: The continuing debate* (pp. 201–232). New York: Teachers College Press.

Schön, D. (1983). *The reflective practitioner: How professionals think in action.* New York: Basic Books.

Seashore Louis, K., Leithwood, K., Wahlstrom, K. L., & Anderson, S. E. (2010). *Investigating the links to improved student learning: Final report of research findings.* Minneapolis: University of Minnesota.

Senge, P. (2006). *The fifth discipline: The art and practice of the learning organization* (2nd ed.). New York: Currency Books.

Senge, P., Smith B., Kruschwitz, N., Laur, J., & Schley, S. (2008). *The necessary revolution: How individuals and organizations are working together to create a sustainable world.* New York: Doubleday.

Sergiovanni, T. (1992). *Moral leadership: Getting to the heart of school improvement.* San Francisco: Jossey-Bass.

Sergiovanni, T. (2005). *Strengthening the heartbeat: Leading and learning together in schools.* San Francisco: Jossey-Bass.

Sinek, S. (2009). *Start with why.* New York: Penguin.

Sparks, D. (2005). Explain, inspire, lead: An interview with Noel Tichy. *Journal of Staff Development, 26*(2), 50–53.

Stephenson, S. (2009). *Leading with trust: How to build strong school teams.* Bloomington, IN: Solution Tree Press.

Stiggins, R., Arter, J., Chappuis, S., & Chappuis, J. (2011). *Classroom assessment for student learning: Doing it right—using it well.* Portland, OR: Assessment Trainers Institute.

Tichy, N. M. (2004). *The cycle of leadership: How great leaders teach their companies to win.* New York: HarperBusiness.

Tichy, N. M., & Cohen, E. B. (1997). How leaders develop leaders. *Training and Development, 51*(5), 58–69.

Tichy, N. M., & Cohen, E. B. (2002). *The leadership engine: How winning companies build leaders at every level.* New York: HarperCollins.

Tosteson, D. C. (1979). Learning in medicine. *New England Journal of Medicine, 301*(13), 690–694.

Vaughan, J. C. (1990). Foreword. In R. T. Clift, W. R. Houston, & M. C. Pugach (Eds.), *Encouraging reflective practice in education: An analysis of issues and programs* (pp. vii–xi). New York: Teachers College Press.

von Frank, V. (2010). Trust matters—For educators, parents, and students. *Tools for Schools, 14*(1), 1–3.

Weinberger, D. (2007). *Everything is miscellaneous: The power of the new digital disorder.* New York: Times Books.

Wheatley, M. (2006). *Leadership and the new science: Discovering order in a chaotic world.* San Francisco: Berrett-Koehler.

White, E. B. (1945). *Stuart Little.* New York: HarperCollins.

White, T. H. (1958). *The once and future king.* New York: Berkley Medallion Books.

Whitten, L., & Anderson, L. (2010). Learning to celebrate and cope with professional success, workplace challenges. *Diverse Issues Higher Education, 26*(25), 19.

Wiggins, G., & McTighe, J. (2005). *Understanding by design* (2nd ed.). Alexandria, VA: Association of Supervision and Curriculum Development.

Wiggins, G., & McTighe, J. (2007). *Schooling by design: Mission, action, and achievement.* Alexandria, VA: Association of Supervision and Curriculum Development.

Wiliam, D. (2007). Content then process: Teacher learning communities in the service of formative assessment. In D. Reeves (Ed.), *Ahead of the curve: The power of assessment to transform teaching and learning* (pp. 183–204). Bloomington, IN: Solution Tree Press.

Wiliam, D. (2007/2008). Changing classroom practice. *Educational Leadership, 65*(4), 36–42.

Wiliam, D. (2011). *Embedded formative assessment.* Bloomington, IN: Solution Tree Press.

Wiliam, D., & Thompson, M. (2007). Integrating assessment with learning: What will it take to make it work? In C. A. Dwyer (Ed.), *The future of assessment: Shaping teaching and learning* (pp. 53–82). New York: Erlbaum.

Wiliam, D., & Thompson, M. (2008). Tight but loose: A conceptual framework for scaling up school reforms. In E. C. Wylie (Ed.), *Tight but loose: Scaling up teacher professional development in diverse contexts* (ETS Research Report No. RR-08-29, pp. 1–44). Princeton, NJ: Educational Testing Service.

Wolff, S., Druskat, V., Koman S., & Messer, T. (2006). The link between group emotional competence and group effectiveness. In V. Druskat, F. Sala, & G. Mount (Eds.), *Linking emotional intelligence and performance at work: Current research evidence with individuals and groups* (pp. 223–242). Mahwah, NJ: Erlbaum.

York-Barr, J., Sommers, W. A., Ghere, G. S., & Montie, J. (2001). *Reflective practice to improve schools: An action guide for educators.* Thousand Oaks, CA: Corwin Press.

INDEX

Solution Tree Author Series: Transformational Learning

Cassandra Erkens

What does deep learning look like? How can educators use quality assessments to promote, enhance, and monitor learning? Cassandra's keynote focuses on the creation of formative cultures in schools to create rich learning experiences for students and teachers alike.

DVF021

The Collaborative Administrator

Austin Buffum, Cassandra Erkens, Charles Hinman, Susan Huff, Lillie G. Jessie, Terri L. Martin, Mike Mattos, Anthony Muhammad, Peter Noonan, Geri Parscale, Eric Twadell, Jay Westover, and Kenneth C. Williams

Foreword by Robert Eaker

Introduction by Richard DuFour

In a culture of shared leadership, the administrator's role is more important than ever. This book addresses your toughest challenges with practical strategies and inspiring insight.

BKF256

Navigating Conflict and Feeling Good About It

Featuring Cassandra Erkens

Many leaders avoid addressing conflict because they fear long-term negative effects. While navigating conflict feels nerve-racking at the outset, there are specific ways leaders can address conflict to elicit respect, improve rapport, and enable progress. Using humor, personal stories, and participant interaction, Cassandra shares strategies, skills, and guidelines to address conflict safely and directly.

DVF037

Learning by Doing
A Handbook for Professional Learning Communities at Work™

Richard DuFour, Rebecca DuFour, Robert Eaker, and Thomas Many

The second edition of *Learning by Doing* is an action guide for closing the knowing-doing gap and transforming schools into PLCs. It also includes seven major additions that equip educators with essential tools for confronting challenges.

BKF416

a division of

Solution Tree | Press

Solution Tree

Visit solution-tree.com or call 800.733.6786 to order.